THE CENTURY STUDIES IN ECONOMICS
WILLIAM H. KIEKHOFER, Editor

ECONOMICS AND PUBLIC UTILITIES

THE CENTURY STUDIES IN ECONOMICS

WILLIAM H. KIEKHOFER, *Editor*

Economics and Public Utilities

By

ELI WINSTON CLEMENS, Ph.D.

Professor of Economics
University of Maryland

NEW YORK
APPLETON-CENTURY-CROFTS, INC.

To

MY MOTHER AND FATHER

Preface

The somewhat unusual title of this book, *Economics and Public Utilities,* reflects the objective of the writer's teaching program in the College of Business and Public Administration at the University of Maryland where the course in public utilities was designed both as a capstone to a curriculum to train economists, accountants, and technicians for public service and as a part of other courses of study. The purpose of the course as well as that of this book was to draw together the lessons of various fields of study including those of economics, accounting, business, law, public administration, and government control into a single integrated study. The objective is not too difficult of attainment. In one way or another public utility economics cuts through numerous segments of economic activity and many opportunities are presented to treat the utility industries virtually as case studies in which lessons of greater import are pointed up. Most chapters carry a concluding section which carries the reader well beyond the strict limits of the field. Obviously these digressions cannot be carried too far in a book designed primarily as a public utilities book, although the way is open to instructors using the book as a text to carry the discussion even further.

On the other hand, "practical men" or those interested for one reason or another in a strictly confined discussion of the conventional and technical phases of the field of public utility economics may hurriedly pass over these sections. Nor is there need to be too apologetic for such a teaching approach. Although few will deny that education must concern itself more with principles than with facts, there are many who might be reluctant to project facts too far into the realm of principles. Moreover facts, even standing alone, have their usefulness. They temper and give content to principles. A certain technical competence and experience is developed through the study of the interplay of details in some limited sphere of human activity that can never be gained from the study of broad principles alone.

The writer has been primarily interested in training men for public service. There is a growing belief that our colleges and universities must accept the positive responsibility of training for such careers if the quality of our corps of public servants is not to be thinned down. A somewhat similar belief was expressed by David Lilienthal, who, in a commencement address at the University of Virginia in 1948, urged that all students plan to give a portion of their lives to public service in some form. If this book can do a small part in giving its readers a realistic knowledge of business and government and in addition contribute to the training of a few practical, yet idealistic, public servants, the writer's purpose will have been accomplished.

The chapters of this book have been designed as integrated units, any one of which can be omitted without unduly affecting the understanding of the others. Those who are skeptical of abstract economic theory can skip parts of Chapter 11 on the Theory of Public Utility Rate Making if they do not want to omit the chapter entirely. Subsections 4, 5, and 6 of Section 2 and all of Section 3 of that chapter can be omitted. On the other hand, those interested in the technical features of rate making or in theoretical economics might choose to enlarge and qualify the material so as to spend much more time on the subject than the allotment of space would indicate. The theory of public utility rate making can be carried with profit into the field of monopolistic competition in a manner which, to the writer's knowledge, has not hitherto been attempted.

Chapter 10 on the Rate of Return constitutes a new approach to the subject which, in the writer's opinion, is worthy of considerably more theoretical and empirical consideration than has been given it so far.

Readers of books in this field are generally interested in the viewpoint of the writer, particularly on the subject of public versus private ownership of the utilities industries. The philosophy underlying this book is delineated in Chapter 1 and embraces a belief in continuous disciplined competition between public and private ownership although not necessarily of the "birch rod" type. Some may disagree with the views expressed; in any event a springboard is provided for further discussion. Views are summarized and the threads of the discussion are brought together in the last chapter on pages 674-680.

The author wishes to express his thanks to several men in the field of regulation who have painstakingly read various parts of the manuscript or have lent invaluable assistance in other ways. Included among these are Charles W. Smith, Melwood W. Van Scoyoc, and Walter H. Beidatsch of the Federal Power Commission; D. B. Emmert of the Securities and Exchange Commission; George O. Gillingham of the Federal Communications Commission; Allyn A. Walters of the Rural Electrification Administration; V. A. McElfresh of the District of Columbia Commission; and Frank Harper, Paul L. Holland, and John C. Masson of the Maryland Commission. Professors D. F. Pegrum and James K. Hall as well as Professor Lionel W. Thatcher, the writer's colleague in the field at the University of Maryland, have also read and criticized various sections. The views of these men (or of the agencies with which they are connected) are not necessarily the same as those expressed in this book, but their criticisms were invariably helpful and constructive. Emerson P. Schmidt, formerly of the University of Minnesota and now with the United States Chamber of Commerce, gave the writer great help in the early stages of writing and indeed started the writer on the project. Thanks must also be expressed to Miss Edna Akers, librarian of the Federal Power Commission, and her staff, and to the long-suffering librarians of the University of Maryland who by their kindness and aid have helped me immensely.

Numerous publishers have graciously permitted the use of copyrighted material. Thanks are particularly due to Public Utilities Reports, Inc., publishers of *Public Utilities Fortnightly;* to the *Southern Economic Journal* for permission to use parts of the writer's article "The Critical Issue of Depreciation in Public Utility Valuation," and to Houghton Mifflin Company for permission to use considerable statistical material from *The Fair Rate Of Return in Public Utility Regulation* by Nelson Lee Smith.

A special debt of gratitude must be acknowledged to the writer's former teachers and associates at the University of Wisconsin and the Wisconsin Public Service Commission. Professor William H. Kiekhofer has given encouragement and spent much time going over the manuscript. Little in this book pertaining to regulation would have been as it is had it not been for the friendly help of various past and present members of the staff of the Wisconsin Commission. To them must go my thanks for many hours of their time. The writer must particularly acknowledge his debt to Professor M. G. Glaeser. Few writers in the field of public utilities can escape the direct or indirect impact of his *"Outlines."* In the case of the author this is especially true, since he had the privilege of studying under Professor Glaeser for several years. However views may differ, if they differ at all, certainly the viewpoint is the same as that which Professor Glaeser, Professor Commons, and others have so aptly summed up as the "Wisconsin Idea"—a belief in the blending of education with government and of pragmatic idealism with a sense of public purpose.

Finally the writer wishes to acknowledge the contribution of his wife, without whose whole-hearted coöperation and forbearance this book would not have been possible.

E.W.C.

COLLEGE PARK, MARYLAND

Contents

ECONOMICS AND PUBLIC UTILITIES

1. The Significance of Public Utility Economics

1. The Student's Interest in Public Utility Economics
2. The Institutional Approach
3. Conclusion

1. THE STUDENT'S INTEREST IN PUBLIC UTILITY ECONOMICS

Public utility economics appeared as a specialized field of study as early as 1907, when Professor Commons taught a class in the subject at the University of Wisconsin. Public utility issues were of great significance at that time. Although the significance of public utility problems has not declined, it is sometimes thought that the field is a specialized one, of interest only to those students who hope for employment in the utility industries or to those students who have already set their lifetime goals in the higher reaches of the professions of law, accounting or public service. This belief is not necessarily true. Even if the transportation, electric, telephone, gas, water, and urban transit industries were not giant industries and important in themselves, the study of public utility economics would be of great significance. For if after studying the various aspects of the public utility industries one extends one's vision ever so slightly, broader vistas come into view which taken together constitute much of the ground of all economic, political, and business activity.

The Lesson of the Public Utility Concept. Few if any problems facing civilization today transcend the problem of reconciling the rights of man with the rights of the state. At one of two polar extremes we find the dictatorial governments which exalt the state at the expense of the individual and at the other our own system of democratic capitalism dedicated to the principle of individual liberty. But even in a democracy we cannot exalt the individual without limit. Somewhere the line must be drawn between the rights of the individual and the rights of the collective group. The line is a shifting one that runs an uneven course across our economic terrain. It is drawn and plotted by the Supreme Court, which in recent years has given more and more of its attention to those conflicts in which the economic interests of individuals are set against those of the state. These conflicts are epitomized by the development of the public utility concept in the theory of our government. Here we find fashioned the law

1

by which public authority steps in and limits individual rights and creates individual duties.

The Administrative Commission. However widely opinions may differ as to how much government control of economic activity is necessary, there is agreement that some control is essential. If we admit the necessity we are immediately brought face to face with another problem, the problem of devising the proper instruments of control. As most students know, our government consists of three branches: legislative, executive, and judicial. Experience has proven that none of these branches in its traditional form is equipped to regulate the complex mechanism of our modern economy. To meet the situation we have developed what is virtually a fourth branch of government—the administrative commission.

Since the early 1930's businessmen have become sharply aware of the fact that this new branch of government has acquired control over the most intimate details of their business activities. In their dealings with the National Labor Relations Board businessmen are learning the rudimentary elements of administrative processes. Tax, social security, workmen's compensation, banking, insurance, labor, and other commissions make businessmen acutely conscious that they are not living in a world that is completely free. This somewhat unpleasant form of knowledge was gained long ago by the railroad and utility companies when the first great administrative commission, the Interstate Commerce Commission, was set up in 1887. Today's businessmen must likewise learn something about this new form of government which so forcibly influences their day by day activities. They will probably learn that the actions of these boards and commissions are not wholly arbitrary and uncontrolled, but rather are subject to a new type of law—administrative law—which is possibly the fastest growing of all law fields. Our study of public utilities should give us some insight into government by commission and of the law which controls it.

Franchises. We learn some more about the nature of our government in the study of public utility franchises. A franchise is a special permit, generally granted by a local government unit, permitting a public utility to operate. Two important problems run through our study of these permits. One lies close to the problem already mentioned, that of balancing individual against public rights. The police power of the state, from which the regulatory power is derived, is inalienable even by express contract. But a franchise is a contract between the state and private parties in which certain rights are granted by the state. Is a state surrendering its power when it grants certain rights to a private corporation by franchise? From a different angle we see the contrast between the contractual rights of individuals, as protected by the Federal Constitution, and the sovereign power of the state.

A second problem inherent in franchise regulation is the problem of centralized or state government versus decentralized or local government. Franchise regulation epitomizes this problem.

Public Utility Finance. The public utility industries, more than any other important industry, use large amounts of capital. It is commonly said that a utility company must make a capital commitment of five dollars to produce an annual revenue of one dollar, while a typical manufacturing industry may produce the same amount of annual revenue from an investment of considerably less than a dollar. The utility industries do a tremendous volume of business; their capital investment is more than proportionately large. It is not surprising then that public utility finance and the regulation of security issues and corporate relations constitute an important segment of the field of corporation finance. Over a long period of years public utility financing has averaged over 40 per cent of all corporate financing. If railway financing were included the percentage would be much higher.

Established principles of public utility finance and security regulation have been incorporated into the general body of financial principles and practices. The study of public utility finance is nothing less than an exceedingly important case study in the field of corporation finance.

Public Finance. When we turn to public utility taxation we must necessarily scan a considerable portion of the field of public finance. The public utility and railroad industries have long been the chief sources of state and local revenues from the property tax; the same industries have contributed a disproportionately large share of their gross revenues in the form of income and excess profits taxes. Indeed the tax collecting capacity of these industries serves to limit the movement towards public ownership.

Public Utility Economics and the Business Student. Students of business must of necessity be interested in problems of management for their own sake; economists find management policies the materials with which they work. Public utility economics touches upon some of the sensitive spots in the science of management. Accountants are much concerned with the theory and practice of property valuation and depreciation. These two matters are among the most complex and controversial in the whole field of accounting. Control of expenses, exemplified here in our study of public utility operating expenses, is almost the gist of business management. The businessman and the business student must take more than a passing interest in the problems of finance, of taxation, of government regulation, of pricing theory, and of other matters touched upon in our study of the public utility industries.

Economic Theory Applied to Public Utilities. In few fields are we able to apply some of the newer principles of economics so aptly as in the field of public utility economics. Utility rate making is an excellent example of the application of the theoretical tools of monopolistic (or imperfect) competition developed by Chamberlin and Joan Robinson. The study of discriminatory pricing even carries us somewhat beyond the main body of their theory. Nowhere are the theories of the late Lord Keynes more pointedly applied than in the utilization of government power projects such as the TVA as new outlets for idle capital resources. The problem of the fair rate of return lies at the heart of our capitalistic system as does the problem of public versus private ownership. Further light is thrown upon the economic problem of balancing savings with investment by our study of utility financing policies.

The Public Utility Industries and Our National Economy. Our study of the public utility industries will show that their development has been integrated into the development of our nation in many complex ways. Much of the theory and practice of government has been shaped by the problems of our public utility industries. The constitutional theory of private versus public economic rights has been hammered out in the development of the public utility concept. The challenge to the constitutional right of free speech appears in our study of the broadcasting industry, an industry which is approaching public utility status. We see new principles of constitutional law and the whole new body of administrative law emerging in the efforts of legal scholars and jurists to formulate rules by which individual rights may be reconciled with governmental necessities.

In still other ways public utility economics touches the political pattern of our nation. The administrative commission, exemplified here by the public utility commission, is emerging as virtually a fourth branch of government. Gigantic electric power projects push the government further and further into public ownership and alter the frontiers of private enterprise. Spanning entire groups of states, these projects tend to create a new geographic unit of government activity, the region. They also create new and previously unheard of spheres of government spending to ameliorate the cyclical fluctuations in business activity.

The perennial problem of monopolistic combinations in our economic society also finds expression here in the problem of the public utility holding company. The much less publicized but conceivably more important problem of conservation of natural resources comes in for some attention in our study of the regional projects and in the study of the regulation of natural gas.

2. THE INSTITUTIONAL APPROACH

1. The Nature of Institutions

Throughout this book an attempt will be made to emphasize the institutional aspects of our problems. There has been controversy and much misunderstanding surrounding the term "institutional." Economic science, if it can be called such, has produced a group of theorists who style themselves institutionalists. The institutional approach to economics primarily constitutes a revolt against orthodox theoretical economics which takes an atomistic approach to economic activity—an approach which views economic activity primarily as the sum total of activities of countless individuals motivated individually and more or less mechanically by the desire for individual monetary gain. With the cultural background and the objectives and assumptions stated and limited, and the means taken for granted, economics thus becomes an almost mathematical science, by which a given result follows automatically from given causes.

In contrast the institutionalists are more interested in patterns of collective action. These patterns are not to be deduced a priori for they depend upon the existing economic and cultural pattern of any particular society. To explain this pattern resort must first be made to history, psychology, philosophy, political science, sociology, and anthropology. Thus we cannot expect the same type of economy to evolve in China as might evolve in the United States, precisely because the present economies (and social cultures) are different. We then must turn to the humanistic forces, the institutions, which shape our economy.

For our purposes, institutions are those humanistic means by which economic forces are made effective. These means fall roughly into five categories:

1. Collective organizations such as labor unions, political parties, corporations, government bureaus, public utility commissions, etc.

2. Patterns of thought or modes of thinking; strong and prevailing beliefs, accepted more or less without question.

3. Codes of working rules through which society or a collective group achieves a certain stability. Working rules may include such formal bodies of law as constitutional or statutory law, rules and regulations for the guidance of a corporation's employees, or even informal methods of procedure accepted by custom.

4. Knowledge or "know-how"—the accumulated knowledge and experience of any individual or group or of society as a whole.

5. Human beings themselves—the human factor in any plan of organized action.

These and perhaps other institutions, taken collectively, constitute the cultural terrain of economic activity.

Our study of public utility economics is particularly adapted to throw light upon the institutional aspects of society. Here we find a group of industries which have been set apart from those other industries which more or less freely work out their destinies according to the laws of competition. In contrast, the utility industries operate within a controlled framework of law (working rules), shaped by prevailing public opinion and knowledge (patterns of thought and knowledge), and administered by a regulatory commission (a collective organization). We find great men, lawyers, jurists, administrators, engineers, managers, teachers, politicians, promoters, and others, who have left their distinguishable marks upon the form and shape of the industries and upon the whole of society. We cannot neglect pure economic theory in our study of any industry or society, but the institutional point of view must be appreciated to attain a realistic understanding of the nature of human activity.

2. Collective Organizations

Any group of people acting as a group is an institution. Collective groups may influence economic activity in ways not encompassed by the principles of pure economic theory. A powerful and monopolistic labor union may modify the distribution of wealth. Its activities may also have to be explained in other terms—in the ambitions of its leaders, in a drive for political power, or in its internal politics. The modern corporation produces a much different form of society from that which we might be led to deduce from the principles of individual enterprise alone. Public utility commissions and other regulatory and administrative bodies are specifically designed to modify the working of economic forces to accord with some concept of public policy.

3. Patterns of Thought

The institutional approach does not take patterns of thought for granted, although certain patterns must be assumed. Thus a pattern of belief in the profit motive is the implied assumption of all theories of capitalism, of democracy, and of orthodox theoretical economics. But the profit motive has by no means a universally uniform appeal. Men may be motivated by the desire for honor, for prestige, for public service and for other reasons. Few if any of a nation's great leaders are motivated by a desire for monetary profit. Thus to a great extent our economics depends upon our assumptions regarding human motives. A widely held belief among great masses of people that security is more important than monetary gain or freedom would materially change the whole nature of economic activity. A growing belief in the rights of posterity would fundamentally alter our utilization of natural resources. Codes of morals and ethics, trust or distrust in our fellow men, including politicians, are the principles by which we live. A shift in our beliefs, a different set of beliefs, would produce different economics.

4. Knowledge or "Know-How"

Economic theory in its pure form involves the assumption of perfect knowledge. It is generally assumed in economic analysis that businessmen are familiar with the most efficient means of production, that workers are familiar with the labor market and will move to those areas or trade where their services are most in demand. Such assumptions are necessary if we are to devise a general theory of economic activity. But, as everyone knows, our knowledge is extremely imperfect and limited rather than perfect and absolute.

Our study of any field of economic activity must give proper consideration to existing states of knowledge. The businessman who knows the value of experience considers this factor all important and commonly speaks of it as the "know-how." It has been said that America's marvelous production record in World War II was not the result of assembly line techniques as much as it was a factor of accumulated production experience or "know-how." We find examples of its significance in the study of the public utility industries. The pattern of the electric utility industry was shaped in large part by the lack of knowledge on the part of the early operators of electric plants. The scarcity of managerial talent and the lack of reliable knowledge about the potential demand for electricity were among the greatest problems the TVA had to solve at the time of its organization. As time went on an efficient working staff was developed and experience was accumulated to add to society's store.

Knowledge, or lack of knowledge, is an important modifying factor in the operation of the pricing mechanism of our society. When two businessmen negotiate a contract or when labor and management bargain over wages, the bargaining parties may arrive at any one of innumerable possible prices. Price is fixed by bargaining power and skill. Bargaining skill depends in part upon each bargainer's knowledge of the alternatives open to the other. Eventually and ruefully the bargainer with the least knowledge will be forced to admit that he made a bad bargain. The utility industries, like all other industries, furnish us with examples of the importance of knowledge in determining economic activity.

5. Codes of Working Rules

In broadest outline, codes of working rules are formal or informal, written or unwritten, bodies of rules of procedure. Codes of working rules appear in many places and are of many kinds. Our constitutional law provides the framework of our government; the law of contracts provides the framework of business. A corporation provides printed regulations for the guidance of its employees. We have unwritten but accepted routines in matters as widely divergent as business practice, political advancement, military sciences—or home economics. Without generally accepted methods and procedures efficiency is impossible. Businessmen find the uncertainty of law much more vexing than its harshness and severity. Man works most effectively when he knows with certainty the manner of procedure of all other men whose activities are related to his own. Individual and group action is also most efficient when it conforms to a pattern, a system, or a code of working rules. Working rules grow from experience and in many instances have nothing more than age to justify their existence. But wise or unwise, they give society or a community or an organization an element of order and stability.

6. The Human Element

Finally we have man himself, the greatest of all institutions. Thus economic activity cannot be plotted accurately without consideration of the human element. An able man succeeds in attaining his objectives, an ineffective man fails. An able man may owe his peculiar abilities to heredity or to environment. Insofar as they are due to the latter they are subject to social control. Great achievements are lengthened shadows of great men; a truism that expresses the concept of man as an institution through which economic, social, or political objectives are achieved. No study of any branch of human activity is complete without a study of its leaders. In this book we will give some consideration to these personalities.

7. Institutional Inertia

The institutional approach recognizes a certain stability and resistance to change in all patterns of human activity. The sheer mass of a collective organization may give it permanency and a certain moment of inertia. Institutions, however, are not dead and frozen. Collective organizations grow or decline as a result of pressures from other institutions or in response to pressures generated within. When we study the public utility commissions, or government bureaus, as institutions, we shall note that they have achieved a degree of permanency. The vested interests of members and employees, their accumulated knowledge and prestige, the desire of the public to have stabilized channels of action—these and many other factors tend to preserve them as going concerns. On the other hand, the growth of public ownership may reduce the significance of the public utility commission and eventually eliminate it from among our institutions. Or the desire for power and prestige on the part of commission members may cause the commission to seek constantly for new ways of enhancing its activities.

Similarly customs and laws may exist long after their reasons for being have passed. In law this is recognized by the rule of *stare decisis* under which courts will adhere to established precedents. Customs, beliefs, working rules, bodies of knowledge, standards of conduct are handed down from generation to generation. Human "know-how" is limited and shaped by experience of the past.

In certain branches of economics institutions are taken for granted. Institutional economics, on the other hand, specifically assumes that our collective organizations and all our other institutions are products of their time and history. They evolve and expand or contract and die from the impact of still other institutions. Thus the institutional economist must draw heavily upon all the other social sciences.

The "Holistic" Approach. No institution can be understood by itself; it must be explained in the light of the other forces which impinge upon it. Thus, the public utility commission to which we give considerable space in this book is the product of political pressures, of laws, of modes of thinking, of statesmanlike leadership. In the words of Professor Gruchy the institutional approach is essentially "holistic" and involves the study of the whole.[1] As a commission is shaped externally by the whole of many forces it is shaped internally by numerous forces which interact upon each other to produce the whole. Like any other institution it is not so much the sum of its parts as it is the product of its parts. Thus given a model law, effective organization, and adequate finances, a regulatory commission might become a complete nullity because of poor administrative leadership.

Cumulative Cause and Effect. Assuming that our problem is the explanation of economic activity, it is to be noted that an institutional approach might lead us to diametrically opposite conclusions from those resulting from analysis in terms of economic theory alone. Our belief, for example, in a free capitalistic economic system is based primarily upon a belief in certain equilibratory economic, social, and political forces by which maladjustments in our society are automatically righted. Inequalities in wages eventually wash out, undesirable conditions automatically set up forces for their remedy, and so on. A study of history shows many examples of cumulative disequilibrium. Institutional adjustments and maladjustments may be self-perpetuating. Ignorance breeds ignorance, low wages create low wages, economic inferiority in the market place tends to increase. Vested interests are created and the resistance to change accumulates. The older the institutions, the more warped may become our society in its attempt to accommodate itself to them. Thus the law of capture, applied a century ago in a more or less offhand manner

---

[1] See A. G. Gruchy, *Modern Economic Thought* (New York, Prentice-Hall, Inc., 1947). The term *holistic* was coined by the South African scholar and statesman, Jan Christian Smuts. The concept also owes much to the Gestalt psychologists.

by the courts to the ownership of underground oil deposits, has given a most unrealistic and anti-social shape to our whole petroleum industry. Private enterprise and socialism create their own mores and customs which serve to make each self-perpetuating in its initial field. To the principle of equilibrating forces we must set opposite the principle of cumulative cause and effect or cumulative disequilibrium.

3. CONCLUSION

Our study will turn around the many institutions which have shaped the history and nature of the utilities industries. We will seek no categorical answers but rather a method of approach to whatever conditions the facts might reveal. Thus we will give no unequivocal answer to the question of the relative merits of public and private ownership, however the advantages might lie with one or the other in specific instances. Rather we will accept each institution as a continuous challenge to the other.

Inherent in this approach is the belief in competition defined in broad terms. The position is taken that the most desirable form of competition is not that competition which results in the survival of the fittest—which may only mean the survival of the best fitted to survive or the emergence of monopoly. Rather it means continuous competition, a continuous challenging of all institutions, and perhaps the preservation of some of them by protective action. In such industries as the public utilities, characterized as they are by both private and public monopolies, special measures may have to be taken to achieve the objectives of competition. These objectives may be attained in part by a system in which public and private ownership co-exist as challenges to each other.

Furthermore, state regulation may be challenged by public ownership —or by Federal regulation. Only in rare instances is society justified in placing its faith in a single method of procedure. No institution should be abandoned entirely unless the superiority of those that remain is overwhelming. By such a system of constant testing and trying each belief, each method, each organization is compared and evaluated. Since competition is inherently unstable, the maintenance of such a system might well require safeguards and controls. Thus our objective becomes not free competition in some absolute sense, but rather controlled or disciplined competition.

We shall also attempt to gain a certain sense of hard-headed realism that will accept none of social instruments or procedures as perfect and also a sense of social craftsmanship that will aid us somewhat more in modifying old institutions than in designing new ones. But whether the institutions are old or new they will be gradually shaped to the new circumstances and conditions of our evolving society. By this means our society can be kept agoing with the least social loss from the frictions of change.

With this background in mind we will now turn to the study of the public utility industries, their regulation, and their position in our national economy. Possibly after the reader has followed this book to the end a rereading of this first chapter might be desirable. Conceivably it might consolidate his thinking. Certainly he will find the chapter clearer than now.

2. The Public Utility Concept

1. The Definition of a Public Utility
2. The Development of the Concept by the Supreme Court
3. The Tests of Public Utility Status
4. Public Utility Status, A Summary
5. The Lesson of the Public Utility Concept

1. THE DEFINITION OF A PUBLIC UTILITY

In a single volume of *Public Utilities Fortnightly,* a journal devoted to public utilities and public utility law, one finds reports of the following, among other, proceedings:

1. The Wisconsin Public Service Commission ordered The Milwaukee Electric Railway & Transport Company, a street-railway company holding an exclusive franchise in the city of Wauwautosa, Wisconsin, to continue to maintain an unprofitable bus service on North Avenue in that city.[1]

2. The Michigan Public Service Commission ordered the Home Telephone Company of Grass Lake to supply 4-party line service rather than multi-party line service to certain of its customers.[2]

3. The Pennsylvania Public Utility Commission denied permission to the Philadelphia Transportation Company to increase street railway rates.[3]

4. The New York Public Service Commission refused to approve a proposed rate schedule of the Brooklyn Union Gas Company offering gas service only to those then using another source of heat.[4]

5. The Wisconsin Public Service Commission, over the protests of certain fuel dealers and railroad employees, considered an application of the Wisconsin Southern Gas Company for a certificate of convenience and necessity to construct a pipe line in that state.[5]

One of these industries was required to extend service to certain customers over its objections. A second was required to give better service than it was then rendering. A third was required to charge particular rates. A fourth was required to refrain from discriminating between customer groups. Another was required to obtain permission to construct facilities to enter a new type of business. Certainly these acts by government agencies seem to do violence to the traditional American concepts

---

[1] *Wauwautosa* v. *The Milwaukee Elec. Ry. & Tr. Co.,* 45 P.U.R. (N.S.) 63 (1942).
[2] *Re Home Telephone Co.,* 45 P.U.R. (N.S.) 107 (1942).
[3] *Pennsylvania Public Utility Commission* v. *Philadelphia Transportation Co.,* 45 P.U.R. (N.S.) 257 (1942).
[4] *Re Brooklyn Union Gas Co.,* 45 P.U.R. (N.S.) 54 (1942).
[5] *Re Wisconsin Southern Gas Co.,* 45 P.U.R. (N.S.) 11 (1942).

of freedom of enterprise. But almost any layman would immediately perceive that these industries are among those commonly considered to be public utilities and would view these actions as not in the least strange and unusual. He would note the four duties common to public utility industries: (1) the duty to serve all comers, (2) the duty to render adequate service, (3) the duty to serve at reasonable rates, and (4) the duty to serve without unjust discrimination. He would also note that the right of entry into the industry and extension of facilities is controlled by public authority by means of a franchise or certificate of convenience and necessity. In the exercise of this right a public utility, like the government itself, has the right of *eminent domain,* that is, the right to take private property with compensation for a purpose deemed to be in the public interest. It also has the right to adequate compensation.

By these rights and duties public utilities are commonly distinguished. These rights and duties are impressed upon them by the state and cannot be acquired or bargained away by contract. They pertain to the industry's status as a public utility. But why should these industries be singled out for such treatment? In short, how is a public utility to be defined?

Many writers have attempted to define a public utility and none perhaps has succeeded to the satisfaction of anyone save himself. It is doubtful that the attempt is worth its while. The reach of the public utility concept may be perceived by the industries it embraces. An important group closely related to urbanization and the subject of most of this text's attention includes the water, gas, electricity, street railway, telegraph, and telephone industries. Another large and old group includes the great transportation industries—rail, motor, air, water and pipe-line carriers. Other industries providing various essential services are given public utility status and made subject to varying degrees and kinds of regulation. These include such businesses as bridges, ferries, wharves and docks, commodity exchanges, grain elevators, stockyards, cotton gins, taxicabs. Another group includes a miscellaneous class of callings that an older and less complex society saw fit to regulate—innkeepers, bakers, grist mills, pawnbrokers, and peddlers. Many of these businesses still remain subject to regulation. Finally there is a large group of industries which in recent years have been made more and more subject to regulation and which, if they have not been given public utility status in all respects, have been treated in somewhat the same way. This group includes such businesses as banking, insurance, housing, coal, and the distribution and processing of milk and other agricultural products.

Some industries may seek regulation and public utility status to escape the rigors of a competitive life. Other industries may prefer the profits of the open market and may be more or less forcibly placed in the public utility category at the discretion of the legislature and with the approval of the courts. The history of price fixing is old. Emperor Diocletian unsuccessfully attempted to fix prices in ancient Rome. This example is used indifferently as proof that price fixing is a natural right of the state and that price fixing must inevitably fall before economic law. During the reign of Charles the First "Bread and Beer Assizes" were held throughout England. Judicial tribunals fixed the prices of these staple commodities for the ensuing year.

The price-fixing regulation of private enterprises such as public utilities involves the invasion of property rights. Legally the problem is one of reconciling the police power of the states or the constitutional powers of the Federal Government with the constitutional protection accorded to individuals by the 14th and 5th Amendments. The 14th Amendment provides that no state shall "deprive any person of life, liberty, or property, without due process of law." A corporation is considered to be a person within the protection of this provision. The 5th Amendment contains a similar restriction upon the Federal Government. Grave considerations of public policy and private rights are thus set against each other.

2. THE DEVELOPMENT OF THE CONCEPT BY THE SUPREME COURT

Munn v. Illinois (1877).[6] The modern history of the public utility concept properly begins with the case of *Munn* v. *Illinois,* decided by the United States Supreme Court in 1877. It has been called one of the twelve most important cases in our constitutional history. It established the foundations of modern public utility regulation and traced roots for the concept that run deep in the past.

The case was an outgrowth of the Granger movement of the 1870's which, in turn, sprang from a secret and fraternal farm organization founded for social and intellectual objectives in 1867. During the farm depression of the 1870's, it became a political organization and an instrument in the agricultural uprising against the new industrialism that was appearing in America. The movement was strong in the southern and middle western states and sought, among other things, the reduction of railroad and warehouse rates which rested grievously upon the farmers.

Pursuant to a new constitution, the legislature of Illinois passed a law in 1871 licensing warehouses and elevators and prescribing maximum rates for them. Munn & Scott, proprietors of a Chicago elevator, refused to take out a license and continued in business as before, charging rates above those prescribed by statute. Action was brought against them and the case reached the United States Supreme Court.

It requires but little perspicacity to grasp the limitations on the eco-

6 *Munn* v. *Illinois,* 94 U.S. 113 (1877).

nomic bargaining power of the many distant shippers of grain confronted as they were by these elevators lined up on the Chicago waterfront and funnelling through them all the grain of the Dakotas and the mid-west to the seaboard and to Europe. It is to be believed that Chief Justice Waite thought the legislation wise and desirable. But could the state of Illinois thus invade private property rights? The Chief Justice gave the answer:

> When one becomes a member of society, he necessarily parts with some rights or privileges which, as an individual not affected by his relations to others, he might retain.... This does not confer power upon the whole people to control rights which are purely and exclusively private; but it does authorize the establishment of laws requiring each citizen to so conduct himself, and so use his own property, as not unnecessarily to injure another.... From this source come the police powers.... Under these powers the government regulates the conduct of its citizens one towards another, and the manner in which each shall use his own property, when such regulation becomes necessary for the public good.[7]

Although Congress as early as 1820 had given the city of Washington the power to regulate the rates of wharfage at private wharfs and the sweeping of chimneys, there was admittedly no precedent for a statute exactly like this one. The Court's necessity was to rationalize this legislation and establish a chain of legal continuity with the past. The majority of the Court found their legal precedents in the words of Lord Chief Justice Hale of England in an almost forgotten work, *De Portibus Maris*, written more than two centuries earlier.

> A man, for his own private advantage, may, in a port or town, set a wharf or a crane, and may take what rates he and his customers can agree for cranage, wharfage, housellage, pesage; for he doth no more than is lawful for any man to do, viz., makes the most of his own.... If the king or subject have a public wharf, unto which all persons that come to that port must come and unlade or lade their goods as for the purpose, because they are the wharfs only licensed by the queen ... or because there is no other wharf in that port, ... in that case there cannot be taken arbitrary and excessive duties ... neither can they be enhanced to an immoderate rate; but the duties must be reasonable and moderate, though settled by the king's license or charter. For now the wharf and crane and other conveniences are affected with a public interest, and they cease to be *juris privati* only; ...[8]

Chief Justice Waite pointed out in this early case that the doctrine that property affected with the public interest ceased to be *juris privati* only had become an essential element in the law of property. Thus when a person submits his property to a use in which the public has an interest, he submits to public control to the extent of that interest. He may with-

[7] *Ibid.*, 124, 125.
[8] *Ibid.*, 127.

draw his property from use, but as long as he maintains the use, he must submit to control.

There were those who dissented on the court. Justice Field could not see that a private building had become a public warehouse: "There is no magic in language, though used by a constitutional convention, which can change a private business into a public one." Nor could he see that the police power extended in any manner to the compensation for the use of property. He thought the right to regulate compensation existed "only where some right or privilege is conferred by the government or municipality upon the owner." [9]

Justice Field was not alone in his opposition to the Court majority. The august New York Times called the doctrine of *Munn* v. *Illinois* "mischievous," "meddlesome," and "vexatious." Many denied the propriety of utilizing a concept taken from the time when "paternalism was in flower." When the *Budd* case, involving a somewhat similar act regulating elevator rates, came before the Court, Justice Brewer said, "The paternal theory of government is to me odious. The utmost possible liberty to the individual, and the fullest possible protection to him and his property, is both the limitation and duty of the government." [10] Justice Brewer was very much afraid that the public was interested in every kind of business. He gave reluctant approval to the doctrine of *Munn* v. *Illinois* but deplored its extension.

The German Alliance Insurance Co. Case (1914). [11] If the concept of "businesses affected with a public interest" gained in content, it lost in tangibility when the Supreme Court upheld the regulation of fire insurance rates in Kansas in the *German Alliance Insurance Co.* case. Here there was little, if any, material property committed to the public use as there was in *Munn* v. *Illinois*. A dissenting judge, Justice Lamar, thought this to be significant. However, the majority of the Court looked to the nature of the business. Fire insurance was necessary to business activity and enterprise. The cost was significant and the purchaser was at a bargaining disadvantage in dealing with large companies whose rates were fixed by agreements among themselves. Nor was it held to be significant that the public did not have the right to demand and receive service.

Wolff Packing Co. v. Kansas Court of Industrial Relations (1923). [12] Here the Court blocked an ambitious attempt to extend the concept of "businesses affected with a public interest" into the far reaches of the economic system. The Kansas legislature declared a large number of

9 *Ibid.*, 146.
10 *Budd* v. *New York*, 143 U.S. 517, 551 (1892).
11 *German Alliance Insurance Co.* v. *Kansas*, 233 U.S. 389 (1914).
12 *Wolff Packing Co.* v. *Court of Industrial Relations of Kansas*, 262 U.S. 522 (1923).

industries, including those of the manufacturing and preparing of food, the production of fuel, transportation, and public utilities, to be affected with a public interest. A Court of Industrial Relations, set up to fix wages and conditions of employment, ordered the Wolff Packing Company to give its employees a substantial increase in wages, although the company was operating unprofitably.

Chief Justice Taft set forth three categories of business affected with a public interest:

(1) Those which were carried on under a public grant implying a duty of rendering service such as railroads, common carriers and public utilities.

(2) Those which had been regulated since the earliest of times, such as innkeepers.

(3) Those which were not public at their inception but had become so in the passage of time.

The Court could not find that the Wolff company fell within any of these classes. The contention that the public had an interest in securing the continuity of these businesses and that wage regulation was necessary to their continuance was swept aside. Apparently there was a difference between a business in which the public had an interest and one affected with a public interest. The legislature could only compel continuity where the obligations of the employer and employees were direct and were assumed when the business was entered. Here there was no obligation on the part of the employees to continue work.

It is interesting to note that Chief Justice Taft recognized the expanding nature of the category of regulated industries by setting up the third classification. It is also noteworthy that legislation similar to that of Kansas has today met with fullest judicial approval.

Tyson & Bro. v. Banton (1927).[13] Here Justice Sutherland, speaking for the majority of the Court, refused to extend the category of "businesses affected with a public interest" to include the theater ticket brokerage business. The state of New York had licensed theater ticket brokers and fixed the resale price of theater tickets. A powerful organization had come to control the sale of all desirable theater seats so that it was impossible to obtain them except at resale and at high prices. The practice was subject to condemnation that was universal among all save the theaters and the brokers. All the lower courts upheld the statute. But still the majority of the Supreme Court could not see that the business was affected with the public interest or was in any sense a public utility. A license was distinguished from a franchise in that the former did not place the proprietor under any duty to furnish entertainment or to serve all who applied. The development of the public utility concept owes

[13] *Tyson. . . . v. Banton,* 273 U.S. 418 (1927).

more to the minority justices who sought to strike away such vague phrases as "affected with the public interest" and base the power to regulate prices upon the existence of bargaining disadvantages of the purchasers.

Ribnik v. McBride (1928).[14] Having laid down the line in the theater-ticket brokerage case, Justice Sutherland determined to hew to it however monstrous the result. The state of New Jersey had refused to grant a license to Ribnik to conduct an employment agency on the grounds that the proposed fees were too high. That the state had the power to license and regulate the business the learned justice did not doubt. Nor did he doubt that the public might conceivably be more interested in this business than in the theater-ticket brokerage business. Extortion, fraud, imposition, discrimination, and the like had been practised with cruel effect upon workmen without jobs. This was magnanimously conceded. Nevertheless, these were grounds for regulation, but not for price fixing. The business did not differ in substantial character from that of real estate broker or ticket broker.

Here again the real contribution to public utility law came from Justice Stone, speaking for a dissenting minority that included Justices Holmes and Brandeis. Justice Stone was concerned with the extortionate fees commonly charged by these brokers, the many malpractices, the inferior bargaining power of the worker, and the larger interest of the state in seeing that its workers find employment without being imposed upon. Thirteen years later the same issue was again squarely presented in *Olsen* v. *Nebraska*,[15] and *Ribnik* v. *McBride* was reversed.

Williams v. Standard Oil Co. (1928).[16] This case was another of Justice Sutherland's decisions. Tennessee had declared the business of selling gasoline to be "affected with a public interest" and had provided for the regulation of its price. Gasoline was considered to be only an ordinary commodity of competitive trade. An important principle was laid down in the declaration that a business does not become affected with a public interest "merely because it is large or because the public are warranted in having a feeling of concern in respect of its maintenance."

New State Ice Company v. Liebmann (1932).[17] Here the ice business was held to be a private one. It constituted the last of a quartet of decisions by Justice Sutherland, who by this time was becoming quite an authority on businesses that were not affected with a public interest. The Oklahoma legislature had declared the ice business to be a public

[14] *Ribnik* v. *McBride,* 277 U.S. 350 (1928).
[15] *Olsen* v. *Nebraska,* 313 U.S. 236 (1941).
[16] *Williams* v. *Standard Oil Co.,* 278 U.S. 235 (1928).
[17] *New State Ice Co.* v. *Liebmann,* 285 U.S. 262 (1932).

one and had set up licensing requirements as conditions of entry. The New State Ice Company brought suit to restrain Liebmann from erecting an ice plant without a license. The Court sustained the contention of Liebmann that the legislation deprived him of property without due process of law.

The Court could only see the ice business as a private one. It could find no elements of necessity or monopoly. On the contrary, it was noted that the effect of the statute was to create artificial monopoly conditions.

Again the minority contributed more to the development of constitutional law. In a masterly dissenting opinion, Justice Brandeis pointed out that the state of Oklahoma had not acted without reason, that obvious evils could and did exist in the distribution of ice, that the product was a necessity, that it was distributed under conditions that tended towards monopoly, and that therefore the Court should grant every presumption of validity to legislation that was primarily a matter for the determination of the state. This case is typical of the repressive force of the Courts upon the upsurgent liberalism that finally broke its bonds under the leadership of President Roosevelt.

Nebbia v. New York (1934).[18] The New York legislature, declaring the milk business to be one affecting the public health and interest, enacted a Milk Law and set up a Milk Control Board charged with the duty of fixing minimum wholesale and retail prices of milk. With the price of milk fixed at nine cents a quart, Nebbia sold two quarts of milk and a loaf of Italian bread for 18 cents. His conviction was upheld by the United States Supreme Court who thus sustained the constitutionality of the New York act.

Material to the Court's decision in this case were the paramount importance of the industry to the state (dairying yielded one half of the total income from all farm products), the demoralization of the price structure of the industry arising from overproduction and unrestricted competition, and the peculiar relationship of the product to the health of the citizens of the state. The Court admitted that the industry was not a public utility in the accepted sense of the word but said in effect that, however that may be, there was no closed category of businesses affected with a public interest.

Thus the minority opinions in the *Tyson* and *Ribnik* cases became the majority opinion and the constitutional law of the land. Should the reasoning of the *Nebbia* case be continued in subsequent cases the governmental power of price fixing may be extended into ever-widening fields of economic activity.

Since *Nebbia* v. *New York* the Court has upheld the constitutionality of the Federal Agricultural Marketing Agreement Act of 1937, by which

[18] *Nebbia v. New York,* 291 U.S. 502 (1934).

interstate prices and activities of the milk industry were regulated.[19] Compulsory inspection of tobacco has been upheld.[20] Although these industries cannot be included within the category of public utility industries without doing violence to the common usage of the term, nevertheless the extension of regulation marks at once the expansion and the obliteration of the boundaries once presumed to exist between the free and regulated spheres of our economy.

Sunshine Anthracite Coal Co. v. Adkins (1940).[21] The vast and chaotic coal industry was virtually brought within the public utility category when the Supreme Court upheld the Bituminous Coal Act of 1937, which provided for the Federal regulation of the sale and distribution of bituminous coal by a National Bituminous Coal Commission. Under this Act coal producers could become members of a Coal Code and agree thereby to maintain certain prices. As members they were exempt from a tax of 19½ per cent on the sale price of coal which applied to non-members. The intention and effect of the Act was to penalize producers who did not maintain prices and to stabilize the industry and prevent unfair competition. The Court considered the chaotic nature of competition within the industry, the strategic significance of the industry to the whole economy and found the Act to be within the powers of Congress under the commerce and tax clauses of the Constitution.

Olsen v. Nebraska (1941).[22] In 1941 the Court was presented with almost the identical issue with which it had been faced in *Ribnik* v. *McBride* in 1928. Speaking for the Court, Justice Douglas dwelt upon the strong and continued drift away from the older case and cited the many cases in which the regulation of an ever-expanding group of industries had been upheld. But most significant of all, Justice Douglas propounded what seems to have become the new doctrine of the Court. In his words:

> We are not concerned, however, with the wisdom, need, or appropriateness of the legislation. Differences of opinion on that score suggest a choice which "should be left where . . . it was left by the Constitution . . . —to the States and to Congress." There is no necessity for the state to demonstrate before us that evils persist despite the competition which attends the bargaining in this field. In final analysis, the only constitutional prohibitions or restraints which respondents have suggested for the invalidation of this legislation are those notions of public policy embedded in earlier decisions of this Court. . . . Since they do not find expression in the Constitution, we cannot give them continuing vitality as standards by which the constitutionality of the economic and social programs of the states is to be determined.[23]

[19] *United States* v. *Rock Royal Coöperative*, 307 U.S. 533 (1939).
[20] *Currin* v. *Wallace*, 306 U.S. 1 (1939).
[21] *Sunshine Anthracite Coal Co.* v. *Adkins*, 310 U.S. 381 (1940).
[22] *Olsen* v. *Nebraska*, 313 U.S. 236 (1941).
[23] *Ibid.*, 246-247.

3. THE TESTS OF PUBLIC UTILITY STATUS

The foregoing cases present no infallible clue to the public utility status. On the contrary, it appears that some industries, once exempt from price regulation, may in the course of time become so affected with the public interest as to become public utilities. Certainly this category of businesses seems to be a growing one and the same tests when applied to different industries seem to have yielded different results. Our next step will be to review these various tests in an attempt to evaluate their significance.

First, it must be pointed out that the terms "affected with a public interest" and "public utility" have not been used with such precision that their boundaries can be clearly demarcated. The former term has the greater legal significance and is more inclusive. The latter term has entered more into common usage. Not all businesses held to be "affected with a public interest" are commonly considered public utilities. The Court in the *Nebbia* case took pains to point this out, saying, "the dairy industry is not, in the accepted sense of the phrase, a public utility," [24] after which the Court found it to be affected with "a public interest."

1. Devotion of Property to a Public Use

The idea of the devotion of property to a public use is as old as the idea of being affected with a public interest. The notion in modern times was established in the *Munn* case. Some doubt remained as to whether the interest of the public was limited to tangible property or whether it was in the business itself. This doubt was set at rest in the *German Alliance* case, although Justice Lamar dissented on the grounds that the power to regulate rates had theretofore only been exercised against a business in which tangible property had been devoted to the public use. The question is really one of whether the business was devoted to the public use.

In medieval England certain "common callings" such as those of innkeeper, ferryman, wharfinger, and carrier were said to be affected with a public interest. At common law these businesses were impressed with a threefold duty of serving all who applied, at reasonable rates, without discrimination.[25] Here is the germ of the modern public utility concept.

[24] *Op. cit.,* 291 U.S. 502, 531.

[25] One legal writer disagrees with the notion that the common callings were so designated because of their peculiar duties to serve the public. His thesis is that the term "common" was originally used to distinguish the habitual followers of a trade from those who practiced it only occasionally. All trades were more or less "common." He thinks that the assumption of the right to regulate by public authority could be traced to an earlier time, to the time of the Black Death in 1348, when all society was disorganized and as a result all labor and trade were regulated. See N. F. Arterburn, "The Origin and First Test of Public Callings," 75 *University of Pennsylvania Law*

Has the firm held itself out to serve either expressly or by implication? If it has, its classification as a public utility may follow automatically along with consequent duties of serving all at reasonable and non-discriminatory rates. In *Tyson* v. *Banton*,[26] it was significant that the entry into the theater business did not put the proprietor under any duty to furnish entertainment or to admit anyone who applied. Regulation of the business was not upheld.

In the modern era the problem frequently presents itself when the validity of rate regulation of particular firms or industries is in question. Courts and commissions are obliged to determine whether a motor carrier is a private, contract, or common carrier. A coal company which operated railway service for its own purposes was held not to be a common carrier.[27] The Court refused to consider a garage call service a public utility, since there was no obligation to sell.[28] The question frequently arises as to whether mutual telephone companies and electric coöperatives hold themselves out to serve all comers. It is sufficient to say that the legislature can make them into public utilities. If an industry is a public utility, the duty to serve naturally follows. But the question is whether there is a duty to serve that creates the status. Intent may be important, but the courts and the legislature may assign the duty beyond the volition of the firm. The pipe-line industry was converted into a common carrier by Congress and the Supreme Court, "by main strength." [29] The Illinois Supreme Court found the Associated Press to be affected with a public interest so as to require it to serve all comers.[30] The Missouri court came to the opposite conclusion.[31] Public utility status with all its duties was denied to the radio broadcasting industry.[32] The Supreme Court upheld a North Dakota law requiring elevator companies to serve all who applied.[33] A related criterion is the right of the public to demand continuous service. In the *Wolff Packing Co.* case the Court refused to include the meat packing industry in the category of public utilities and pointed out that such status exists only where:

> ...the obligation to the public of continuous service is direct, clear, and mandatory, and arises as a contractual condition, express or implied, of entering the business either as owner or worker.[34]

Review 411 (1927). This is not the notion that has been incorporated into our regulatory law.

26 *Op. cit.*, 273 U.S. 440-41.

27 *Railroad Comm.* v. *Bozeman and Park Railroad Co.*, P.U.R. 1927C, 225 (Mont.).

28 *Terminal Taxicab Co.* v. *Kutz*, 241 U.S. 252 (1916).

29 *The Pipe Line Cases*, 234 U.S. 548 (1914).

30 *Inter-Ocean Publishing Co.* v. *Associated Press*, 56 N.E. 822 (Illinois, 1889).

31 *State* v. *Associated Press*, 60 S.W. 91 (Missouri, 1900).

32 *Pulitzer Pub. Co.* v. *F.C.C.*, 94 F. (2d) 249 (1937).

33 *Brass* v. *Stoeser*, 153 U.S. 391 (1894).

34 *Op. cit.*, 262 U.S. 522, 541.

There is no reason why a shopkeeper cannot abandon his business whenever it pleases him to do so. But a railroad cannot discontinue service without express permission. On the other hand, fire insurance companies are under no obligation to continue business or to serve all who apply.[35]

Thus we can say that the continuous duty to serve all comers at reasonable rates without discrimination is a hallmark of public utility status. The duty may spring from custom or it may be impressed upon the business by the courts or the legislature if public interest so requires. Once within the public utility category, the business becomes affixed with these duties. They arise from status of a public utility, not from a contract volitionally entered into.

2. The Historical Test

If a business has been regulated in the past, there is a presumption that it continues to be subject to regulation. But we cannot confine public utility status to the inns, the cabs, and the grist mills that were regulated by Parliament and early colonial governments. The category of utility industries is an expanding one. As a first expedient the judges reasoned by analogy. Stockyards were thought to be public businesses because they were similar to warehouses.[36] A cold storage business was held to be public because it was linked to transportation, the Adam of all public utilities.[37] To borrow from a phrase of Professor Cabot, it is as if the judges had separated the sheep from the goats by constructing a historical model of a sheep to be compared with the animal before them. The test however was obviously imperfect. The common carrier concept could be extended with ease to the telegraph and pipe-line industries, but not to those of coal and milk. On the other hand, such occupations as baking, brewing, tailoring, and milling are no longer regulated as they were by the English Parliament, nor are surgeons considered public servants as they were in the eighteenth century. The warehouses whose rates were regulated by Illinois in the 1870's are not now defined as public utilities in thirty-eight states, although all states subject them to some regulation.

A calling once private may become public. Those who embarked upon a business when it was still labelled private cannot thereby escape the regulatory power of public authority. There can be no vested private interest against the public in any rule of common law. The warehouse of Munn and Scott was private antecedent to the legislation of the state of Illinois. In *Nebbia* v. *New York,* the Court swept aside the contention that it was only property voluntarily committed to public use that was

---

[35] See *German Alliance Insurance Co.* v. *Kansas,* 233 U.S. 389 (1914).
[36] *Ratcliff* v. *Wichita Union Stockyards Co.,* 86 Pac. 150 (Kansas, 1906).
[37] *Pub. Util. Comm.* v. *Monarch Ref. Co.,* 108 N.E. 716 (Ill., 1915).

subject to price regulation. "It is clear," the Court said, "that there is no closed category of businesses affected with a public interest." [38]

Thus we cannot look to history to limit the category of public utility industries. There is significant force in the legal notion emphasized by Professor Glaeser of a public utility as a fixed concept with a changing content. [39]

3. The Franchise Test

Entry into many public utility industries depends upon the possession of a franchise permitting the utility to use the streets and public property. To some extent the state controls the entry into all industries. The corporation charter, although freely granted, establishes the corporation's existence and thus, to a degree, may control entry. Licenses are necessary in many professions and occupations. The franchise represents a greater privilege and is issued less freely. Two basic lines of policy determine the issuance of franchises. First, it is believed that the industry serves a public purpose and that its private pursuit should be permitted and even encouraged. The franchise may thus carry with it unusual rights. Second, it is believed necessary to control entry into the industry. To this extent the number of franchises is restricted and those firms that do possess them have partial freedom from competition.

Justice Field, dissenting in *Munn* v. *Illinois,* expressed the view that the police power of price regulation extended only to those instances where some right or privilege was conferred upon the owner of property. [40] Justice Field's views received but little subsequent recognition and in the *Wolff* case, Chief Justice Taft included those industries operating under a grant of public authority as but one of three classes of business affected with the public interest. [41] However, in *Tyson* v. *Banton,* [42] the Court pointed out that the power to license and regulate may not extend to the control of prices.

The franchise is thus an instrument of public policy which confers a privilege upon its recipient. If the franchise is exclusive, monopoly is created and the privileges are measurably increased. Possession of a franchise or even of a license carries with it some measure of public utility status. However, the franchise is not a cause of public utility status. Rather it is an instrument of public policy towards businesses in which the public is concerned because of their economic, social, or political characteristics. It is, in short, the effect of public utility status.

38 *Op. cit.,* 291 U.S. 502, 536.
39 M. G. Glaeser, *Outlines of Public Utility Economics* (New York, The Macmillan Company, 1927), p. 179.
40 *Op. cit.,* 94 U.S. 113, 146.
41 *Op. cit.,* 262 U.S. 522, 535.
42 *Op. cit.,* 273 U.S. 418, 430.

4. Necessity, a Fundamental Test

Necessity and monopoly are almost prerequisites of public utility status. In *Munn* v. *Illinois,* the service of grain elevators was thought to be absolutely necessary to the farmers of the Northwest. Fire insurance was thought to be necessary to business activity in the *German Alliance* case. The services supplied by water, gas, electric, telephone, transportation, and other utility industries are necessities of life under modern conditions, although they might not have been in the past. On the other hand, the Court did not think very much of the necessity of the services supplied by theaters, although Justice Holmes in a dissenting opinion thought that the public might well consider them necessary to maintain the cultural standards of the community. The Court did not believe that ice was a necessity in the state of Oklahoma. The same service could be supplied by mechanical refrigeration. Competition from beyond the industry served to remove the consumer's disability even if he was dealing in a monopolistic market. Considerably less rational was the Court's failure to regard the necessary nature of the services provided by employment agencies in *Ribnik* v. *McBride*. Later this decision was overruled in *Olsen* v. *Nebraska*.

Conditions of inadequate supply may make a particular service a necessity. Thus the wartime regulation of rents in the national capital was sustained.[43] Time is another factor. The services of particular hotels may be necessities since the traveler has no time to shop for accommodations. Meat and gasoline may be necessary to our modern way of life, but here the consumer goes into the competitive market and is at no bargaining disadvantage. Hence, we may say that necessity of the service is one of the several prerequisites of public utility status.

5. The Test of Monopoly

Public concern with a business increases with monopoly. Where competition prevails, rivalry between firms "will strip profit of its excess." If there is free entry into the industry, no single firm can long enjoy unusual profits before competitors will appear. Correspondingly, the less efficient firms will be weeded out and, as if by an unseen hand, industry will be regulated to the public's benefit. So runs the argument.

In almost all of the early cases in which a business was declared to be "affected with a public interest," the conditions of monopoly were present. Grist mills and grain elevators, railroads and stockyards, all met the consumer under conditions where he had no alternatives. On the other hand, competition was still possible in the meat-packing, ice, and gasoline businesses. We may conclude without further discussion that

[43] *Block* v. *Hirsh,* 256 U.S. 135 (1921).

monopoly conditions are closely allied with public utility status. Public faith in competition died slowly. For a long time it was not perceived that many monopolies were not made so by man's avaricious nature but were inherently made in that nature by economic facts. If a railroad charged extortionate rates, the remedy was to charter another one to the injury of both. If one electric utility gave bad service, the remedy was to establish another one and allow both to go bankrupt. Finally it became apparent that competition was fundamentally unstable and monopoly inescapable. It is now our purpose to review the forces that work irresistibly to make certain industries monopolies.

Conditions of Space and Geography. Monopoly may arise from mere limitations of space. Our streets and alleys cannot be clogged up with several sets of telephone poles nor the space under them given to the separate pipes and mains of several gas or water companies. Streets hold space for the rails of but one streetcar company. Competition would become a public nuisance. The limitations of waterfront space restricted the number of grain elevators in Chicago, while the dearth of passes across the Rockies limited the number of western railways.

TABLE 1

PHYSICAL PROPERTIES COMPARED WITH ANNUAL REVENUES
SOME TYPICAL UTILITY COMPANIES, 1947 *

	Population Served	Value of Physical Property (Before Depreciation)	Gross Operating Revenues
		MILLIONS OF DOLLARS	
Consolidated Gas, Electric Light and Power Company of Baltimore			
Gas Service	1,200,000	62.0	16.2
Electric Service	1,400,000	127.0	45.1
Lowell Gas Light Company (Mass.)			
Gas Service	140,000	4.6	1.4
Toledo Edison Company			
Electric Service	490,000	76.6	20.4
American Telephone and Telegraph Company	Most of		
Telephone Service	the Nation	7,348.8	2,224.6
Huntington Water Corporation (W. Va.)			
Water Service	83,000	4.2	.7
Cincinnati Street Railway Company			
Street-Railway Service	567,000	32.8	12.9

* Moody's *Public Utilities*, 1948.

Large Capital Investments. The large capital investment required in the utility industries may practically preclude the entry of competitors. Thus the Potomac Electric Power Company serving Washington and the vicinity has physical property to the amount of $125,000,000. The Toledo Edison Company serving Toledo, Ohio, and the area adjacent to it with electricity has more than $76,000,000 of property. The gigantic American Telephone and Telegraph Company has over $7,000,000,000 of physical properties.

The absolute figures of property investment become more significant when they are compared with the revenues they produce. The capital requirements of electric, gas, water, street-railway, and telephone utility companies are normally from four to six times their annual income. Even a so-called high-capital industry such as the steel industry does not normally require capital in excess of its annual revenue. In most manufacturing industries the ratio between total assets and annual revenues is one to one or less. Table 2 presents these ratios for some industries.[44]

Economies of Decreasing Costs. It is not merely that the large capital requirements of the utility industries make prospective entrants more hesitant about entering the field. Competition between firms already in the industry is destroyed. A large capital investment makes for high fixed costs, the total of which does not vary with any changes in output. This puts pressure upon firms to reduce prices to gain a larger volume of business over which these fixed costs may be spread. Price cutting tends to become cut-throat and competitors are driven to bankruptcy to be replaced by a single monopoly.[45]

Technical Limitations of the Market. In the telephone industry technical conditions of demand necessitate a single enterprise. Customers will demand facilities to communicate with all other customers. Competition cannot be otherwise than expensive and inconvenient. To the same end Congress recently found that a merger of Western Union and Postal Telegraph companies was in the public interest. A single urban transportation company will better serve the public interest than several.

The Franchise. It has already been pointed out that in theory the franchise is the result and not the cause of public utility status. For the reasons discussed here competition is considered to be undesirable, and as a matter of public policy franchises are usually exclusive. The Illinois court has said, "It is the policy in this state to provide the public with efficient service at a reasonable rate by compelling an established public utility occupying a given field to provide adequate service and

[44] Care must be taken in interpreting these figures, for the degree of integration affects the amount of the ratio. A highly integrated industry which controls production from raw materials to the finished product will show much more capital per dollar of revenue than one which purchases its raw materials in a semi-finished state.

[45] Further attention is given this subject in Chapter 11.

at the same time protect it from ruinous competition." [46] Thus, to the economic and technical barriers to competition is added an extremely important legal one.

TABLE 2

INVESTMENT IN FIXED PLANT REQUIRED TO PRODUCE $1.00 OF
NET SALES PER YEAR, VARIOUS INDUSTRIES, 1940 *

Utility Industries	
Class 1 railroads	$6.13
Electric	5.80
Manufactured gas	4.63
Urban transportation	4.57
Natural gas	4.31
Mixed gas	4.08
Bell telephone system	4.06
Telegraph	3.38
Greyhound bus	1.40
Air lines	.87
Other Industries	
Anthracite and bituminous coal	2.70
Petroleum	2.50
Non-ferrous metals	1.90
Railway equipment	1.88
Iron and steel products	1.66
Chemical manufacturing	1.15
Tires and rubber goods	.72
Electrical equipment	.49
Farm implements	.45
Automobiles and parts	.37
Aircraft parts	.35
Retail stores	.32
Meat packing	.25

* Ernest R. Abrams, "The Product of the Dollar in Various Types of Business," 35 *Pub. Util. Fort.* 795 (June 21, 1945).

There are other factors, common to industries in general and too familiar to mention, that lead to monopoly and large-scale enterprise. Whatever may be the reasons, the existence or absence of monopoly conditions weighed heavily in the minds of judges in the many cases that have been cited. These conditions were reason to bring grain elevators within the scope of the concept and their absence was sufficient to exclude the sale of gasoline, ice, food, and fuel. The fire insurance business was not monopolistic, but rates were fixed by agreement. Monopoly and necessity seem to be two prime requisites for utility status. Yet we cannot be sure. The motor carrier industry is highly competitive, yet it is a public utility. The expanding category of utility industries will shortly include the coal and milk businesses, where competition has been found to rule. The test of monopoly is not a complete one.

[46] *Bartonville Bus Line* v. *Eagle Motor Coach Lines,* 157 N.E. 176 (Ill., 1927).

6. Excessive Competition

It is apparent that excessive competition may be closely allied with monopoly. Large amounts of specialized capital may first produce excessive competition in which prices are driven below average costs and down to variable or marginal costs. Competition becomes "cut-throat." Firms face bankruptcy. Finally, in self-preservation, they unite to form a monopolistic combination. Public authority, invoking the anti-trust statutes, may step in to enjoin the combination, or it may confer a degree of utility status on the combination.

Regardless of any tendency towards monopoly, excessive competition brings its own evils with it. Resources are wasted, rivals and labor will be exploited, consumers will be faced with discriminatory pricing. In the *Carter Coal Company* case [47] Justice Cardozo spoke of free competition being degraded into anarchy. However, the majority of the Court was still unwilling to approve the thoroughgoing regulation of wages and prices contemplated by the Act.

Finally in the *Sunshine Anthracite* case, in which virtual public utility status was extended to the coal industry, the Court said, "Overproduction and savage, competitive warfare wasted the industry. Labor and capital alike were victims. Financial distress among operators and acute poverty among miners prevailed even during periods of general prosperity." [48] "Restrictive and demoralizing competitive conditions" were made much of by the Court in upholding the regulation of the price of milk in New York.[49] The case was specifically compared with *Brass* v. *Stoeser*,[50] in which the Court upheld the regulation of grain elevators in the face of uncontradicted proof that the business was keenly competitive.

It can be concluded that the protection that is extended the consumer when he is at a bargaining disadvantage may also be extended to other groups in society. Not only monopoly but excessive competition creates a public interest.

7. The Test of Emergency

The Court has clearly recognized the existence of the public power to regulate industries as if they were utilities in cases of great and temporary emergency. The regulation of rents in Washington, D. C. during the first World War was upheld in *Block* v. *Hirsh*.[51] In the second World War regulation was carried much further under the Emergency Price

[47] *Carter* v. *Carter Coal Co.*, 298 U.S. 238 (1936).
[48] *Sunshine Anthracite Coal Co.* v. *Adkins*, 310 U.S. 381, 395 (1940). The Court was citing Justice Cardozo in *Carter* v. *Carter Coal Co.*
[49] *Nebbia* v. *New York*, 291 U.S. 502 (1934).
[50] *Brass* v. *Stoeser*, 153 U.S. 391 (1894).
[51] *Block* v. *Hirsh*, 256 U.S. 135 (1921).

Control Act. On the other hand, general price regulation as a depression measure under the National Industrial Recovery Act was struck down by the Court in the famous *Schechter Poultry Company* case ostensibly on the grounds that the Act transcended the powers of Congress under the commerce clause of the Constitution and because the price-fixing power was an unconstitutional delegation of legislative power.[52]

It is unthinkable to deny to a sovereign state the power to deal with an emergency. If the emergency is great enough the police power of the states, and the commerce, war, and other powers of the Federal government are likely to be found sufficient to the situation.

8. Competition with Regulated Industries

The regulation of industries affected with a public interest may bring the regulation of other industries in its wake because of competition between the two. The Court upheld the power of the Texas Railroad Commission to prescribe minimum rates for contract carriers operating without franchise and under conditions of competition both among themselves and with the regulated common carriers.[53] The highly competitive taxicab industry has been regulated in part because of competition with the buses and street railways. There can be little doubt that regulation to be effective must span the area of competition.

9. The Test of Conservation of Resources

In 1607 all the judges of England assembled at Sergeants' Inn set forth the public interest in the nation's supply of gunpowder. In the language of Sir Edward Coke: "Yet inasmuch as this concerns the necessary defense of the realm, he (the King) shall not be driven to buy it in foreign parts; and foreign powers may restrain it at their pleasure, in their own dominions."[54] This is perhaps the earliest recorded legal recognition of the principle of conservation. Although it would appear that the conservation of our natural resources would be a primary test of the public interest, our spendthrift habits born of an era of impetuous expansion have yielded but slowly to the demands of public policy.

Some efforts have been made to conserve the public lands and resources pertaining to them. But the exploitation of most of our resources have been marked by unbridled waste and economic chaos. In 1934 a billion cubic feet of gas were blown into the air daily in the West Texas field. Fires in the Smackover and El Dorado oil and gas fields were allowed

---

[52] *Schechter Poultry Corp.* v. *U.S.,* 295 U.S. 495 (1935).

[53] *Stephenson* v. *Binford,* 287 U.S. 251 (1932).

[54] As cited by C. C. Williams, Jr., "Conservation of Mineral Resources, A Brief Survey," 47 *West Virginia Law Qtly.* 247 (1941). Considerable use is made of this article in this section as well as that of Northcutt Ely, "The Conservation of Oil," 51 *Harvard Law Rev.* 1209 (1938).

to burn unchecked for weeks. The United States Bureau of Mines estimates that we lose 35 per cent of the coal in our working coal seams in comparison with 5 to 10 per cent in western Europe. The avoidable loss in coal mining is said to total 150,000,000 tons a year. In the East Texas oil fields, 13,000 of the 24,000 wells are said to be unnecessary.

Our mineral resources are not unlimited. Some of the best coal seams in the East are substantially worked out. The large reserves of low quality coal and lignite in the West are but inadequate substitutes. The first as well as the second World War took a tremendous toll of our resources of coal, iron, oil, copper, aluminum and other minerals. War and waste together make a portentous and foreboding picture.

Much of this waste has been due to the medieval law of capture, bequeathed to us in *Acton* v. *Blundell* by England who promptly set it aside once the development of a petroleum industry appeared.[55] The discovery of the gushing Seminole, Oklahoma City, Kettleman Hills, and East Texas fields between 1926 and 1931 at the onset of the depression presented the oil conservation problem with striking impact. Martial law was used in Texas and Oklahoma to limit production and stabilize prices.

State pro-rationing of oil production has been upheld by the United States Supreme Court.[56] The interstate compact has been used with moderate success as a regulatory device. State quotas are allotted and then distributed within the states. The states' rights to conserve their natural resources for their own inhabitants is, however, constitutionally limited. This may be both an interference with private property and an unlawful restraint upon interstate commerce. Thus an Oklahoma law prohibiting the sending of natural gas outside the state has been held to be unconstitutional, although its stated purpose was the conservation of a natural resource.[57]

An ambitious attempt at Federal regulation came to naught when certain sections of the National Industrial Recovery Act authorizing the President to prohibit transportation in interstate commerce of oil produced in excess of state quotas was held to be an unconstitutional delegation of power.[58]

The Guffey Act of 1937, upheld in the previously mentioned *Sunshine Anthracite Co.* case, represented an attempt at stabilization and conservation in the coal industry by the Federal Government. For these reasons

[55] The West Virginia court has refused to consider the necessity of mining upper seams of coal before lower ones. *Continental Coal Co.* v. *Connellsville By-Product Co.*, 138 S.E. 737 (W. Va., 1927). The Pennsylvania court has held that a landowner has a legal right to allow gas to escape in thin air. *Hague* v. *Wheeler*, 27 Atl. 714 (Penn., 1893).

[56] *Champlin Refining Co.* v. *Corporation Commission*, 286 U.S. 210 (1932).

[57] *Oklahoma* v. *Kansas Natural Gas Co.*, 221 U.S. 229 (1911). See also *Pennsylvania* v. *West Virginia*, 262 U.S. 553 (1923). But see Chapter 13.

[58] *Panama Refining Co.* v. *Ryan*, 293 U.S. 388 (1935).

the theory has already been advanced that coal mining should be confined to a carefully limited number of large-scale companies with ample capital. Thus Howard N. Eavenson, an outstanding mining engineer, has advocated that coal mining companies be consolidated and the less efficient mines closed.[59]

Although the transmission and distribution of natural gas has been brought within the public utility category, production remains largely unregulated and subject to unchecked waste. The necessity for regulation is apparent, but the economic problems are so momentous that little has been done to set up the necessary regulatory machinery. Justice Jackson of the United States Supreme Court has discussed the problem at length in two opinions.[60] The Court could, however, find no delegation of power to the Federal Power Commission under the Natural Gas Act of 1938 to meet the conservation problem.

Most conservation legislation is really designed to stabilize if not to raise prices. There can be little doubt that industrial leaders who favor some form of rationalization are actually more interested in the elimination of competition. Ranged against these interests will be other producers who are restive under quota restrictions on output and a general public that is downright antagonistic to higher prices. There will be few to speak for future generations. In short, there will be a most serious divergence between national policy and the public will.

However, regardless of the motive, it seems to be inescapable that public control is the most hopeful means by which resources can be conserved under private ownership. Otherwise competition and the law of capture make waste inevitable.

The problem of conservation of resources arises in another manner. Competition tends to disappear in decreasing cost industries, but where it persists it leads to higher prices and the wasteful utilization of capital and labor. The competition of two firms where one could serve as well supplies an argument for the intervention of public authority. Justice Brandeis was willing to concede to the state of Oklahoma the right to license ice plants to prevent waste.[61] The same situation is found in the milk industry. Professor Mortenson estimates that the consolidation of milk companies could reduce the price of milk from $1\frac{1}{2}$ to $2\frac{1}{4}$ cents per quart and effect a saving of from $11.00 to $15.00 a customer annually.[62] This is an appreciable item in the budget of poorer families with growing children.

59 119 *A.I.M.E. Transactions* 391 (1936), as cited by Williams, *op. cit.*

60 1. *Federal Power Commission* v. *Hope Natural Gas Co.*, 320 U.S. 591 (1944); *Colorado Interstate Gas Co.* v. *Federal Power Commission*, 324 U.S. 581 (1945).

61 Dissenting opinion in *New State Ice Co.* v. *Liebmann*, 285 U.S. 262, 282 (1932).

62 W. P. Mortenson, "Legal Possibilities and Limitations of Milk Distribution as a Public Utility," 16 *Jnl. of Land & Pub. Util. Econ.* 60, 70 (1940).

In conclusion, we can say that the principle of conservation has received but scant recognition within the play of the doctrine of "affection with a public interest." Old legal institutions have served us grievously and we have not been wont to replace them with new.

10. The National Interest in the Welfare of the Industry

The public interest goes beyond a concern for the interests of those who meet at the market place. In times of war the welfare of almost all industries is closely related to national security. The development of the Tennessee River Valley was originally premised upon national defense. There can be little doubt but that the conservation of strategic minerals for national defense and for future generations can and should be grounds for public intervention. Here the national interest transcends that of both the consumer and the producer. In the *Sunshine Anthracite Coal Co.* case the Court gave great weight to the strategic importance of the coal industry in the national economy. The declaration of policy in the Agricultural Marketing Agreement Act, upheld in the *Rock Royal Coöperative* case, states that:

> ... the disruption of the orderly exchange of commodities in interstate commerce impairs the purchasing power of farmers, thus destroying the value of agricultural assets to the detriment of the national public interest.[63]

11. The Test of Legislative Discretion

An important question remains. Can the legislature make an industry into a public utility by legislative fiat? Who is to define the content of the public utility concept, the legislature or the courts? The Supreme Court, as final arbitrator, is in the position of being able to take or deny this power to itself. The whole question is bound up inextricably with the judicial philosophy of the Court. To this question the next chapter will be devoted. To anticipate the conclusion we can say that the Court has swung from a position in *Munn* v. *Illinois*, in which it ascribed extreme powers to the legislatures, to a position in which it claimed for itself the powers of judicial review with greater and greater insistence. Then in the late 1930's and 1940's a new Court broke sharply with the precedents established by its forebears to permit to the states and to Congress the widest of legislative discretion. We may assume that should a legislature find by any of the preceding tests, or by still other tests unmentioned, that a substantial public interest exists in any industry, such legislation would not be invalidated by the Court. The dissenting opinion of Justice Holmes in *Tyson* v. *Banton* has almost become the law of the land. In that case he said: "I think the proper course is to recognize that a state legislature can do whatever it sees fit to do unless it is restrained

[63] *Op. cit.*, 307 U.S. 533, 543.

by some express prohibition in the Constitution of the United States or
of the state...." [64]

4. PUBLIC UTILITY STATUS, A SUMMARY

The question may well be asked, "Just what can we take hold of in
determining public utility status?" Unfortunately no answer can be precise. The definition of a public utility is primarily to be derived from the
decisions of the Supreme Court. Since the attention of the Court is given
to but one case at a time, the concept is but slowly marked out. Case by
case the field of the public utilities is demarcated. Surrounding and including this group is the field of those industries "affected with a public
interest." Beyond lie the industries which are private only. The limits
of these fields are not matters of definition but of the judgment of the
Court, dealing with the facts of single cases in the light of their conception of public policy within the framework of the Constitution. It is this
Court that Professor John R. Commons has spoken of as the only authori-
tative faculty of political economy in the world.

The layman recognizes a public utility by certain rights and duties
assigned to it—the duty to render adequate service to all comers at reasonable rates without discrimination—the right to reasonable compensation and the right to use the power of eminent domain—the privileges
and obligations of the franchise. These rights and duties cannot be acquired or bargained away by contract. They arise out of the status of
being a public utility. Hence, it is said that a public utility is a creature
of status and not of contract.

The classification of public utilities and the manner of their regulation has changed from time to time. But however the businesses have
changed, however the manner of regulation has differed, there is always
running through our legal and political institutions the belief that the
interest of the public transcends that of the individual. At times the
doctrine has been pressed with vigor, for other long periods of time an
apathetic public has allowed it to lie inert and ignored. But the belief
in the doctrine and in the public power that comes from it has never
been relinquished. Whatever the business, the lesser private interest
must yield to a greater public interest. "Public utility" is a fixed concept,
with a changing content.

Of the several tests of public utility status, the tests of necessity and
inadequate competition appear more frequently than others. Inadequate
competition is a larger term than monopoly, for it may include its opposite. No doubt there should be other reasons of equal importance. But
these tests are salient points in marking the outlines of the concept.

[64] *Op. cit.*, 273 U.S. 418, 446.

5. THE LESSON OF THE PUBLIC UTILITY CONCEPT

Throughout this text an attempt will be made to treat the public utility industries as case studies in business, economics, and social control. The lessons of the utility industries may be integrated into the more extensive body of our social knowledge. There will be scarcely a phase of our studies that will not carry with it broader implications for our whole economy.

From earliest colonial times until late in the nineteenth century, we have had an "American system," a society dedicated to freedom of enterprise, where the rights of the individual and of property were, by and large, untrammeled and unrestrained. The importance of freedom to the early colonists, the boundlessness of the natural resources that were only waiting to be taken, the self reliance of the frontiersmen who looked to themselves for all they needed, the very simplicity of life itself, all created in America a tradition of freedom in which the rights of the individual were exalted. In England, the Industrial Revolution created new economic opportunities and released the same forces and energies to establish similar traditions. Adam Smith and the Manchester school became the prophets of a new order, of a laissez faire philosophy, which was eagerly accepted by the many who could profit from it. Across the channel on the continent, the French Revolution destroyed old concepts, rights, and institutions, and substituted a new democratic order of liberty, equality, and fraternity.

But such beliefs and concepts did not take root everywhere. They were strange and unreal in an emerging Germany in which the state was glorified even in its weakness. They were unheard of in Russia and in the many countries that the western nations considered benighted and backward. Feudal traditions, the ways of the guilds, and the rights of kings and manorial lords against the people prevailed in universality. Even in England could be found vestigial remnants of these institutions as well as those of Mercantilism.

Thus it is the lesson of history that the roots of individual rights run neither deep nor wide. In two countries two revolutions still called modern and a new society in a third and younger country created those legal institutions which establish the rights of the individual against society. Well to the fore of those individual rights is the right of property. It is the coercive, monopolistic right of the individual to use his own as he sees fit, against all comers, and against even the state itself.

The Granger movement of the 1870's expressed a consciousness of the growing coercive power of property. The frontier with its free lands was disappearing or becoming more difficult of access. Resources were no longer free except for the labor of taking them, nor was food free except for the labor of raising it. Transportation was not by horseback or privately owned vehicle but by a corporation-owned railroad. Individual specialization of production increased the dependence of one upon the other. The individual was not a self-contained unit, resourceful and reliant upon his own abilities for all he needed. Between him and his needs stood the complex market from which he bought at a price from those who possessed. Here the laws of scarcity prevailed, rather than the laws of abundance. Vaguely, at first, but later with almost explosive force, the individual realized the coercive force of property and his own economic inferiority in the world of the market place.

Thus it was that the legislature, expressing the mass will of the people, sought to limit the rights of property. With fumbling hands the Court groped for precedents and finally with an amazing sureness of grasp fastened on the words of a Lord Chief Justice in England. Two hundred years, covering the brief interlude of laissez faire, were spanned in its reach. A bridge-head to the past was created, the interests of justice were served, a legal precedent for an obvious necessity was found. If we are to predict the future of the public utility concept we can rest assured that the laws of property will not stand in the way of public necessity. It may perhaps be comforting to know, however, that there are legal precedents of strong and prevailing force.

It is not sufficient to justify regulation by references to legal history. The practical, pragmatic social problem remains, for all the past words of the Courts. The category of regulated industries has grown steadily and will continue to grow.[65] Some industries will be made into public utilities over their violent protests. Others will seek utility status to escape the rigors of a competitive economy. Then the question will be whether the regulated and collectivist segment will grow so monstrous and the unorganized, competitive segment so dwarfed that the latter can no longer carry the former.

What will remain to the unorganized consumer, the unorganized business, the unorganized worker when larger collective groups, with government approval, take the first and preferred share of the national income? What remains of private enterprise and a free economy when the distribution of wealth is by legislative or judicial fiat?

The question remains for the future. The concept of "businesses affected with a public interest" is not yet so all-pervading that we can deny general validity to the precepts of free competition. Although the private collectivist controls of labor unions and monopolies have been increased

65 See Myron W. Watkins, "Business and the Law," 42 *Journal of Political Economy* 178 (1934) for a humorous and concise article which lists and discusses the regulatory adventures of many industries.

and tightened, government controls need not be so rigid that free enterprise cannot be carried on within their framework.

One student of the subject, Professor Gray, has coupled the increase in the scope of regulation with a professed belief in its breakdown to argue for the abandonment of the whole public utility concept. As an alternative, socialization is suggested.[66] The premise that regulation has broken down can be questioned. It has many faults, but little can be gained by comparing regulation in practice with socialization in theory. It is quite likely that the weight of wisdom lies in that philosophy of government which utilizes experience and precedents to build new institutions upon old, to devise and improvise as our economy moves along to whatever destiny there is in store for it. If this philosophy is sound, the public utility concept will remain a reasonable basis of classification to group certain industries to which may be applied a more or less unified and coherent set of controls.

[66] H. M. Gray, "The Passing of the Public Utility Concept," 16 *Journal of Land & Public Utility Economics* 8 (February, 1940).

3. The Nature of Commission Regulation

1. TYPES OF REGULATION

An understanding of the nature and economics of the utility industries requires a knowledge of regulation within the framework of which utility companies must operate. Regulatory commissions in turn operate within the ambit of their statutory powers. Their orders are subject to review by the courts. This chapter deals with the administrative and legal nature of regulation.

We may distinguish five types of regulation to which public utilities have been subject, namely (1) direct regulation by the courts, (2) direct regulation by state legislatures, (3) regulation by local government units, (4) regulation by state commissions, and (5) regulation by the Federal Government.

Direct Regulation by the Courts. Even before the establishment of regulatory commissions and in the absence of statutory or legislative control, certain industries or callings were subject to a semblance of regulation by the courts. Under common law they were required to give adequate service to all comers at reasonable rates without discrimination. Individual grievances were handled by the courts. The many deficiencies of this type of regulation are obvious. Individuals often were in no position to know when they were aggrieved. There was no machinery for concerted action. Regulation was intermittent and spasmodic, and came into action only after the injury had occurred. The judiciary lacked the technical competence and experience that comes from continued contact with utility problems.

Direct Regulation by State Legislatures. In the past, attempts were made to regulate public utilities directly through statutory enactments enforced by the courts. Rates and service conditions were fixed by law, or by charter or franchise provisions. This type of regulation proved clumsy and inefficient at the best. Legislatures, however able, did not possess the time or ability to handle the specialized problems that were presented constantly for attention. Furthermore, they were too close to the people and too mindful of political pressure from lobbies and the electorate. Today only general legislation is enacted; administration is delegated to administrative commissions or to municipalities as agents of the state.

Regulation by Local Government Units. Municipalities, counties, and other local government units may regulate their own local utilities within the powers granted them by the state. The right of a utility to use the city streets and to do business is conditioned upon the possession of a franchise or permit granted it by the city. Regulatory provisions are frequently incorporated in the franchise. Where the franchises are subject to revision, this type of regulation may be effective. Although it is one of the earliest forms of modern regulation, it is still favored in many states such as Minnesota, Ohio, Iowa, Nebraska, and others.

Regulation by State Commissions. Today public utility regulation is largely in the hands of appointed or elected, semi-judicial administrative commissions which prescribe reasonable rates, service, etc., within the powers given to them by the state legislatures. Forty-seven states and the District of Columbia have public utility commissions. Delaware alone has none. The orders of these commissions are subject to judicial review for conformity to Federal and state constitutions and to the appropriate statutes.

Regulation by Federal Commissions. The interstate activities of a large number of utilities are subject to regulation by Federal commissions under Federal legislation. The Interstate Commerce Commission is the oldest of these commissions. The Federal Power Commission, the Federal Communications Commission and the Securities and Exchange Commission have been established more recently and have been given increasing powers. The Civil Aeronautics Board regulates air transportation; the Maritime Commission regulates shipping. In general, the scope of Federal regulation has increased very rapidly in the last two decades.

2. THE DEVELOPMENT OF COMMISSION REGULATION

Of the several types of utility regulation, regulation by state and Federal commissions is by far the most important. The commission, a device for regulating all manner of economic activity, has gained a still-expanding place within the framework of our government. Nowhere is it more firmly entrenched than in the field of public utility regulation. A study of utility commissions may be regarded as a case study in a substantial part of the great field of administrative government that has recently become so important.

The First Commissions. Regulation of the early railroads by charter proved ineffective. As early as the 1830's, temporary and permanent railroad commissions were set up in some of the New England states to check abuses and to aid in the enforcement of statutes. Rhode Island and New Hampshire established railroad commissions in 1844, Connecticut set up a commission in 1853, Vermont in 1855, and Maine in 1858. The movement spread to the west, and Ohio set up a commission in 1867. These commissions were of the "weak" type. They had limited authority and functioned largely to gather information and make recommendations. Publicity was relied upon for a small amount of control. On the whole there was a strong belief in competition as a social regulator. The courts remained in the background to enforce certain statutory and common law duties.

The Granger Commissions. The public attitude against the railroad monopolies stiffened after the Civil War. Rates were high, service was unsatisfactory, and discrimination was rampant. The promises which had led small investors to contribute their funds for securities and legislatures to grant franchises failed to materialize. It was thought that the railroads avoided their just share of the taxes. Farm unrest swept the country and settled in the great midwest to create the Granger movement of the 1870's.

"Strong" or mandatory commissions with control over rates were established as part of the movement in Illinois, Minnesota, and Wisconsin between 1871 and 1874. In the South, Georgia led the movement by establishing a commission in 1879 consisting of an "experienced" railroad man, a lawyer, and a man of affairs. These commissions were given strong powers over railroads and some other businesses. The laws had "teeth." The constitutionality of much of this state legislation was established in a series of cases, of which *Munn* v. *Illinois* (1877) was the first and the most famous. This regulatory movement, however, did not develop roots and thrive. Minnesota, Wisconsin, and Iowa repealed their laws before the end of the decade, and the nation entered upon another of a succession of railroad-building booms.

Federal Regulation. The Federal Government entered the field of utility regulation with the enactment of the Interstate Commerce Act of 1887. For a time the Interstate Commerce Commission, created by the Act, shared the burden of regulating railroad rates with the state commissions. It took some time for the ICC to win the confidence of the Supreme Court. Its orders were so frequently upset and its statutory powers were so restricted that it failed to exercise any appreciable power in the field of railway regulation. However, the framework of administrative law was devised. Later the Commission was given more power and it gained the confidence of the judiciary.

The Shreveport Case. No court decision was more important than that of the *Shreveport Case*.[1] The Texas Commission had fixed lower rates from Houston and Dallas eastward toward Shreveport, Louisiana, than the interstate rates westward from Shreveport into Texas. This was to the detriment of Shreveport shippers and to the advantage of Texas shippers. The Supreme Court held that the ICC could require a change in the local Texas rates to remove discrimination against interstate commerce. The principle of the superiority of the powers of the Federal Government in regulating interstate commerce over the powers of the states in regulating local commerce has been extended until the state regulation of railroads has become a mere appendage of the Federal system.

State Regulation of Local Utilities. The first serious attempt to subject the emerging local utilities to commission regulation was made in 1885 when Massachusetts created the Board of Gas Commissioners. Interestingly enough the commission was set up primarily to regulate not rates but rather competition, and was set up at the request of the gas companies. The commission had rather comprehensive powers including those of ordering improvements in gas service and reductions in rates. In 1887 it was given jurisdiction over electric light companies.

The real movement to subject local utilities to state commission regulation and the third period of regulation began in 1907. New York, Wisconsin, and Georgia in rapid succession set up strong mandatory commissions in that year. Extensive investigations in Wisconsin and in New York had made it apparent that the rapidly expanding local utilities were growing beyond the power of local control. Abuses were widespread. In New York, Governor Charles Evans Hughes, later a candidate for President and a Chief Justice of the United States Supreme Court, was responsible for the movement. In Wisconsin the crusading Governor La Follette ("Old Bob") led the movement. The noted economist, John R. Commons of the University of Wisconsin, contributed in drafting the law which served as a model for many years for other states.

The movement was not as violent as that of the 1870's, but it was more firmly established and made rapid headway. By 1913 there were 28 state commissions. In practically all instances these new commissions replaced older railroad commissions.

The Modern Period. The modern period, which began about 1930, was marked by two significant developments. First, the Federal Govern-

[1] *Houston, East and West Texas Ry.* v. *U.S.*, 234 U.S. 342 (1914). Also important in this respect are the *Minnesota Rate Cases*, 230 U.S. 352 (1913) and the *Wisconsin Passenger Fare Cases*, 257 U.S. 563 (1922).

ment enlarged the scope of its regulatory activities to such an extent that it was feared by many that the state agencies would be forced from the field as they virtually were in the field of railway regulation. Second, state commissions were strengthened by new legislation designed to meet abuses that had become apparent.

Federal regulation of local utilities had been growing steadily. The Federal Power Commission had been set up in 1920 with jurisdiction over the nation's hydro-electric resources. The Federal Radio Commission had been set up in 1927 to bring order to the nation's turbulent radio broadcasting industry. The real participation of the Federal Government had to wait the "New Deal." Growing dissatisfaction with state commissions and the expanding scope of the utilities industries contributed to Federal expansion. In 1934 the Federal Communications Commission was established to succeed the Federal Radio Commission and to take general jurisdiction over interstate telecommunications. The Securities and Exchange Commission was set up in 1934. Its powers over utility industries and those of the Federal Power Commission were vastly expanded in 1935. In 1938 the Federal Power Commission was given jurisdiction over the interstate natural gas industry. The Federal Government also subjected electric utilities to pressure and indirect regulation through competition from Federally owned and aided power projects scattered across the nation.

State Reforms. The deficiencies of utility regulation that developed during the 1920's did not go unnoticed by the states. In attempts to shore up regulation, commissions were reorganized and laws were revised. Commissions were given increased powers over securities and financial practices, over holding company relations, over depreciation, and over accounts and records. In some instances they were given new rate-making powers. Their financial resources were frequently increased. There was a tendency to give regulatory commissions more of the characteristics of public defenders and less those of judicial bodies. Thus the Oregon law charged the commissioner to protect ratepayers from "unjust and unreasonable exactions and practices." The Arkansas Commission was directed to furnish legal assistance to cities and towns in litigation involving rates.

Not all changes increased the power and prestige of state commissions. Financial stringency brought with it a reduction in commission personnel and frequent curtailment in appropriations. Oregon, Indiana, Utah, Illinois, North Carolina, and Rhode Island reduced the size of their commissions.[2] Later state commissions were drained of some of their ablest administrators by the expanding Federal agencies.

[2] D. L. Marlett and O. F. Traylor, "Public Utility Legislation in the Depression," 11 *Jnl. Land & Pub. Util. Econ.* 290 (August, 1935).

3. REGULATION WITHIN THE CONSTITUTIONAL FRAMEWORK

In the first chapter we considered the nature of those industries which were public utilities or businesses affected with a public interest and were made subject to price and other regulation. The power to regulate is not a power without limits. Both the state and Federal governments are limited by constitutional restrictions as interpreted by the United States Supreme Court.

Our Constitution distributes powers between the Federal and state governments and limits their use against individuals. The Federal Government has only those powers specifically delegated to it by the Constitution or reasonably implied from those powers. State governments are entitled to all powers not granted to the Federal Government or not expressly or implicitly denied to them by the Constitution. Where there is a conflict the powers of the Federal Government are supreme over those of the states.

Under the American system of government the courts are the final interpreters of the constitutionality of statutes as well as of the constitutionality of acts of administrative and executive officers. The courts also have the function of interpreting the application of statutes to particular situations. State courts interpret and apply the acts of their respective state legislatures and determine the constitutionality of state legislation under state constitutions. In these matters their decisions are final. The United States Supreme Court is the final arbiter of the constitutionality of all legislation, both state and Federal, under the United States Constitution.[3]

1. The Police Power

When a state acts to regulate its utilities it generally acts under the police power. This power is so difficult to define that it is known as the "Dark Continent" of American law. It does not arise from any constitution, in fact it is not even mentioned in the United States Constitution. It was originally considered to be the residuary sovereignty of the States not surrendered to the General Government of the United States. Later the exercise of the power came to be justified as reasonably required for the protection of public health, safety, and morals. It has been said that the very existence of government depends upon it—the security of the social order, the life and health of the citizens, and the use of property. It is the essence of sovereignty. It is the power that a legislature exercises over matters involving public welfare and by which it forces

[3] This was established in respect to Federal legislation in *Marbury* v. *Madison,* 1 Cranch 137 (1803) and in respect to state legislation in *Fletcher* v. *Peck,* 6 Cranch 87 (1810).

the observance by each member of society of duties which it owes to the community at large. The nature of the police power is perhaps best put by Justice Holmes:

> It may be said in a general way that the police power extends to all great public needs. It may be put forth in aid of what is sanctioned by usage, or held by the prevailing morality or strong and preponderant opinion to be greatly and immediately necessary to the public welfare.[4]

The police power is admittedly not subject to precise definition and no one can foresee the ever-changing conditions which might bring it forth. "With regard to the police power, or elsewhere in the law, lines are pricked out by the gradual approach and contact of decisions on the opposing sides." [5]

The scope and extent of the police power is limited only to a degree by the Constitutional prohibition against impairing the obligation of contract, taking property without due process of law or denying the equal protection of the laws. As the Court said in one case:

> It is established by repeated decisions of this court that neither of these provisions of the Federal Constitution (the due process and contract clauses) has the effect of overriding the power of the State to establish all regulations reasonably necessary to secure the health, safety, or general welfare of the community; that this power can neither be abdicated nor bargained away, and is inalienable even by express grant; and that all contract and property rights are held subject to its fair exercise. And it is also settled that the police power embraces regulations designed to promote the public convenience or the general welfare and prosperity, as well as those in the interest of public health, morals, or safety.[6]

It is to be noted that the Court indicated that the power extends beyond that of protecting the public health, morals, and safety.

The police power of the states extends only to intrastate matters. The line between intrastate and interstate business is hard to draw, and the powers of the state frequently come into conflict with the powers of the Federal Government as they did in the *Shreveport Case*. Where they do, the power of the state must yield to the power of the Federal Government.

Under police power, property rights are cut down and taken without pay. In this it is to be distinguished from the right of eminent domain, which is the right to take private property for a public purpose with compensation. Price fixing cannot help but take property, for the measure of a property's value is its earning capacity.

---

[4] *Noble State Bank* v. *Haskell*, 219 U.S. 104, 111 (1911).
[5] *Ibid.*, 112.
[6] *Chicago & Alton R.R.* v. *Tranbarger*, 238 U.S. 67, 76 (1915).

2. The Powers of the Federal Government Under the Commerce Clause

Since the commercial disorders among the states contributed largely to the fall of the early confederacy, the need for uniform regulation of commerce by the central government was apparent when our Constitution was adopted. The power delegated to Congress to "regulate commerce with foreign nations and among the several States, and with the Indian tribes" [7] constitutes one of the greatest, if not the greatest, of the national government's powers. The full scope of the power was not utilized, if it was even comprehended, until almost a hundred years later, when Congress enacted the Interstate Commerce Act. Significantly enough this was the first great public utility law. Practically all Federal public utility legislation as well as a large portion of other social and economic legislation is enacted pursuant to this power. The Federal Water Power Act of 1920, the Federal Power Act of 1935, and the Natural Gas Act of 1938, under which the Federal Power Commission regulates certain activities of electric and natural gas utilities; the Securities Act of 1933, the Securities Exchange Act of 1934, and the Public Utility Act of 1935, under which the Securities and Exchange Commission regulates certain financial and accounting practices of electric and gas utilities; and the Federal Communications Act of 1934, under which the Federal Communications Commission regulates the communications industries; all constitute the exercise of the commerce power.

Under the commerce clause and within the field of interstate commerce, the power of the Federal Government is supreme and is akin to the police power of the states. Regulation of commerce may be similar in all important respects to police regulation for the general welfare. It is, however, subject to the limitations of the Fifth Amendment, and by other constitutional restrictions and by the reserved powers of the states. Ours is a dual system of government, and the powers of Congress are not so great as to extend to matters within any one state that are purely local, internal, or intrastate in nature. On the other hand, in the exercise of police power the states cannot burden or interfere with interstate commerce. Thus a state may regulate the business of a peddler who carries his goods from door to door, but it cannot regulate the business of a salesman who takes orders for delivery from another state. The regulatory powers of both the state and Federal governments are each limited and restricted by the powers of the other as well as by specific constitutional limitations.

[7] Article I, Section 8, Clause 3.

3. The Due Process Clauses

The powers of both state and Federal governments are restricted by the so-called "due process clauses." The Fifth Amendment of the Constitution provides that no person shall "be deprived of life, liberty, or property without due process of law," and is a restriction upon the Federal Government. The Fourteenth Amendment is worded similarly and is a limitation upon the states.

The due process clauses limit but do not prohibit government regulation for the public welfare. Thus all the great delegated powers of Congress including the war power, the taxing power, the bankruptcy power, the power to regulate commerce, and the power to exclude aliens are subject to it. Correlatively, the police power of the states, the power of eminent domain, the power of taxation and of assessment are also limited by the due process clause. The due process clauses do not prohibit the taking of property. This must be accomplished, however, by methods consistent with due process. That is, it must not be done in a manner contrary to settled usages and modes of procedure as without notice and hearing. Laws must not be unreasonable, capricious, or arbitrary, and the means selected must have a real and substantial relation to the objective sought.

4. The Equal Protection of the Laws Clause

The Fourteenth Amendment also contains the provision that no state shall "deny to any person within its jurisdiction the equal protection of the laws." The due process and equal protection clauses have been regarded as coterminous. More recently the Court has taken the position that the second provision is more specific than the first. Whereas the due process clause secures a required minimum of protection, the equal protection clause specifically requires equality of treatment even if something more than the minimum protection is accorded.[8]

This clause has been said to mean that no person or class of persons shall be denied the same protection of the laws which is enjoyed by other persons or classes under like circumstances. It is not necessary that the laws affect everyone alike, but there must be equal operation upon persons in like circumstances. This creates the power and duty of classification, which has been construed rather liberally. The Court has held that a city tax upon a private utility does not violate the equal protection clause merely because the city is also engaged in the utility business in active competition with the privately owned utility.[9] Can a state regu-

[8] *Truax* v. *Corrigan*, 257 U.S. 312 (1921).

[9] *Puget Sound P. & L. Co.* v. *Seattle*, 291 U.S. 619 (1934). Other notable regulatory cases in which this clause has been at issue include the *German Alliance* case, 233 U.S. 389 (1914) and *Frost* v. *Corporation Commission*, 278 U.S. 515 (1929).

latory statute distinguish between barbers in New York City and in Saratoga Springs? The New York court said that it could.[10]

Is a Corporation a Person? The due process and equal protection clauses protect the rights of persons. Is a corporation a person? There is some reason to believe that those who drafted the Fourteenth Amendment never intended that its protection should be extended to corporations. Certainly the corporation entity was not nearly the important institution in our economic structure at that time that it is today. In an obiter dictum in the *Slaughter House Cases*,[11] Justice Miller expressed doubt whether the Fourteenth Amendment would ever be used for any purpose but to protect the Negro. This opinion was unjustified. Thirteen years later, without dissent, the Supreme Court said that the Amendment did apply to corporations.[12] Thus a corporation was converted into a person by judicial fiat.

The Court's interpretation of the scope and meaning of the word has often been challenged. Justice Black in a dissenting opinion in *Connecticut General Life Insurance Company* v. *Johnson* stated flatly, "I do not believe the word 'person' in the Fourteenth Amendment includes corporations."[13] Justice Black went on to demonstrate that the Court had built up such a doctrine by stare decisis and marshalled strong historical reasons to show the lack of any such intention on the part of the people and the statesmen of the time when it became a part of the Constitution.

5. Obligation of Contracts Clause

Article 1, Section 10 of the Constitution provides that "no State shall ...pass any...law impairing the obligation of contracts." This is not a restriction upon the Federal Government. Public utility companies frequently call upon this clause to protect certain contractual rights gained under a franchise or contract. It may be said in general, however, that the legitimate exercise of the police power of the state cannot be abridged by this clause. Otherwise, all manner of reform legislation could be forever precluded by the mere use of the contractual device. As in other instances, the police power must be exercised for a public purpose.

[10] *People* v. *Havenor,* 149 N.Y. 195 (1896).

[11] *Slaughter House Cases,* 16 Wall. 36 (1873).

[12] *Santa Clara Co.* v. *Southern Pacific R. Co.,* 118 U.S. 394, 396 (1886). "This court does not wish to hear argument on the question whether the provision in the Fourteenth Amendment to the Constitution, which forbids a State to deny to any person within its jurisdiction the equal protection of the laws, applies to these corporations. We are all of the opinion that it does."

[13] *Connecticut General Life Insurance Co.* v. *Johnson,* 303 U.S. 77, 85 (1938).

6. The Rights of Citizens

The Privileges and Immunities Clause. Article 4, Section 2, Clause I of the Constitution provides: "The citizens of each State shall be entitled to all privileges and immunities of citizens in the several States." The Supreme Court has held that a corporation is not a citizen within the meaning of the term used here. The Court pointed out that a corporation is a mere creation of local law and can have no existence or right to existence beyond the limits of the sovereignty which created it. That being the case, other states "may exclude the foreign corporation entirely; they may restrict its business to particular localities, or they may exact such security for the performance of its contracts with their citizens as in their judgment will best promote the public interest." [14]

It is apparent that such an interpretation of this clause opens the way for a state to place certain restrictions upon out-of-state corporations, such as utility companies, doing business within the state. In so doing, however, they may not burden interstate commerce, nor may they impair any obligations of contract or regulate them in ways repugnant to the 14th Amendment.

Access to the Federal Courts. Confusingly enough, a corporation is deemed to be a citizen under the provisions of Article 3, Section 2, Clause 1, which extends the judicial power of the United States to controversies between citizens of different states and between a State and a citizen of another state. The effect of this clause is to permit a utility corporation access to the Federal courts under relevant circumstances.

The preceding discussion is summarized in Table 3.

4. SUBSTANTIVE PROTECTION AND JUDICIAL REVIEW

It has been pointed out that the police power of the states and certain specific powers of the Federal Government are limited by the 14th and 5th Amendments, both of which contain the due process clause. What is due process of law? It is no overstatement to say that within this question lies the basic problem of our American form of government. For it represents the clash between the power and rights of all the people, as expressed in the acts of their government, and the rights of individuals standing alone.

1. Development of Due Process

Procedural and Substantive Protection. There are two possible interpretations of the due process clause. One is the procedural interpreta-

14 *Paul* v. *Virginia*, 8 Wall. 168, 181 (1869).

tion that a person may be deprived of life, liberty, or property only in accordance with a formally established administrative, legislative, or judicial procedure. Under such an interpretation, the rights of a public utility might be exhausted if a regulatory commission, acting within the bounds of the powers granted it by the legislature, investigated the company, gave it adequate notice of its suggested action, and accorded it an opportunity to be heard. Administrative orders may be attacked on these procedural grounds. Constitutional protection, however, extends much further than this and covers the substance of the administrative order as well as the procedural form adopted. The utility is protected against confiscation. This is the substantive interpretation.

It might be thought that a commission in reducing a rate and the earnings of a utility is taking property. This, however, is not necessarily confiscation. As long as a utility is allowed a reasonable return there is no confiscation; anything below the zone of reasonableness is confiscation. Over the course of time, the doctrine has developed that a legislature or a commission is the judge of reasonableness, while the courts are the judges of confiscation. A nice balance is presumably struck between the individual's rights of property and the public's interest in the business, and between due process of law and the police power of the state. We will now trace the development of this doctrine.

TABLE 3

REGULATION UNDER THE CONSTITUTION

	Powers of Regulation Derived From:	Powers of Regulation Limited By:

State Governments and their Agencies	Police Power	1. Powers delegated to the Federal Government
		2. 14th Amendment
		  1—Due Process Clause
		  2—Equal Protection Clause
		3. Obligation of Contracts Clause
		4. Privileges and Immunities Clause

Federal Government and its Agencies	Commerce Clause	1. Powers retained by the States 2. 5th Amendment

The Slaughter House Cases (1873).[15] In the exercise of its police powers, the state of Louisiana passed an act chartering a company with the exclusive right of operating stockyards and slaughter houses in the city of New Orleans and provided that all animals intended for food be slaughtered there. Certain butchers of New Orleans brought suit, contending, among other things, that they were deprived of liberty and

[15] *Slaughter House Cases,* 16 Wall. 36 (1873).

property without due process of law in contravention of the Fourteenth Amendment. The majority of the Court, however, gave but scant consideration to the due process clause and held the Act to be within the powers of the State. Justice Bradley, in dissenting, was equally certain that the measure had none of the attributes of police regulation, although it was admitted that some provisions allowing for inspection and location of the buildings did have.

Munn v. Illinois (1877).[16] The high tide of the states' powers of regulation was reached at its veritable inception. Here again *Munn* v. *Illinois* serves as a benchmark. Reading the case one would conclude that the power of the state in setting rates charged by public utilities was virtually untrammelled. Upholding the right of the Illinois legislature to fix warehouse charges the Court said: "Rights of property which have been created by the common law cannot be taken away without due process; but the law itself, as a rule of conduct, may be changed at will, or even at whim, of the legislature, unless prevented by constitutional limitations." The due process clause seemed to grant only procedural protection. The Court concluded with brutal frankness: "We know that this is a power which may be abused; but that is no argument against its existence. For protection against abuses by legislatures the people must resort to the polls, not to the courts." The advice to resort to the polls was not too well given, for the railroads and utilities had already seen the wisdom of having themselves well represented in the legislative halls of the nation.

Stone v. Farmers' Loan & Trust Co. (1886).[17] The Court was soon ready to abandon the position established with such resounding words in *Munn* v. *Illinois*. In 1886, in a case involving the Mobile and Ohio Railroad, the Court upheld the rate-fixing power of the Mississippi Commission with a proviso that "it is not to be inferred that this power of limitation or regulation is itself without limit. This power to regulate is not a power to destroy, and limitation is not the equivalent of confiscation." The Court thus warned the commissions and set itself on record as being mindful of confiscation.

Chicago, Milwaukee & St. Paul Ry. v. Minnesota (1890).[18] By 1890 six judges of the Court which had rendered the *Munn* decision had been replaced by others. The new Court was much more in sympathy with the position of Justice Field who had dissented in that case. Now the Court was to be presented with the clear-cut issue of judicial review. The effect of a Minnesota statute was to make the rates fixed by a Railroad and Warehouse Commission final and conclusive, and to deprive the courts of the state of any power to stay the hand of the commission except

16 *Munn* v. *Illinois,* 94 U.S. 113, 134 (1877).
17 *Stone* v. *Farmers' Loan & Trust Co.,* 116 U.S. 307, 331 (1886).
18 *Chicago, Milwaukee & St. Paul Ry.* v. *Minnesota,* 134 U.S. 418 (1890).

on procedural grounds. This the Supreme Court held to be in conflict with the Constitution. "The question of the reasonableness of a rate ... is eminently a question for judicial investigation." Justice Bradley expressed sharp dissent, saying that the case overruled *Munn* v. *Illinois,* and that the question of reasonableness was a legislative question and not a judicial one. Thus the majority of the Court expanded the meaning of due process so as to give the courts the power to block state and national legislative action. "Due process" was held to mean reasonableness as determined by the judiciary. The conclusions of whatever judges there may be, acting in accordance with whatever notions they may hold, is, in the name of constitutionality, substituted for legislative policy. No less an authority than Justice Holmes has said that this makes the sky the limit of judicial power to declare legislative acts unconstitutional.[19]

2. The Rule of Smyth v. Ames

Having thus placed both substantive and procedural rights within the ambit of the Court's review, the next question to be dealt with was that of the proper standard for reasonable rates. This came in the famous *Smyth* v. *Ames* case in 1898. This case is ranked with *Munn* v. *Illinois* as one of the two great cases in public utility regulation.

Smyth v. Ames.[20] In 1893 Nebraska passed a law fixing maximum freight rates to be charged by railroads operating in Nebraska. The law was challenged by the Union Pacific and other railways on the grounds that the rates would so reduce the earning power and value of their property as to deprive them of property in violation of the Fourteenth Amendment of the Constitution. It was brought out that the Union Pacific Railway had been built in a period of high prices during and following the Civil War at a cost of approximately $103,000 a mile, an amount unusually high, moreover, because of graft and chicanery on the part of its management. The property, according to testimony, could have been reproduced for $20,000 a mile, or $30,000 including chicanery, in the existing period of low prices. The state of Nebraska through no less an attorney than William Jennings Bryan contended first, that rates fixed by the state were constitutionally valid as long as they permitted the railroad to earn something more than operating expenses and, second, that if the Court should pass upon the reasonableness of the earnings, the proper basis of comparison was the present cost of reproduction rather than the original cost.

The counsel for the company thought that the railway was entitled to revenues sufficient to meet operating expenses, interest, and dividends and that any amount less than that would deprive it of property. This

[19] In *Baldwin* v. *Missouri,* 281 U.S. 586, 595 (1930).
[20] *Smyth* v. *Ames,* 169 U.S. 466 (1898).

the Court thought to be unsound for it excluded from consideration the fair value of property, and the right of the public to be exempt from unreasonable exactions and made the interests of a corporation maintaining a public highway the sole tests of the reasonableness of the rates established between itself and the public. "We hold, however, that the basis of all calculations as to the reasonableness of rates to be charged by a corporation maintaining a highway under legislative sanction must be the fair value of the property being used for the convenience of the public." Forthwith the Court set forth the "Fair value" rule of *Smyth* v. *Ames.*

The Rule of Fair Value. The famous "Fair value" rule provided that rates to be constitutional must yield a fair return on the fair value of the property. After admitting that the exact determination of this compensation would "always be an embarrassing question," the Court set forth six matters for consideration, all of which were contradictory:

1. The original cost of construction.
2. The amount expended in permanent improvements.
3. The amount and market value of its bonds and stock.
4. The present as compared with the original cost of construction.
5. The probable earning capacity of the property under particular rates prescribed by statute.
6. The sum required to meet operating expenses.

And the Court added, "We do not say that there may not be other matters to be regarded in estimating the value of the property." There were many other matters and one notable omission. There was no mention of depreciation. This factor received its first consideration in the *Knoxville Water Company* case of 1909.

Rate-making Procedure. At this point it is desirable to outline the rate-making procedure by which the rule is applied. First, the depreciated value of the physical property is determined in accordance with the present fair value rule. To this figure is applied a rate of return to obtain the return to those who committed capital to the enterprise, whether bondholders or stockholders. To the return is added the estimated operating expenses. The total represents the amount that the rates should yield. Expressed as a formula:

$$R = E + (V - D) r$$

Where R is the revenue to be obtained from the rates in question:
  E is the operating expenses
  V is the value of the physical property new
  D is the depreciation to be deducted
  r is the rate of return expressed as a percentage.

Each of the factors in the formula raises a host of questions which are at once the despair of administrators and the delight and livelihood of lawyers. The most difficult issue to reconcile was whether original cost (claimed by the Union Pacific Railway in this case) or present cost (urged by the state) was to be given the greatest weight in determining present fair value. The Court was silent at the time on the weight to be given to each, but subsequently, with rare selectivity and precision of touch, the Court settled upon the worst possible interpretation; that fair value meant almost—but not quite—present value. However, we are not concerned at this point with the peregrinations of the Court after that most elusive will-o-the-wisp, "present fair value."

It is apparent that the numerous and complex factors, any one of which is a matter of subjective judgment, cannot be compounded into a single quantitative and ascertainable fact. As one writer puts it, "The whole doctrine of *Smyth* v. *Ames* rests upon a gigantic illusion. The fact which for twenty years the court has been vainly trying to find does not exist. 'Fair value' must be shelved among the great juristic myths of history, with the Law of Nature and the Social Contract. As a practical concept, from which practical conclusions can be drawn, it is valueless." [21]

However, with both procedural and substantive rights firmly encompassed within the purview of the courts, this clumsy rule became the touchstone against which all administrative orders were to be tested. No commission knew exactly what it meant; it is doubtful whether the Court did. Constitutionally, substantive due process became a complicated matter of law, accountancy, engineering, and economics. If, in the Court's mind, these matters were not handled aright by the technical experts on commission staffs, it would handle them itself. If the Court realized its own lack of capacity, as it did more and more, it soon developed a device to escape its own infirmity. A master would be appointed to examine matters anew, virtually ignoring (if it suited his purpose) all the work previously done by an administrative commission. On this report the Court could base its decision. This became substantive due process in action.

3. The New Attitude

Long and oft-repeated attacks on the process of judicial review brought a momentous reshaping of constitutional law in the hands of a new Court in the late 1930's and early 1940's. Justice Holmes' position, presented without avail in *Tyson* v. *Banton*, became the new constitutional law of the land.

Federal Power Commission v. Natural Gas Pipeline Co. (1942). In the *Natural Gas Pipeline* case the Supreme Court prepared to abandon its position in the field of public utility regulation. Upholding a rate-fixing order of the Federal Power Commission, the Court said:

[21] G. C. Henderson, "Railway Valuation and the Courts," 33 *Harvard Law Review* 1031, 1051 (1920).

The Constitution does not bind rate-making bodies to the service of any single formula or combination of formulas. Agencies to whom this legislative power has been delegated are free, within the ambit of their statutory authority, to make the pragmatic adjustments which may be called for by particular circumstances. Once a fair hearing has been given, proper findings made, and other statutory requirements satisfied, the courts cannot intervene in the absence of a clear showing that the limits of due process have been overstepped. If the Commission's order, as applied to the facts before it and viewed in its entirety, produces no arbitrary result, our inquiry is at an end.[22]

The mere requirement that the Commission's order should produce no arbitrary result marked a considerable abrogation of judicial power and a more liberal attitude on the part of the Court.

Federal Power Commission v. Hope Natural Gas Co. (1944). A short time later, the Supreme Court swung even further from its old position. Rates fixed by the Commission were challenged as unreasonable under the Natural Gas Act which provided that all rates "shall be just and reasonable...." The Court said significantly: "Under the statutory standard of 'just and reasonable' it is the result reached not the method employed which is controlling. It is not theory but the impact of the rate order which counts.... The fact that the method employed to reach that result may contain infirmities is not then important.... (The order) is the product of expert judgment which carries a presumption of validity."[23]

At once this decision made sweeping concessions to the doctrine of administrative finality and substituted a new rule of "the end result" for the fair value rule of *Smyth* v. *Ames*. In short, if the final result of a commission's order is fair, and it is to be presumed that it is, then the utility has been accorded substantive protection regardless of the method used to reach that result.

With this we must let the problem of valuation stand until in a later chapter it will be taken up in more detail.

5. THE NATURE OF REGULATORY PROCEDURE

In General. Members of a public utility commission are elected or appointed for limited terms. The commission has the power to hire a permanent staff to assist it. The staff, made up of engineering, accounting, legal, clerical, and other help, may range in size from a few employees to several hundred, or to thousands in the case of the Federal commissions.

A regulatory commission is sometimes referred to as a semi-judicial

[22] *Federal Power Commission* v. *Natural Gas Pipeline Co.*, 315 U.S. 575, 586 (1942).
[23] *Federal Power Commission* v. *Hope Natural Gas Co.*, 320 U.S. 591, 602 (1944).

body. In truth it has characteristics of all three branches of government, judicial, legislative, and executive. It holds hearings, makes findings, and issues orders in a manner similar to a court. Complainants appear before it, respondents are summoned. Rules of evidence, however, are much less strict and proceedings are less formal. Controversies are often determined by administrative discretion. Yet a commission cannot enforce its orders. For this it must go to the courts.

A commission acts in a legislative capacity when it makes rules to be applied to future transactions. It may issue accounting rules, establish service standards, etc. It has only the powers the legislature has given it and it is not, like a legislature, a policy-determining body. A commission is without power to order a company to institute a rate schedule that is unreasonable by judicial standards merely because it would be a wise policy to do so. The Idaho Public Utilities Commission could not order a utility company to grant a 33⅓ per cent discount to hospitals and religious institutions.[24] The legislature, however, could authorize a discount. Such matters are matters of policy and are beyond the scope of the commission's discretion.

A commission acts in an executive capacity when it applies the law. Carrying out a legislative requirement that rates must be just and reasonable, it may order a reduction in charges. Commissioners are responsible to the executive and in some instances may be removed by the governor or the president.

In a rate hearing a commission may have evidence presented to show that existing rates are unreasonable and that new rates are reasonable; it may find old rates unreasonable and new rates reasonable; and it may order the new rates to be placed in effect. This makes it seem that a commission is prosecutor, judge, and jury. This procedure, however, is in full accordance with principles of administrative law. A Doctor Brinkley, a goat-gland specialist of renown a few years ago, was subject to proceedings by a medical board that sought to revoke his license. Brinkley complained that certain members of the board who had made the original complaint also had a part in conducting the investigation. The Court pointed out that this challenged combination of functions had never been held unconstitutional in an administrative tribunal.[25]

This procedure may be rationalized if it is remembered that the commission is only administering a law already laid down by the legislature. Due process requires that the utility be accorded a hearing. Evidence in the hearing is presented by the commission's staff; the decision is made by the commission. There is thus a dual division of responsibility. Commissioners are generally chosen for their legal training and for their

[24] *Idaho Power Co.* v. *Thompson*, 19 F.(2d) 547, 580 (1927).
[25] *Brinkley* v. *Hassig*, 83 F.(2d) 351 (1936).

objective attitude. They gradually gather around themselves all the appendages and appurtenances of judges, if they do not already possess them. They are fully conscious of the fact that they must work within the framework of administrative law and that their orders are subject to appeal to judicial tribunals.

Statutory Limits of a Commission's Powers. A utility commission possesses only those powers conferred upon it by statute, either expressly or by implication. A provision giving it jurisdiction over electric utility companies would not give it jurisdiction over electric coöperatives.

A legislature cannot delegate its legislative powers either to the executive or to administrative commissions. What it does do is make laws establishing general standards. A commission functions to determine the facts which will make the law apply to specific cases. Thus a legislature may enact a law requiring gas utility rates to be just and reasonable. A utility commission, after investigating the facts, determines the reasonableness of the particular rates or orders specific rates found reasonable to be placed in effect.

A commission has no jurisdiction over private matters between a public utility and individuals. It would have no control over wage contracts. A commission cannot make rules affecting substantive rights. A rule of the Alabama Public Service Commission to the effect that an electric utility could not assume any obligation or responsibility for the condition of the customers' apparatus and appliances was held to deal clearly with substantive law and be beyond the commission's authority. Nor could the commission make a rule that no statement of a utility employee or officer would be binding upon the company unless it was in writing and was signed.[26]

Regulation versus Management. Commissions have given powers of regulation but they cannot encroach upon the field of management. The line between the two is sometimes difficult to draw. In the past the courts have been watchful to prevent commissions from enlarging their powers. The Maryland court has ruled that a commission cannot determine the salaries of utility officers except where there has been a flagrant abuse of discretion.[27] The Wisconsin Supreme Court upheld the prerogatives of management when it overruled a Commission decision which excluded from the rate base certain excess capacity that had been added before a depression.[28] In an older case it was held that the Missouri Commission could not disallow more than a half of a fee of 4½ per cent of gross revenues paid by the Southwestern Bell Telephone Company as a rent

[26] *Compton* v. *Alabama Power Co.*, 114 S. 46 (Alabama, 1927). See 51 *Corpus Juris* 44.

[27] *Havre de Grace & Perryville Bridge Co.* v. *T.*, 103 Atl. 319 (1918). For a discussion of the problem see F. X. Welch, "Is Utility Regulation Encroaching on Management?" 46 *W. Va. Law Qtly.* 122 (1940).

[28] *Wis. Tel. Co.* v. *Pub. Serv. Comm.*, 287 N.W. 122 (Wisconsin, 1939).

and license fee to the American Telephone & Telegraph Company, its holding company. The Commission thought the fee excessive, but the Court noted that there was no evidence of bad faith.[29]

More recently commissions have received greater powers to check the acts of management. Although they cannot control the expenditures they can refuse to allow unreasonable expenditures in operating expenses. An Oregon law goes further and places the burden of proving reasonableness of certain expenditures on the utility. Under this law the Oregon Commission refused to recognize almost $20,000 of a $78,000 budget for executive salaries.[30]

Complaints. Much of a commission's work originates from complaints about rates, service, practices, etc. These may be handled formally or informally. In 1936, forty-five state commissions handled 17,120 formal cases, 73,106 informal cases, and 796,230 miscellaneous inquiries.[31] On this basis we can say that the average state commission handles about 380 formal cases, 1,600 informal cases, and about 18,000 miscellaneous inquiries a year.

Informal Procedure. Informal procedure is used to handle a large number of minor complaints involving meters, service, voltage regulation, and such matters. Adjustments are secured almost immediately by informal contact with the utility concerned. If an adjustment cannot be obtained, the matter may become a subject for formal procedure before the commission.

In recent years many more important matters such as rate adjustments have been handled to an increasing extent by informal procedure. In fact "negotiational rate making" has become virtually as important as formal rate making.

Formal Commission Procedure. Formal procedure is outlined by statute and by rules set forth by the commission itself. Rules of procedure are not as strict as those for judicial proceedings. Proceedings may be expensive and time consuming. A formal investigation of the Wisconsin Telephone Company by the Wisconsin Commission was commenced July 29, 1931, and the final order was not rendered until March 24, 1936. The Commission's order was appealed to the courts, and the final decision did not come until 1939.[32] The decision was unfavorable to the commission. The Illinois Commission began proceedings against the Illinois Bell Telephone Company in 1921. Commission proceedings and litigation dragged on until 1934. The utility company alone spent more than

29 *Southwest. Bell Tel. Co.* v. *Pub. Serv. Comm.*, 262 U.S. 276 (1923).

30 *Re Pacific Tel. & Tel. Co.*, 2 P.U.R. (N.S.) 384 (Oregon, 1933).

31 H. S. Spurr, "A Bit of Jaywalking in the Regulatory Highway," 19 *Pub. Util. Fort.* 742, 745 (June 10, 1937).

32 *Re Wisconsin Telephone Co.—State Wide Case.*, 13 P.U.R. (N.S.) 224 (1936). *Wis. Tel. Co.* v. *Pub. Serv. Comm.*, 287 N.W. 122 (Wis., 1939).

$1,200,000 in preparing its case for presentation to the commission.[33] In these cases the issues were important and the utility companies were willing and financially able to fight to the last. They are exceptional, but they are indicative of the delay and expense that can be forced upon commissions in rate litigation. In practically all instances delay is immaterial if not actually desirable to the companies. The expenses can always be recovered from the ratepayers. The reader may have justifiable doubts whether under these circumstances regulation is effective.

Initiating Formal Proceedings. Formal action may be initiated on a commission's own motion or on the complaint of municipal officials, public, or semi-public bodies, corporations, or a certain number of persons specified by statute. The Wisconsin law provides that a complaint may be made by "any mercantile, agricultural, or manufacturing society, or by any body politic or municipal organization, or by any twenty-five persons." [34] Maryland limits the right of complaint to officials of a municipality or not less than one hundred customers.[35]

The right of a commission to begin proceedings on its own motion, that is, on its own initiative, is an important adjunct to regulation. Many matters will require corrective action before they are apparent to ratepayers. A commission should have information not easily available to the public. Many times action on a broad and sweeping front beyond the scope of individual complaints is necessary. However, many commissions have found their limited time and personnel so occupied with routine duties that they have had little or no occasion to make more work for themselves by starting proceedings on their own initiative.

Notice. Before serving a complaint upon a utility a commission may conduct a preliminary investigation to determine whether formal action is necessary. The notice will specify the exact nature of the complaint and the time of a hearing. Minimum notice may be ten, twenty days or longer, depending upon the importance and complexity of the case. In some instances a pre-hearing conference will be held between representatives of the complainants, the utility, and the commission to clarify issues. It is to be noted that the utility is entitled to adequate notice and a hearing.

What Constitutes Notice and Complaint? A utility appearing before a commission is entitled to notice of the specific complaint to be made against it, and the order can be rendered only on the basis of the complaint. Under the Packers and Stockyards Act, the Secretary of Agriculture fixed rates for a stockyard. The examiner in the case had refused

---

[33] For a summary of this case and others and a vigorous criticism of judicial review of administrative procedure see Justice Brandeis' dissenting opinion in *St. Joseph Stock Yards v. U.S.*, 298 U.S. 38, 73 (1936).

[34] *Wisconsin Statutes*, 1945, Section 196.26.

[35] *Maryland Statutes*, 1910, Chapter 180, Section 36.

to prepare a tentative report of the government's contentions and proposed findings. The Supreme Court said, "The right to a hearing embraces not only the right to present evidence but also a reasonable opportunity to know the claims of the opposing party and to meet them." [36]

The Hearing. After a date and place of hearing have been specified, it will be placed on the commission's docket. By that time both the utility and the commission staff will have had time to prepare evidence. The hearing will be held before one or more commissioners or before an examiner or commission employee acting in the place of the commission. Final action, however, will be taken by the commission itself. By statute a commission must afford interested parties a right to be heard, which includes the right to introduce evidence and to object to evidence offered. Commissions are given power to summon witnesses and to compel the submission of records, documents, and other relevant material. Evidence will be presented by the commission staff, by the utility, and by other interested parties. A commission is bound only to a limited extent by the laws of evidence and it has liberal discretion in passing upon its competency. Briefs and exhibits will be submitted. A stenographic record of the proceedings will be kept and will become the basis for the final decision.

Proceedings are less formal than in court cases. Questions may be asked and answers given "off the record." The record may be developed almost as if by informal discussion. Lawyers and witnesses may have been long familiar with each other and with the commission. Commissioners may question witnesses. Sometimes they fall asleep.

The First Morgan Case.[37] In the previously mentioned Morgan cases the price-fixing order of the Secretary of Agriculture was based upon a transcript of oral testimony of some 13,000 pages and more than a thousand pages of exhibits and written briefs. The proceedings were carried on under a trial examiner, but the Secretary of Agriculture issued the order allegedly without either having heard or read the evidence or the arguments. This the Court decided did not constitute a full hearing as required by statute. The Court said:

> The "hearing" is designed to afford the safeguard that the one who decides shall be found in good conscience to consider the evidence, to be guided by that alone, and to reach his conclusion uninfluenced by extraneous considerations which in other fields might have play in determining purely executive action.[38]

The Court was apparently laying down the rule that "The one who decides must hear." Haste was made to qualify it. It was noted that

[36] *Morgan v. U.S.* (*The Second Morgan Case*), 304 U.S. 1, 18 (1938).
[37] *Morgan v. U.S.* (*The First Morgan Case*), 298 U.S. 468 (1936).
[38] *Ibid.*, 480.

assistants may prosecute inquiries, evidence may be taken by an examiner, and may be sifted and analyzed by competent subordinates. But the officer who makes the order must consider and appraise the evidence. This, it was admitted, may be an "onerous duty."

Considering the mass of evidence and the number of cases before a commission, the onerous duty may well be an impossible task. Perhaps the Court was aware of this, for on a second appeal the Court was satisfied when it appeared that the Secretary had kept the record on his desk for a while, and "dipped into" it from time to time. He had read the appellants' briefs and the transcript of the oral argument and had discussed the matter with those who had conducted the investigation.[39]

Findings of Fact. A commission will make findings of fact based on the evidence developed in the record. A commission has no power to consider evidence developed by its own experts if the parties to the case were not informed of it and given the opportunity to controvert it. Findings of fact must be specific and must be based upon the evidence. In the so-called *Orient Division* case an order of the Interstate Commerce Commission was set aside because the findings were based in part upon materials taken from annual reports filed with the Commission but not introduced as evidence. It was not sufficient that the examiner had stated that the Commission would refer to these reports.[40] Commissions may take "judicial notice" of facts of common knowledge such as a business depression and a decline in market values of property. But a company appearing before it has the right to demand an opportunity to explain or rebut the assumptions involved.[41] However, a utility does not have the right to challenge or rely on evidence that was not offered or considered.[42]

Findings clearly contradictory to the evidence are invalid. The sufficiency of the evidence may be determined by judicial review; but if the evidence is sufficient and substantial and not clearly contradictory to the findings, it will be conclusive on the commission and the courts in most instances.

Many of the basic principles of administrative law were formulated in cases where orders of the Interstate Commerce Commission were presented for review. The basic restrictions upon commission action were summarized in one of the most important of these cases as follows:

> Administrative orders, quasi judicial in character, are void if a hearing was denied; if that granted was inadequate or manifestly unfair; if the finding was contrary to the indisputable character of the evidence . . . the Commissioners cannot act upon their own information, as could jurors in primitive

39 *Morgan v. U.S.* (*The Second Morgan Case*), 304 U.S. 1, 17 (1938).
40 *U.S.* v. *Abilene & Southern Ry.*, 265 U.S. 274 (1924).
41 *Ohio Bell Tel. Co.* v. *Pub. Util. Comm.*, 301 U.S. 292 (1937).
42 *F.P.C.* v. *Natural Gas Pipeline Co.*, 315 U.S. 575, 584 (1942). *New England Division Case*, 261 U.S. 184, 201 (1923).

days. All parties must be fully apprised of the evidence submitted or to be considered, and must be given an opportunity to cross-examine witnesses, to inspect documents, and to offer evidence in explanation or rebuttal. In no other way can a party maintain its rights or make its defense. In no other way can it test the sufficiency of the facts to support the finding; for otherwise, even though it appeared that the order was without evidence, the manifest deficiency could always be explained on the theory that the Commission had before it extraneous, unknown, but presumptively sufficient information to support the finding.[43]

Commission Practice. In practice a commission takes considerably more latitude to itself than a strict reading of administrative law would indicate. Whereas courts are concerned only with the rights under the law of the parties appearing before it, a commission must be ever mindful of the general interest of the public and of the interests of many not appearing before it. The interest of the general public, for example, in a railroad rate tariff may be enormous in the aggregate, but only a few would find the opportunity to become parties to commission action. A commission exists to protect public rights and to determine, within statutory limits, lines of public action. Inevitably it will be required to draw upon its familiarity with conditions, statistics, reports, rate schedules, and other materials that cannot be presented as evidence: such material, it has been said, is, "as the air the commission breathes."

It might be argued that a commission should carefully investigate all aspects of a case before presenting its material at a hearing. In practice this would be a task of insuperable magnitude for most commissions. Furthermore, the real issues may not be defined until the hearing has sifted out the critical questions. To some extent the situation can be met by reopening the hearing if new material is developed. Another method is that of incorporating new evidence in a proposed report to which parties to the case can take exception.

It is undoubtedly true that many commission orders are based upon nothing more solid than a general impression or conjecture. Certainly there is a long jump from the shifting and uncertain ground of "evidence" to the firm and precise "finding of facts." Yet a commission must make it. As a practical matter, an ordinary sense of fair play is probably more important than the strict adherence to the letter of the law.

Enforcement. Ordinarily, commissions have no power to enforce their own orders, restrain violations, or impose fines or penalties. Instead they must institute proceedings in the courts. They can seek appropriate court orders such as writs of mandamus or injunction to compel or restrain.

---

[43] *ICC* v. *L. & N. R.R.*, 227 U.S. 88 (1913). Citation paraphrased. See also *ICC* v. *Delaware, Lackawanna & Western R. Co.*, 220 U.S. 235 (1911); *Pennsylvania Co.* v. *U.S.*, 236 U.S. 351 (1915); *ICC* v. *Union Pacific Ry. Co.*, 222 U.S. 541 (1912); *ICC* v. *Illinois Central R.R. Co.*, 215 U.S. 452 (1910).

Judicial Review. Statutes must also provide for judicial review of commission decisions. The Supreme Court has held that a state law authorizing an administrative officer to require railroads to eliminate grade crossings without provision for notice, hearing, and judicial review violates the due process clause of the Constitution.[44] A person aggrieved by a commission ruling may appeal it to a designated court. Thus the orders of the Wisconsin Commission may be appealed to the Circuit Court of Dane County. Decisions of this court may in turn be appealed to the State Supreme Court. If a Federal law or a constitutional issue is involved, or if there is a controversy between citizens of different states or between a state and a citizen of another, there may be an appeal to a Federal court and finally to the United States Supreme Court. State statutes cannot limit the right to appeal to a Federal court on such issues.

The courts have formulated a doctrine of exhaustion of administrative remedies as a prerequisite to judicial review. On appeal, the orders of utility commissions are generally made prima facie reasonable with the burden of proof thrown upon the aggrieved person to show that they are unreasonable or unlawful. If new evidence is developed in the court, the case must be remanded to the commission. If any other procedure were followed, parties to the commission proceedings might deliberately withhold evidence to present it to a court that they might think more favorably disposed towards their claims. In contrast, consumers have practically no rights to judicial review of administrative orders.[45]

The Johnson Act. Limitations on Judicial Review. Under certain circumstances a utility company may appeal from commission orders to either state or Federal courts. The ability to choose between the two procedures is a great advantage to the company. Federal courts may be less sympathetic to state commissions than state courts. Appeals to state courts must be brought within certain periods of time. This is not true of appeals to the Federal courts. While most state courts are bound by commission records, hearings in the Federal courts may be conducted as a trial *de novo*. A master may be appointed to take new evidence and the whole procedure repeated at enormous expense. The utility can charge this expense to the ratepayer, but the commission cannot. In the least, the company, if it so desires, can prolong litigation almost endlessly.

In an attempt to meet this situation Congress passed the Johnson Act in 1934 providing that no Federal district court should have jurisdiction to restrain the enforcement of any state commission order on the grounds of diversity of citizenship or repugnance of the order to the Constitution of the United States where the order:

[44] *Southern Ry. Co.* v. *Virginia,* 290 U.S. 190 (1933).
[45] R. T. Witmer, "Consumers' Appeals from Public Service Commission Rate Orders," 8 *U. of Chicago Law Rev.* 258 (1941).

(1) Affects rates charged by a public utility.
(2) Does not interfere with interstate commerce.
(3) Was made after reasonable notice and hearing.
(4) Where a plain, speedy, and efficient remedy can be had by law or in equity in the courts of such state.[46]

It is difficult to show any significant effect of this law. One Supreme Court decision limits the scope of the Act. The Court held that a Montana statute prohibiting the issuance of an injunction prior to the final determination of the reasonableness of rates in the courts does deny the utility a "plain, speedy, and efficient relief." [47]

6. PROCEDURAL PROTECTION AND JUDICIAL REVIEW

To what extent is a utility, or an individual, entitled to judicial review of administrative decisions? The problem is one of judicial review versus administrative finality. Much of the form and shape of our government depends upon the areas to be cleft by the line between the two. The somewhat clumsy rule of *Smyth* v. *Ames* was hit upon by the Court as a test of substantive due process. Can the Court give us a happier or a more adroit rule of procedural due process?

Will a Court Attempt to Weigh the Evidence? Will a court attempt to weigh the evidence upon which a commission bases its orders? A principle early laid down is the "substantial evidence rule":

The determination whether a rate is unreasonable or discriminatory is a question on which the finding of the Commission is conclusive if supported by substantial evidence.[48]

In another case the Supreme Court said that it would review the findings of a commission in so-called questions of mixed law and fact only to see if there was evidence upon which the conclusion could have been reached by reasonable men and that the "courts will not examine the facts further than to determine whether there was substantial evidence to sustain the order." [49] For example, the court would not pass upon the creditability of witnesses or upon the conflict of testimony.[50]

For many years the Court was satisfied to adhere to the "substantial evidence" rule. Then came the significant *Ben Avon* case.

[46] 48 Stat. 775 (1934), 28 U.S.C. 41.
[47] *Mountain States Power Co.* v. *Pub. Serv. Comm.*, 299 U.S. 167 (1936).
[48] *Western Paper Makers Chemical Co.* v. *U.S.*, 271 U.S. 268, 271 (1926). The rule was established in *ICC* v. *Louisville & Nashville R.R.*, 227 U.S. 88 (1913).
[49] *ICC* v. *U.P.R. Co.*, 222 U.S. 541, 548 (1912).
[50] *ICC* v. *L. & N. Ry.*, 227 U.S. 88, 92 (1913).

Ohio Valley Water Co. v. Ben Avon Borough (1920).[51] The Pennsylvania Commission fixed certain rates for the utility against which the company appealed, as provided by statute, to the state Superior Court. Evidence presented at the hearing was transmitted to the court. The court evaluated it, reversed the commission order, and ordered higher rates. The commission then appealed to the state Supreme Court, contending that the lower court, in passing on the evidence, had merely substituted its own judgment for that of the commission. The state Supreme Court noted that there was ample evidence to support the commission and reversed the lower court. The case then went to the United States Supreme Court which reversed the Pennsylvania Supreme Court on the ground that "the Supreme Court interpreted the statute as withholding from the courts their power to determine the question of confiscation according to their own independent judgment. . . ."

In short, this decision meant that where the constitutional issue of confiscation of property was involved the courts must have the opportunity of determining the issue upon "its own independent judgment as to both law and facts."

In its effect in crippling and emasculating commission regulation during the 1920's, this case must be ranked with the long line of valuation cases interpreting the rule of *Smyth* v. *Ames.* It is not too much to say that every utility rate case involves confiscation in a degree. It is true that a working distinction between confiscation and reasonableness was developed. Rates might be low, but still not so unreasonable as to involve confiscation. But all too often commissions became evidence-gathering bodies. The actual weighing of the evidence came to rest more and more in the hands of the courts. The practice soon developed of appealing to the courts on every minor detail of the rate-determining process. At its worst, the whole regulatory process was repeated under less favorable circumstances and conditions in the court rooms. In other instances the court would appoint a master to take new evidence.

Jurisdictional Facts. To the doctrine of "constitutional facts" of the *Ben Avon* case must be added the doctrine of "jurisdictional facts" of *Crowell* v. *Benson.*[52] Suppose an administrative order is attacked on the ground that the agency, by the Constitution, did not have jurisdiction. The Federal Longshoremen's and Harbor Workers' Compensation Act applies to workers on navigable streams. Who is to determine what is a navigable stream? The Supreme Court said that the navigability of certain streams is a question of fact that can be reviewed and tried *de novo* of

---

[51] *Ohio Valley Water Co.* v. *Ben Avon Borough,* 253 U.S. 287 (1920).
[52] *Crowell* v. *Benson,* 285 U.S. 22 (1932). It has been argued that this doctrine has been considerably modified in *R.R. Comm. of Texas* v. *Rowan & Nichols Oil Co.,* 310 U.S. 573 (1940).

facts, since navigability must be found to establish the existence of congressional power.

Regardless of how able regulatory commissions might be, regulation was made less effective and more uncertain by the possibility that a court, wary and distrustful of administrative processes, might find a constitutional or jurisdictional fact lurking in the background and take for itself the function of reviewing the facts to set the commission's work at naught.

There is considerable evidence of a growing liberality of attitude on the part of the Court towards commission orders. The "end result" doctrine of the *Hope Natural Gas* case considerably narrows the substantive protection to be accorded to utilities under the due process clause. In the *West Ohio Gas Company* case the Court said that if there was no confiscation there was no denial of due process, although "the proceeding is shot through with irregularity and error." [53]

This series of cases leaves much to be desired. It is uncertain as to what circumstances will call forth judicial review of evidence presented in administrative hearings. Cautiously the situation might be summarized as follows: Findings of fact, if supported by substantial evidence, will be accepted by the courts as conclusive to the extent that the constitutional issues of confiscation and jurisdiction are not involved.

7. THE SIGNIFICANCE OF THIS CHAPTER

The preceding pages must be regarded as more than a study in public utility law and commission procedure. It is in the field of public utility law more than in any other field that the balance is struck between the rights of private property and the power of public authority. It is here that the principles of administrative law are being worked out even today to create working rules for a new and fourth branch of our government. So rapidly have administrative commissions multiplied, and so far have their powers expanded, that it can well be said that administrative tribunals, although subordinate to, must still rank with the legislative, executive, and judiciary branches of our government.

The rapid expansion of state and Federal administrative agencies is not confined to the field of public utility regulation. The advance has been on such a wide front as to virtually reform and reshape the manner of our government. Many have viewed the trend with disquiet and alarm. Around no term in all the lexicon of government has there clustered such a mass of connotations of dislike, fear, and abuse as around the term "bureaucracy." The man in the street may have little respect for Congress or the state legislature, but he has little fear of them. But "bureaucracy" is almost universally hated and feared. It is regarded as the antithesis of

[53] *West Ohio Gas Co.* v. *Pub. Util. Comm.*, 294 U.S. 63, 70 (1935).

all that is to be admired in the American system of government. Its orders rest with peculiar force and irritation upon the businesses to whom they are directed. Business feels itself baffled and helpless before an administrative tribunal that is isolated from the forces that play upon and soften a legislative body. To those unacquainted with the broader dictates of public policy its orders may appear capricious and arbitrary—as indeed they often are.

But governmental regulation of business is now accepted as an integral part of our American system. As its scope has expanded its nature has changed. It was once thought that the purpose of government was to aid the natural working of economic laws. This sophistry is scarcely creditable today. For better or for worse the government makes economic laws. Property rights are created and taken away by a government in action. A regulatory commission determining reasonable value by administrative fiat, a labor relations board restricting and limiting the employer's intangible property in the good-will of his working force, a legislature fixing minimum wages are examples that are but picked at random. In a curious twist of terminology the "economic liberal" of the nineteenth century who believed in the efficacy of economic laws if they were only left to work unimpeded is now replaced by the "economic liberal" who would go far in replacing uninhibited individual action with social action.

The basic questions are two in number. To what extent may the powers of the legislature, the executive, and the judiciary be shared by an emerging fourth branch of our government—the administrative tribunal? To whom should go the final voice in determining public purpose and policy—the judiciary or the legislature? The answers to both questions are being worked out in the field of public utility law and economics, but the implications of both go far beyond that limited compass.

Dean Landis of the Harvard Law School has written:

> The most fascinating branch of American constitutional law relates to judicial review over legislative action. Here one is presented with decisions that speak of contest between two agencies of government—one, like St. George, eternally refreshing its vigor from the stream of democratic desires, the other majestically girding itself with the wisdom of the ages. Similarly, in the field of administrative law judicial review over administrative action gives a sense of battle.[54]

1. The Question of Administrative Finality

The regulatory commission is the instrument by which the coercive power of the state, roughly shaped in statutes and expressions of legislative intent, is brought to bear with fine precision upon the diverse

[54] James M. Landis, *The Administrative Process* (New Haven, Yale University Press, 1938), p. 123.

particles of the economic system. For the purpose of administering this power in a systematic way, a vast body of administrative law has grown up. The basic principles were set forth by the Courts in reviewing the early orders of the Interstate Commerce Commission. Administrative law, like constitutional law, has not become stabilized. Where will the line be drawn between the power of the administrative tribunal and the power of the courts?

Administrative agencies are fact-finding bodies. Are their findings of facts to be regarded as conclusive and final, or may they be, in general, subject to review? It is admitted that the findings might be erroneous, arbitrary, prejudiced, or faulty for other reasons. On the other hand, is anything to be gained by substituting the judgment of the courts for that of the commissions?

The argument for judicial review was well put by Chief Justice Hughes in the *St. Joseph Stock Yards* case:

> Legislative agencies, with varying qualifications, work in a field peculiarly exposed to political demands. Some may be expert and impartial, others subservient. It is not difficult for them to observe the requirements of law in giving a hearing and receiving evidence. But to say that their findings of fact may be made conclusive where constitutional rights of liberty and property are involved, although the evidence clearly establishes that the findings are wrong and constitutional rights have been invaded, is to place those rights at the mercy of administrative officials and seriously to impair the security inherent in our judicial safeguards. That prospect, with our multiplication of administrative agencies, is not one to be lightly regarded.[55]

One can agree with Chief Justice Hughes in principle without accepting the doctrine of the *Ben Avon* and *Crowell* cases. To claim more than this for judicial review would presuppose the existence of a body of facts which exists with certainty and can be found with definity. It presupposes judicial omniscience. To upset commission orders because the findings are clearly wrong is one thing, to upset them where there is substantial evidence to support them as the Court has done is something entirely different.

To a greater and greater extent the administrative tribunal will become the only effective means by which the government can exercise that degree of control over our economic activity demanded by prevailing public sentiment. While the courts have a bounden duty to safeguard the rights of the individual against the unwise and overzealous bureaucrat, they cannot go so far as to emasculate such a vital branch of our government. The practical arguments are strong ones.

The Infirmities of Judicial Review. The courts are not equipped with technical competence or time to weigh the vast masses of evidence that are

[55] *St. Joseph Stock Yards* v. *U.S.*, 298 U.S. 38, 52 (1936).

presented in utility rate cases before commissions all over the country. The transcript of the original evidence and arguments in the Chicago telephone rate case before the Illinois Commerce Commission ran to 4,500 pages, and 3,000 more pages of testimony were presented before the District Court. A second hearing involved a record of over 16,000 pages.[56] The time consumed in the reëxamination of much less evidence than this would make regulation a complete nullity and would leave the courts little time for anything else. Fair appraisal of technical evidence might be beyond the court's competence. The facts for which commissions and courts profess to search so diligently are likely to be no more than matters of judgment—reasonable assumptions compounded from a mass of inferences and other assumptions. In the determination of such facts little can be gained by substituting the judgment of the judiciary for that of competent, technical experts. A high degree of conclusiveness must be attributed to the findings of administrative commissions.

Justice Brandeis' Rules. Justice Brandeis in his concurring opinion in the *St. Joseph Stock Yards* case set forth the conditions under which he believed the Court was justified in setting aside a commission order.[57] It is believed that these principles are adequate to safeguard the rights of those appearing before administrative bodies while permitting regulation to be carried on with speed and dispatch.

Paraphrasing Justice Brandeis, commission orders may be set aside:

1. If the rates prescribed are confiscatory on the facts found.
2. If there is an error of substantive or procedural law.
3. If what purports to be a finding of fact is so involved with and dependent upon questions of law so as to be a decision of the latter, the Court will examine the entire record.
4. If the order lacks findings to support it.
5. If the findings are made without evidence to support them.
6. If the evidence was such "that it was impossible for a fair-minded board to come to the result which was reached."
7. If the order was based on evidence not legally cognizable.
8. If facts which ought to have been considered were excluded.
9. If facts or circumstances were considered which could not legally influence the conclusion.
10. If the commission applied a rule thought wrong for determining value.

Judicial Strengthening of Commissions. In the past attempts have been made to undermine the prestige of commissions by deliberately withholding evidence at a hearing only to introduce it before the courts. Some courts, distrustful or jealous of commissions, have abetted the practice from time to time. In its early days the Interstate Commerce

[56] As cited by Justice Brandeis in the *St. Joseph Stock Yards* case, 89.
[57] *Ibid.*, 74.

Commission lacked the confidence of the courts. Today its orders are treated with a high degree of respect and its prestige has increased accordingly. The Federal Trade Commission was likewise plagued by judicial suspicion for many years.

Justice Brandeis has wisely pointed out that the courts must consider the effect of their decisions not only upon the function of regulation but upon the administrative tribunals as well. "Responsibility is the great developer of men. May it not tend to emasculate or demoralize the rate-making body if ultimate responsibility is transferred to others?" [58] There are few who are conversant with administrative procedure who would be willing to deny that the ultimate determinant of administrative efficiency is the human factor. As Joseph B. Eastman, one of our ablest administrators, has said, "the personnel which does the administering is more important than the wording of the statute. Good men can produce more with a poor law than poor men can produce with a good law." [59]

In the past the courts' confidence or lack of confidence has contributed to the success or failure of certain types of administrative regulation. The courts can also take a positive, constructive attitude and build up the prestige of the commissions.

The Rule of Substantial Evidence. The weight of the argument seems to lie with Justice Brandeis. Judicial review is necessary. But it should be simple, quick, and limited. Otherwise regulation becomes a nullity and a fraud upon the taxpayers. The doctrine of "constitutional facts" rests upon the naïve belief that the facts exist as an abstraction determinable beyond all revocation. The implications of the doctrine of "jurisdictional facts" are so grotesque as to make a mockery of both regulatory administration and judicial review. The rule of "substantial evidence" seems adequate to protect individual rights from star chamber proceedings. It should lend certainty to administrative action, speed judicial review, and protect individual rights.

2. The Question of Judicial Review of Legislation

In *Munn* v. *Illinois* the Court conceded sweeping and untrammeled power to the legislatures of the states. Fourteen years later, in the *Chicago, Milwaukee and St. Paul Railway* case a Court of somewhat different judges reclaimed much of these powers by reading into the due process clause the concept of public purpose to be judicially determined. As time went on the Court developed what Professor John R. Commons called the doctrine of "Reasonable Value," which was to be accorded both procedural and substantive protection. As judicial philosophy of "reasonable value" firmed and hardened, the Court gave its attention to devising

[58] *Ibid.,* 92.

[59] In an address before the American Bar Association, 30 *A.B.A. Journal* 266 (1944).

working rules within which administrative tribunals must operate in effectuating public purpose. Only recently this hard shell of judicial philosophy has been broken by a new court that presumably reflects more accurately the political spirit of the times. So violent has been the breaking of old traditions, so far apart are the several new concepts into which the old has been split, that the Court has made but slow progress in fashioning them into a new and unified doctrine of public purpose and procedure.

Uncertain Foundation of Judicial Review. The doctrine of judicial review rests on an uncertain foundation compounded from obiter dicta and stare decisis. The police power under which public authority takes property without compensation for public purposes has been confounded with the power of eminent domain under which property is taken with compensation. By converting a corporation into a person the entire reach of our national economy has been brought within the play of the Fifth and Fourteenth Amendments and insulated in part from the power of public authority. Substantive protection has been imputed to these constitutional amendments where conceivably only procedural protection was intended to exist. Under the guise of interpreting the law the Court has taken unto itself the expert function of finding the facts thus limiting and restricting the functions of administrative tribunals.

Historically the judiciary has been conservative and has lent the weight of tradition and its own prestige against innovation and change. Changes in the law and in legal institutions have come about, but they have come from without rather than from within. In the eyes of the impatient later-day liberals the courts are seen as obstacles to progress. In the eyes of others they are left as the last remaining bulwark of individual rights, of liberty and property, against the growing forces of collectivism. Both the courts and their critics are likely to regard themselves as exclusive curators of the social wisdom that is to be expressed in public policy.

Can we look to the legislature as the proper and ultimate custodian of public policy? Too much is not to be expected. The legislative halls are not always the forum in which arguments are weighed and balanced against abstract conceptions of the public good and driven to conclusions to be expressed in law. Legislatures are rather arenas where pressure groups push and logroll and jockey for political advantage. From time to time, in one field or another, dominance may rest with labor, agriculture, business, industry, war veterans, or with some small groups that make up for the paucity of their numbers by the efficiency and discipline of their organization. It is truly said that the legislature is closest to the voice of the people, but often the only voice is that of the people who are organized to be heard. As Dr. Herring has said, "The 'voice of the people' sometimes suggests the squeal of pigs at the trough." In bursts of momentary enthusiasm or under pressure from powerful groups, wise and unwise legislation may be enacted. Matters of pressing concern may be left unattended for want of an advocate. Public welfare cannot always be regarded as the inevitable synthesis of these many divergent forces, just as it is not to be compounded from the devious workings of unrestrained economic laws.

It is hardly possible to balance precisely the rights of the individual against the claims of all society in scales that measure ultimate good or bad. Our government is a system of checks and balances. In the long run we may perhaps most closely approximate public wisdom from the composite action of the legislature, executive, judiciary, and administrative tribunals. Each in a degree must be controlled by the others.

In asserting the doctrine of judicial review the judiciary has claimed for itself the position of being the first arbiter of the governmental terrain that is to be allocated to each. But as recent and past political history has indicated, the courts can not too long run counter to the plain and apparent sentiment of the mass of the people and prevailing political mores. As our economic society grows more complex, it seems inevitable that more and more individual rights will have to be surrendered for the common good. To a lesser and lesser extent will the court find reason to assert itself as the protector of the rights of the individual, either private or corporate. Such a doctrine will not be accepted by all with good grace. It is sufficient to say that these are the legal institutions which our society is fashioning for itself. There may be better. There are certainly many worse.

4. Regulation by Franchise and Permit

1. THE RIGHT TO ENGAGE IN THE UTILITY BUSINESS

Significance of the Franchise. The right to engage in the public utility business, unlike most other businesses, exists only with the permission of public authority. Proper authority may be conveyed by:

1. The corporate charter
2. The franchise
3. Certificates, permits and licenses
4. The certificate of convenience and necessity.

It has been the experience of regulatory history that both price and service regulation break down without the regulation of entry into the industry. The three types of control are mutually dependent upon each other. The regulation of taxicab charges has frequently broken down without the regulation of the number of taxicabs. An excessive number of cabs will frequently enough bring very low rates, but it may also reduce the quality of service as competition becomes more severe. By franchises, permits, licenses, etc., public authority retains the necessary control over competition.

The Corporate Charter. The corporate charter is issued by the state and creates the corporation. In return for the right to be a corporation with all the privileges and advantages that go with it, the state may logically subject the grantee to various burdens and restrictions. In the early days of the last century, when corporate charters were issued only by special acts of the legislatures, attempts were made to subject some public utilities such as bridge, canal, ferry, wharf, and railroad companies to regulatory restrictions by charter.

The Franchise. The franchise is a right granted by a municipality under authority conferred upon it by the state to private parties to engage in the public utility business and to use public property for private profit. A utility can construct and operate facilities on public highways which but for the franchise would constitute trespass.

In the absence of provisions to the contrary, franchises can be transferred. One of the features of the consolidation movement, by which many small and competing utilities were put together into larger systems, was the financial, political, and legal maneuvering to acquire as many franchises as possible. The franchise of the old United Railways and Electric Company of Baltimore was made up of some 75 independent street-railway franchises. Back in the 1890's promoters frequently secured street-railway franchises with only the intent of selling them at as high a nuisance value as possible to other promoters.

Some mention should be made of the easement which in Maryland conveys the right to use public streets and is similar to a franchise. In general an easement is a permanent right in realty without an interest in ownership.

Licenses, Permits, and Certificates. Licenses, permits, and certificates do not achieve the dignity of a franchise. They may be required of non-utility businesses or of professional men such as doctors and lawyers. They represent a personal privilege, are of temporary and revocable nature, and carry with them none of the contractual elements of the franchise. They are commonly granted, non-exclusive, and do not create monopoly property rights as franchises frequently do. A permit might be issued to a utility to issue securities or to construct a dam. A contract carrier might be required to obtain a permit to do business; a common carrier might be required to obtain a certificate of convenience and necessity while only an ordinary license might be required of a private carrier. Permits and licenses, then, do not involve such a great degree of regulation.

The Certificate of Convenience and Necessity. The certificate of convenience and necessity is a special permit, commonly issued by a state commission rather than by a municipality, which authorizes a utility to engage in business, construct facilities, or perform some other service. It supplements the franchise, and like the franchise it is used to control competition and secure a more orderly extension of service. It might be required of an electric utility to extend its lines to a new community, or to erect a new generating plant. It finds very frequent use in the control of motor transportation service.

These certificates differ from franchises in that they do not generally confer property rights. There is no right of transfer. They are not contracts with the state, but a privilege conferred by the state. A new law subjecting an industry to regulation generally contains a so-called "Grandfather" clause which automatically gives a certificate to firms already in the business.

Extent of Franchise Regulation. Regulatory powers may be allocated between the utility commission and the municipalities of the state as the state legislature deems wise. Although centralized regulation is generally assumed in this text, direct regulation has its proponents and many states have retained the older method. In some states virtually all regulatory powers over certain utilities are given to the municipalities. This is true of Iowa, New Mexico, and Texas in respect to telephone utilities. In Iowa, Michigan, New Mexico, Texas, Washington, and Wyoming, commissions have no control over street railways. The commissions of Florida, Iowa, Minnesota, Mississippi, Texas, and South Dakota have no control over electric rates. In Colorado, cities of more than 2,000 population may become "Home Rule" cities and fix their rates exclusive of the state commission. By action of the legislature, New Orleans, Louisiana, regulates its own utilities. In some states such as Ohio and Michigan, regulatory jurisdiction is given to municipalities subject to appeal to the commission. Most states have given their commissions such comprehensive powers that few matters are left for local control. The franchise becomes little more than a permit to use the streets.

2. THE FRANCHISE AS AN INSTRUMENT OF REGULATION

1. Types of Franchises

It has been shown that a state can call upon either of two methods of regulating utilities. If the franchise method is adopted, municipalities contract with their utilities.

Franchises may be classified according to their duration as perpetual, long term, short term, and indeterminate. The duration of a utility's franchise is an important factor in determining the desirability of its securities in the financial markets.

The Perpetual Franchise. In the early days of public utility development many franchises were made perpetual or were construed to be perpetual by the courts. If the general laws of a state impose no restriction upon the duration of a franchise and the franchise itself is silent, the Federal courts have construed the franchise to be perpetual.[1] Before this federal rule was pronounced, state courts generally considered a franchise to be terminable at will if there were no specific provisions to the contrary.

State statutes or constitutions almost invariably prohibit perpetual

[1] *Owensboro* v. *Cumberland T. & T. Co.,* 230 U.S. 58 (1913); *Ohio Pub. Serv. Co.* v. *Ohio,* 274 U.S. 12 (1927); *Northern Ohio Traction & L. Co.* v. *State,* 245 U.S. 574 (1917).

franchises today. At any rate, few communities would make the mistake of granting such a franchise now. Burdened with a franchise carrying special privileges, the municipality may be virtually helpless to oust the utility if it becomes dissatisfied with rates or service. The perpetual franchise is inflexible and cannot be made to fit into the needs of a growing community or into the demands of changing technology. Under the terms of a perpetual franchise a horse car continued to operate on the streets of Manhattan until after 1915. The franchise is particularly obnoxious if it is exclusive and precludes competition from the city or from another utility.

The Long-Term Franchise. The long-term franchise may run for twenty-five years or more within the maximum period prescribed by the legislature or by the state constitution. If the perpetual franchise is bad, the long-term franchise is little better. It is of almost no use as a regulatory device. Once the franchise is granted the utility is normally beyond the control of the municipality. It may take only a few years to make the best-devised regulatory provisions obsolete. The value of some provisions prescribing rates, voltage, street car routes, and the heating content of gas has often failed to outlast the next technological or economic development. In practice long-term franchises may not be quite so bad. They are frequently restricted in terms and provide for frequent revisions in rates and conditions of service without the surrender of the franchise. To the utility, the long term franchise is, of course, highly desirable. Long-range construction plans can be made, financing is easier, and there is little fear of competition.

The Short-Term Franchise. Short-term franchises run for twenty years or less. The expiration of the franchise gives the municipality an opportunity to oust the utility if service is unsatisfactory or to renegotiate rate and service provisions. The short-term franchise was devised to meet the failures of the long-term franchise but it brought with it a batch of evils of its own. It may be unsatisfactory to the city and utility alike. The utility will be reluctant to expand facilities, particularly as the expiration date approaches, as in the case of Toronto, where a street-railway company allowed service to deteriorate until it was the worst-served city on the continent. In Des Moines the city had to improvise service when the utility declined to continue service after the date of expiration.[2] Since there is no assurance that a buyer can be found for the properties if the franchise is not renewed, the utility will seek to recapture its investment during the life of the franchise. Rates will be excessive. If the franchise is renewed, the utility will be in a position of having its cake after having eaten it as well.

[2] Cited by M. G. Glaeser, *Outlines of Public Utility Economics* (New York, The Macmillan Company, 1927), pp. 1-2.

As the expiration of the franchise approaches, the utility will be tempted to go into politics to secure its renewal if it has not already taken that step. No utility is likely to overlook the value of friendly councilmen. It is probably true that most utilities regard participation in politics as highly undesirable, but many of them regard it as a necessary evil. Such participation, even if it is open and aboveboard, is not consistent with the public interest; yet utility management feels obliged to do everything possible to safeguard its investment.

The short-term franchise makes financing difficult and raises the cost of capital and service. Finally, it may be said that the franchise offers little real flexibility anyway. The necessity of adjusting rates and service may arise at any time. Whether the franchise is for five or fifty years, the city and the utility are under immediate and odious contractual burdens that cannot be escaped.

The Indeterminate Permit. In its simplest form the indeterminate permit is nothing more than a franchise that can be revoked at will without compensation to the utility. Franchises granted by Congress in the District of Columbia and in Porto Rico are of this type. The more common type is modelled from the Wisconsin law and may be defined as a franchise that may be terminated at any time, the property of the utility being taken with fair compensation as determined by the state commission. If service is unsatisfactory, the commission has the power to grant a certificate of convenience and necessity to another utility to render competing service. The hoped-for effect of the indeterminate permit is to put the utility upon its good behavior.

Underlying the theory of the indeterminate permit are several basic considerations:

1. As a franchise it becomes a mere permit to use the streets, although municipalities may retain some powers to determine the nature of service, to require extensions and impose other conditions subject to review by the state commission.

2. Regulatory power is transferred from the municipality to the state commission.

3. The utility operates as a protected monopoly, subject to the conditions that it must render satisfactory service and that its permit may be terminated by the purchase at a fair price.

Special Franchises. "Sliding-scale" and "service-at-cost" franchises represent a special and further development of contractual regulation. Under these franchises rates and profits are automatically adjusted by formulas determined in advance. The former type offers incentives for rate reductions while the latter is a device to keep rates continuously adjusted to the cost of service. They will be discussed in detail in a later chapter.

2. The Development of Franchise Regulation

The *Dartmouth College* Case. In 1819, in a dispute between the trustees of Dartmouth College and an officer of the State of New Hampshire for the control of the college, the Supreme Court laid the cornerstone for the somewhat shaky and uncertain edifice of franchise law. Before the Revolution, a Reverend Eleazer Wheelock had secured a corporate charter from the King of England to establish a religious school for Indians. By 1819 the Indians had ceased to haunt the academic halls of that venerable institution, although it is said that attempts were made to import a canoe-load of Indians for the special purpose of proving that it was still an Indian school. However that may be, the Supreme Court found the College's charter to be an inviolable contract, binding upon the state, and as such subject to Article 1, Section 10 of the Constitution, which says, "No State shall ... pass any ... Law impairing the Obligation of Contracts." [3]

The doctrine of the *Dartmouth College* case may appear somewhat strange. Is not a franchise, as normally granted by an act of legislation, similar to any other piece of legislation that may be repealed with or without cause? At the best, is a franchise anything more than a permit which may be revoked at will? The answer has already been given. A more telling criticism remains. May a state, by virtue of a franchise grant, contract away its normal police powers which are the essence of its sovereignty?

The *Charles River Bridge* Case. The Court itself may have been inclined to look somewhat askance at what it had done. Some years later in *Charles River Bridge* v. *Warren Bridge*,[4] the Court formulated the doctrine of strict construction. Here it was held that a specific grant of the right to build a toll bridge across the Charles River at Boston did not bar the state from making a similar grant to another competing bridge company, although the new franchise would probably destroy the value of the first grant. The franchise had not been made exclusive by any specific proviso. That was the point. "No rights are taken from the public or given to the corporation beyond those which the words of the charter ... purport to convey." In short, all doubts as to the subject matter of the franchise, and as to the subsequent rights of the state, were to be resolved in favor of the state. As time went on this principle of franchise law acquired a significance and force that fully equaled that of the older and more famous *Dartmouth College* case. Many utility corporations

[3] *Dartmouth College* v. *Woodward*, 4 Wheat. 518 (1819).
[4] *Charles River Bridge* v. *Warren Bridge*, 11 Peters 420 (1837).

were later to find out a franchise did not protect them from many and surprising laws that legislatures subsequently enacted.

The scarcity and timidity of capital and the demand for public services which came with insistent clamor from new and growing communities gave all the bargaining advantages to early corporate promoters. Over the course of years the turnpike, canal, railroad, water, gas, traction, and electric companies followed each other in turn in wrangling lucrative franchises and charters from Federal, state and local politicians who never seemed to realize the value of what they gave—or in some instances realized too well. Thus the city of St. Paul guaranteed a return of eight per cent to a gas company in a charter issued in 1856, while Minnesota was still a territory. Rights of way that embraced large acreages of public lands, generous rates and the privileges of tax exemption, freedom from competition, and other favors and emoluments were granted by compliant legislators without stint or consideration. Fortified by the *Dartmouth College* case and warned by the *Charles River Bridge* case, the promoters moved fast behind the courts to nail these rights down by binding contractual obligations within their franchise grants. Later, public representatives realized the value of the rights which they had so casually and magnanimously granted and sought to recapture some of the monopoly profits by selling franchises or subjecting franchise holders to special taxes. But in general the early promoters proved themselves more sharp witted than the politicians, not to say statesmen, with whom they dealt.

During the Granger movement franchise law disintegrated before the consuming force of public anger over corporate abuses. Even the Court in its citadel was reached by the fiery outburst of public outrage. Attempts were made to break franchise and charter grants with some success. The supremacy of the state's police power was upheld in *Munn* v. *Illinois* in 1877.

The Traction Franchise Scandals. The Granger movement had hardly subsided when the evils that brought it into being appeared again in another quarter. After Frank J. Sprague had completed the first commercial electric street railway in Richmond, Virginia, in 1888, trolley systems popped up over night in every important city in the United States. Almost eight hundred systems were set up in two years. If the early horse-car franchises were luscious plums, they were as nothing compared with the fruits that might be expected from a street railway franchise. With the traction franchises and largely because of them came a period of municipal corruption, the odors of which were never surpassed in the history of American municipal government. When the denouement came it brought into being a whole new school of journalism whose votaries were somewhat derisively termed "the muckrakers."

As horseless carriages captured the fancy of the riding public, the traction promoters proved themselves just as successful in capturing those permits which gave them the right to "lay, operate, and maintain" their tracks on city streets. These privileges could be had for a price that found its way into the pockets of the councilmen of the period. In defiance of any sense of decency promoters openly haunted the halls and lobbies of city halls, their pockets conspicuously stuffed with bills which disappeared in the course of the evening. "Boodle" and "boodlers" became standard terms in the American vocabulary. After a few years' service, councilmen acquired palatial homes and magnificent carriages in ways that were not entirely mysterious even to the general public.

Lincoln Steffens, one of the most famous of the "muckrakers," reported that "the graft of Pittsburgh falls conveniently into four classes: franchises, public contracts, vice, and public funds." [5] The same writer reported that in St. Louis in 1899 a promoter spent nearly $300,000 in bribes to secure a blanket street-railway franchise, the generosity of which was not equalled by any franchise then in existence in the city. Two separate attempts were necessary, as the first attempt failed when the mayor vetoed the measure. Two thirds of the councilmen then passed the measure over the mayor's veto. Not all the members received the $50,000 fee given to one man whose honor came somewhat high. Within a week the franchise was sold for $1,250,000 to other promoters who, without owning a single foot of rail or a single streetcar, forced all the other streetcar companies in the city, save one, to contribute their stock and right of way to a merger. [6]

It is a mistake to assume that all these traction barons were completely devoid of a sense of ethics. On the contrary, they complained bitterly of the venality and foul practices of the politicians who came to them with open palms and watering mouths. With some measure of justice it can be said that the politicians took the lead in seeking out wealthy corporations for financial favors. Business men were all too often obliged to meet the legislators on their own terms or forego the privilege of engaging in business. At least their competitors would do so if they didn't. The question may be raised as to which of a conniving pair is more subject to censure—he who offers the bribe or he who solicits it. Little can be gained by attempting to assess the comparative morals of either group. Such was the venality and corruption of the period that there was ample dishonor for all.

On the other hand, the more public-spirited members of the city councils, fully realizing the value of the grants they were making to private individuals, sought to recover or retain as much for the city as possible. Franchises frequently were granted to the highest bidder or contained provisions requiring a large annual payment into the coffers

[5] Lincoln Steffens, *The Shame of the Cities* (New York, McClure, Phillips, 1904), p. 165.
[6] *Ibid.,* p. 52.

of the city. Although such provisions were designed to recapture some of the profits made by the favored corporation, they probably had the effect of increasing the rates charged to consumers. However laudable the motives of those who sought such protective provisions, the wisdom was circumspect. It was a needless burden on the ratepayers and represented a far too inflexible method of dealing with monopoly profits.

Decline of Franchise Regulation. It was hardly necessary for the muck-rakers to demonstrate that the franchise had proven inadequate as an instrument of regulation. The public turned to other methods. Investigations and reform movements in New York and Wisconsin paved the way for the first public utility commission laws in 1907. Other states followed in rapid succession. With approval of the courts the newly established commissions were able to recapture in large measure those regulatory powers that had been so easily surrendered by the municipalities. State constitutions were amended specifically to reserve to the legislatures the right to amend charters and franchises. Legislatures looked more closely to the powers granted their municipalities. Indeterminate permit laws led many utilities more or less voluntarily to surrender their franchises in exchange for the new permits. In some instances this was a clear gain for the public. In other instances the franchises were undesirable to the utilities, or were about to expire in any event.

Franchise abandonment was speeded when the rising prices of the first World War brought the utilities on their knees to the people, begging to be released from fixed rate provisions. Columbus, Ohio, refused to allow a utility to surrender its franchise and gain release from rates fixed by ordinance for 25 years in 1901. In other instances utilities were permitted to escape from contractual rate provisions by surrendering their franchises for indeterminate permits. Rates were generally increased. The five-cent fare on which the street-railway industry had been founded before the century began became an economic anachronism.

3. THE LEGAL PROBLEMS OF THE FRANCHISE

The problem of franchise law is a difficult one because it involves a welter of conflicting rights arising under different circumstances. The principal parties that may be involved in franchise litigation include the following:

1. The state, whose rights are determined and limited by the police power, the Federal constitution, the state constitution and state statutes.

2. The municipality, whose jurisdiction is established by its own charter and by the state constitution.

3. The public utility commission, whose powers are established by state law and by the state constitution.

4. The utility, who in addition to its constitutional rights gains certain contractual rights by virtue of its franchise.

Beginning with the *Charles River Bridge* case, the Supreme Court has steadily limited the theory of franchise rights as protected by the obligations of the contract clause of the constitution and correspondingly enhanced the police powers of the state, which cannot be contracted away. To state the basic problem of much of the following discussion succinctly: Is a state (or its municipalities) contracting away its police powers of regulation or is it exercising them, when it fixes rates for the future by enactments pursuant to a franchise?

What Regulatory Rights Are Embraced by the Police Power? In a case in which the city of Goldsboro, North Carolina, attempted to regulate the speed of trains within the city, the Supreme Court said, "it is settled that neither the 'contract' clause nor the 'due process' clause has the effect of overriding the power of the State to establish all regulations that are reasonably necessary to serve the health, safety, good order, comfort, or general welfare of the community; that this power can neither be abdicated nor bargained away, and is inalienable even by express grant; and that all contract and property rights are held subject to its fair exercise." [7] The railway had claimed that the city ordinance impaired its charter, which granted it a right of way through the city.

For our purposes we can say that if the public interest is substantial a municipality retains the right to impose reasonable conditions looking to public safety, health, and morals upon franchise holders. The power to alter franchise rates, however, stands on a different footing.[8]

Can It Be Assumed That a Municipality Has the Right to Fix Utility Rates? An Illinois law of 1872 authorized municipalities to "contract for a supply of water for public use for a period not exceeding thirty years," and authorized private persons to construct waterworks "and maintain the same at such rates as may be fixed by ordinance, and for a period not exceeding thirty years." Do these provisions give a municipality the right to enter into a thirty-year rate contract? The Illinois Supreme Court said no and the United States Supreme Court accepted this interpretation.[9]

[7] *A.C.L.* v. *Goldsboro*, 232 U.S. 548, 558 (1914). See also *Southern Wisconsin Ry.* v. *Madison*, 240 U.S. 457 (1916); *Springfield* v. *Springfield St. Ry.*, 64 N.E. 577 (1902). For cases limiting the rights of the city see *Grand Trunk Western Ry.* v. *South Bend*, 227 U.S. 544 (1913); *Welch* v. *Swasey*, 214 U.S. 91 (1909).

[8] *Beer Co.* v. *Massachusetts*, 97 U.S. 25 (1878); *New Orleans Gas Co.* v. *La. Light Co.*, 115 U.S. 650 (1885).

[9] *Freeport Water Co.* v. *Freeport*, 180 U.S. 587 (1901). For other cases holding that a municipality has no inherent or implied power to regulate rates or contract away the police powers of the state see *Detroit* v. *Detroit Citizens Street Ry.*, 184 U.S. 368 (1902);

The right to fix rates by ordinance for thirty years is not the right to fix them by a thirty-year contract. The reasoning is precise and fine.

The legal principles involved are well set forth in the more recent case of *Railroad Commission of California* v. *Los Angeles Railway Company*.[10] The railway operated under franchises granted by the city which specified a maximum fare of five cents. These rates were apparently confiscatory. The company appealed to the state commission for an increase which the commission refused to grant in the belief that the franchise provisions were binding. The United States Supreme Court, however, failed to find any specific delegation by the state to the municipality of the power to fix rates and thus held the rates subject to commission jurisdiction.

Can a State Consent to be Bound? By ordinance the city of St. Cloud, Minnesota, had early granted the predecessors of the St. Cloud Public Service Company the right to construct and maintain gas works for thirty years and had authorized it to sell gas at a rate not exceeding $1.35 per thousand cubic feet. By 1917 conditions had so changed that a rate of $3.39 was necessary to give the company a fair and non-confiscatory return. The company threatened to raise the rates.

The Court examined the constitution, statutes, and court decisions of Minnesota to determine whether the city was authorized to enter into a contract as to gas rates. This was the basic issue, for as the court said, "It has been long settled that a State may authorize a municipal corporation to establish by inviolable contract the rates to be charged by a public service corporation for a definite term, not grossly unreasonable in time, and that the effect of such a contract is to suspend, during its life, the governmental power of fixing and regulating rates." The court concluded that the city had the right to contract and that this right was not limited by a charter proviso that the city council should have the right to regulate. Finding the ordinance a valid contract, the court held the utility to be bound by it.[11]

Ohio has sometimes been cited as a state whose municipalities have the power of making inviolable rate contracts. The Ohio constitution does give municipalities comprehensive powers, but recent interpretations

---

Cleveland v. *Cleveland City Ry.*, 194 U.S. 517 (1904); *Vicksburg* v. *Vicksburg W.W. Co.*, 206 U.S. 496 (1907); *Home T. & T. Co.* v. *Los Angeles*, 211 U.S. 265 (1908); *Puget Sound Traction Co.* v. *Reynolds*, 244 U.S. 574 (1917); *City of Englewood* v. *Denver & S.P. Co.*, 248 U.S. 294 (1919).

[10] *R.R. Comm. of Cal.* v. *Los Angeles Ry. Co.*, 280 U.S. 145 (1929).

[11] *Pub. Serv. Co.* v. *St. Cloud*, 265 U.S. 352 (1924). See also *Ga. Ry. & Power Co.* v. *Decatur*, 262 U.S. 432 (1923); *Ga. Power Co.* v. *Decatur*, 281 U.S. 505 (1930); *Southern Utilities Co.* v. *Palatka*, 268 U.S. 232 (1925); *Opelika* v. *Opelika Sewer Co.*, 265 U.S. 215 (1924).

have held that a municipality has no authority to make an irrevocable contract for a period of more than ten years.[12] Virginia has held that its cities do not have the power of making such contracts.[13] It has been held that under the "Home Rule" provisions of the Colorado constitution, rate contracts cannot be abrogated.[14] The same rule applies to a limited extent to New Jersey [15] and Louisiana.[16]

These cases illustrate several principles of franchise law. The power to fix rates must be delegated specifically to the municipality by the legislature. It is possible for a state to authorize a municipality to establish rates for a limited term of years, "not grossly unreasonable in time," and thereby suspend the regulatory power in the interim. A contract made under these conditions is binding even if rates are unduly high or low. The United States Supreme Court will be bound by the decisions of the highest state court in interpreting the power of each state's municipalities. All doubts are to be resolved in favor of the state and any grant or authority to surrender power is not to be inferred.

Are Old Franchise Rates Valid After a New Commission Is Created? The conflict between the police powers of the state and the contractual rights of municipalities or utilities is most frequently presented where a franchise antedates the establishment of a regulatory commission. Can a new commission set these old franchise rates aside?

Before the formation of a state public utilities commission, the borough of West Chester, Pennsylvania, entered into a franchise agreement with the Philadelphia Electric Company by which the utility supplied free steam heating service for the firehouses in return for the right to place a system of pipes under the streets. Later the utility began charging the borough its regular filed rates for this service. The Pennsylvania Commission held that the contract must give way before the exercise of the police power of the state through the establishment of a regulatory commission.[17]

In general, provisions of municipal franchises relating to subjects within the jurisdiction of the state commission are void upon the exercise of the commission's powers.[18] State constitutions and state laws will control. The New York law is an example. The New York court held that a

---

[12] *Interurban Ry. Co.* v. *Pub. Util. Comm.,* 120 N.E. 831 (Ohio, 1918); *Columbus* v. *Pub. Serv. Comm.,* 133 N.E. 800 (Ohio, 1921).

[13] *Victoria* v. *Victoria Ice Co.,* 114 S.E. 92 (Va., 1922).

[14] *Pueblo* v. *Pub. Util. Comm.,* 187 Pac. 1026 (Colo., 1920); *Golden ... Co.* v. *Colorado Sprs. P. C.,* 192 Pac. 493 (Colo., 1920).

[15] *Federal Shipbuilding Co.* v. *Bayonne,* 141 Atl. 455 (N.J., 1928).

[16] *Baton Rouge Water Co.* v. *La. Pub. Serv. Comm.,* 100 So. 710 (La., 1924).

[17] *Borough of West Chester* v. *Phila. El. Co.,* 44 P.U.R. (N.S.) 127 (Penna., 1942).

[18] *C. B. & Q. Ry.* v. *Nebraska,* 170 U.S. 57 (1898); *The Milwaukee Ry. & L. Co.* v. *Railroad Comm. of Wis.,* 238 U.S. 174 (1915).

state commission can change all franchise rates except those over which it had no delegated authority.[19]

May a Franchise Bind a Utility Without Binding the City? In the Los Angeles case the court interpreted the California law to the effect that a city had no right to bind itself in a manner which would prevent it from exercising its regulatory powers. Since the city was not bound, it was reasoned, the utility was not bound either.

The charter of the city of Texarkana, Texas, contained the provision that all franchises granted by the city council should expressly reserve to the city the right of regulating public utilities. By franchise agreement the city stipulated that the rates of the gas company should be no higher than those in the adjoining city of Texarkana, Arkansas. Arkansas rates were lowered and the Texas city brought suit to have its rates lowered accordingly. By its own charter the city obviously could not be bound, but under these circumstances could the utility?

The court thought that the action of the city of Texarkana was an exercise and not an abdication of its regulatory power, since it used the Arkansas rates as a "mere measuring rod, as though the rate fluctuated with temperature or consumption." Under decisions of the Texas courts, contract and regulatory powers could be exercised concurrently. Thus the city had both powers. The contract was binding upon the utility, but not on the city, since it could still exercise regulatory power.[20]

What Rights and Duties Exist After a Franchise Has Expired? A water company serving Carthage, Missouri, and the city failed to agree on purchase terms after the franchise of the company had expired. The city then went ahead with plans to build a municipal water system and attempted to make the private company continue its service while the city plant was being constructed. The utility company got an injunction restraining the city from interfering while it removed its pipes from the city streets.[21] This is an extreme case and is hardly controlling, but it illustrates the general principle that both the right and the duty to serve expire with the franchise. An attempt to force service is an impairment of the property and contract rights of the utility.[22]

This principle is subject to considerable modification. Courts will consider not only the interests of the utility and the city but the general interest of the people in continuity of service.[23] However, the city cannot

[19] *Quinby* v. *Pub. Serv. Comm.,* 119 N.E. 433 (N.Y., 1918); *People ex rel. Village of South Glen Falls,* 121 N.E. 777 (N.Y., 1919).

[20] *Texarkana* v. *Arkansas Louisiana Gas Co.,* 306 U.S. 188 (1939) For an older decision involving the Texas law which is no longer controlling see *San Antonio* v. *San Antonio Public Service Co.,* 255 U.S. 547 (1921).

[21] *Laighton* v. *City of Carthage,* 175 F. 145 (1909).

[22] *American Express Co.* v. *U.S.,* 212 U.S. 522 (1909).

[23] *Seaford* v. *Eastern Shore Public Service Co.,* 194 Atl. 92 (Del., 1937). Commented upon by P. H. Ford in 12 *Southern California Law Review* 98 (Nov., 1938).

compel service after a reasonable period of time has elapsed after the utility has served notice.[24] If the utility voluntarily continues to serve and the city acquiesces, a franchise of indefinite duration is implied. The arrangement may be terminated at will by either party after reasonable notice.[25] If the utility makes costly improvements with the consent of the city after the franchise has expired, the period of reasonable notice is lengthened.[26] Utility patrons must pay a reasonable compensation for service as long as the utility gives it and the city accepts it.[27]

The *Carthage* case was an attempt to force continuance of service after a franchise had expired. Attempts to oust a utility may create situations just as difficult. In general, a utility does not become a trespasser until it has had a reasonable time to dispose of its property or secure a new franchise.[28] A city is under no obligation to purchase the plant,[29] nor can it take possession of facilities or grant them to another utility with compensation.[30]

4. AN EVALUATION OF THE FRANCHISE

Basis of Criticism. An evaluation of the franchise may be made from several viewpoints. First, it may be considered a mere instrument for the control of utility rates and service—an answer to the problem of regulation. Second, it may be placed in somewhat broader perspective and considered the focal point of public utility economics—an instrument by which the controls of competition, monopoly, and regulation are shaped. Finally, it can be considered in the light of a case study in local versus state government.

What is a good franchise? In the first place it must be pointed out that in many states franchise standards would be meaningless, since most, if not all, regulatory powers are vested in the state commissions. Even in these states, however, the utilities must come to the municipalities for the right to use the city streets and to this privilege the city can attach special conditions. The preceding discussion should have made it abundantly clear that a municipality's power to regulate are closely circumscribed by its own charter, by the state constitution and general statutes, and by the specific powers conferred upon the state commission.

---

[24] *East Ohio Gas Co.* v. *Akron*, 90 N.E. 40 (Ohio, 1909).

[25] *Denver* v. *Denver Union Water Co.*, 246 U.S. 178 (1918). Commented upon in 23 *Harvard Law Review* 646 (1910).

[26] *State* v. *Des Moines City Ry.*, 140 N.W. 437 (Iowa, 1913). Noted, 46 *Harvard Law Review* 1028 (1933). See also *Detroit United Ry. Co.* v. *Detroit*, 255 U.S. 171 (1921).

[27] *Toledo* v. *Toledo Rys. & L. Co.*, 259 Fed. 450 (1919); *Toledo Rys. & L. Co.* v. *Doherty* v. *Toledo Rys & L. Co.*, 254 Fed. 597 (1918).

[28] *State* v. *Des Moines Ry. Co.*, 140 N.W. 437 (Iowa, 1913).

[29] *Cincinnati* v. *Cin. & Ham. Traction Co.*, 245 U.S. 446 (1917).

[30] *Cleveland Electric Ry. Co.* v. *Cleveland*, 204 U.S. 116 (1907).

Even under indeterminate permit laws, municipalities do not always lose all their powers of control. In California the grantee can be made to pay annual franchise taxes. In Ohio municipalities have comprehensive regulatory powers. They have considerable power in Louisiana, Massachusetts, and Oklahoma. In Wisconsin, on the other hand, most municipal rights, including that of requiring the payment of certain taxes, were swept away by court decisions.[31] The Indiana courts followed the interpretation of the Wisconsin courts.

Continuous Regulation. We may say in general that municipalities should retain the right of continuous regulation. Attempts to make utilities behave by confining them within a system of contractual obligations are likely to defeat their own purpose as experiences with five-cent fares and horse-car regulations have so amply proven. Certainly it would seem desirable to keep the utility continuously subject to municipal ordinances. On the other hand, regulatory powers can be used with such lack of restraint that service will suffer from the overburdening of the utility.[32]

Franchises should be limited in such a manner as to permit the municipality to order specific changes in service or facilities as they become necessary. A check on unwise action on the part of the municipality may be provided by making municipal orders subject to review by the state commission. A further reason for review is to secure more or less uniform control in all communities served by the utility. Unreasonable service or costs placed upon a utility in one community may impair service in others.

Whatever policy is adopted, a clear line of distinction must be drawn between the conditions imposed by the municipality under its regulatory powers and those imposed by contract. The former are subject to the usual restrictions on the police power including those imposed by the 14th Amendment. The latter are contractual and binding.

Regulation of Service and Rates. To the degree that state statutes are permissive, a municipality may wisely retain control over service standards. Such matters as the location of lines and facilities, motive power, operating schedules and routes of street-railways, candle power and heating standards of gas service, voltage standards and extension rules of electric utilities, and all other safety and service matters should be subject to continuous control by ordinance or order of city officials. Such matters cannot be regulated by contractual provisions inserted in the franchise. There is even less excuse for including long-term and binding rate provisions in the franchise. Even ten years is too long to fix rates by contract.

---

[31] See *LaCrosse* v. *LaCrosse G. & E. Co.*, 130 N.W. 530 (1911); *Calumet Serv. Co.* v. *Chilton*, 135 N.W. 131 (1912); *T.M.E.R. & L. Co.* v. *Milwaukee*, 181 N.W. 298 (1921).

[32] For a further discussion of franchise standards see John Bauer, *The Public Utility Franchise* (Chicago, Public Administration Service, 1946).

Accounts and Reports. A crucial line of distinction between a purely private business and a business affected with the public interest pertains to privacy of management. Not only is publicity necessary in a public utility enterprise, but the franchise should contain provisions for standard accounting reports and forms that reveal rather than conceal the actual results of operations in such a manner that they can be compared with standard ratios. Unfortunately, few utilities set up their accounts in this manner and such requirements are likely to be burdensome.

Special Burdens. Municipalities may impose various burdens upon franchise holders. Utilities may be required to pay a certain portion of the revenues gained within municipal limits into the municipal treasury. Telephone companies may be required to furnish municipal offices with telephone service without charge. Street-railway companies may be required to carry policemen and firemen while in uniform. Water companies may be required to furnish water for fire protection and to flush the streets without charge.

There can be little question of the desirability of requiring a utility to meet the cost of special paving made necessary by utility service. A franchise tax to pay the cost of a municipal golf course or recreation center or any other burden unrelated to the cost or inconvenience occasioned by utility service is hardly justifiable. Like the sales tax, the franchise tax is inequitable in that it rests with undue weight upon the persons with lower incomes; but, like the sales tax, it is an easy means of raising revenue. On the whole there is little to warrant such special burdens in the form of either taxes or services.

Recapture of Excess Earnings. A different aspect of somewhat the same problem appears when a municipality attempts to recapture excess earnings by franchise provisions. Cities sometimes realize belatedly the value of the privileges they have conferred upon their utilities and demand a share in utility earnings. Taxation of this nature is not a suitable substitute for regulation, but if regulation has broken down otherwise, there is little that can be said against this attempt to salvage what can be saved by contractual franchise provisions. Professor Burkhead has advocated this policy.[33]

The Adjustment of Labor Disputes. There are far too many cases that can be called upon as illustrations of the crippling effects of street railway, electric, telephone, and other utility strikes. Hence it has been suggested that a good franchise should provide machinery for the arbitration or conciliation of labor disputes. There is strong reason why the settlement of labor disputes should not be left to the pulling and hauling of contending parties while the public waits for service. Some provisions

[33] Jesse V. Burkhead, "The Changing Incidence of Public Utility Taxation," 15 *Jnl. Land & Pub. Util. Econ.* 383 (1939).

for conciliation, mediation, or arbitration are desirable; but it must be remembered that with the growth and integration of labor organizations there is little a single municipality can do towards settling a public utility strike locally.

Provisions for Public Ownership. Public ownership as an alternative should never be abandoned in any regulatory system. A good franchise should contain provisions for acquiring utility property at any time at a fair price. Probably something is gained if the franchise is non-exclusive. Many states have laws or constitutional provisions prohibiting the issuance of exclusive franchises. Whether it is desirable for a municipality to use a right to establish a competing plant is another question. Regardless of the use of the right to purchase utility property or to establish a competing plant, the privilege alone strengthens the municipality's bargaining power in rate negotiations and other matters.

5. THE SPECIAL PROBLEM OF THE INDETERMINATE PERMIT

The indeterminate permit system originated in Wisconsin when that state passed its original public utility legislation in 1907. Provisions for some form of the indeterminate permit have been included in the laws of Arkansas, California, Indiana, Louisiana, Massachusetts, Minnesota, Ohio, Oklahoma, New York, and some other states. Some cities, such as Kansas City, Missouri; Detroit, Grand Rapids, Dallas, Des Moines, Chicago and other cities enjoying the rights of "Home Rule," have also granted franchises of the indeterminate permit type.

The Wisconsin Experience. The indeterminate permit has not won universal acclaim. In Wisconsin it has been subject to criticism both from within and from without the state. Criticism came from municipal groups and from public ownership advocates, the former attacking it because it removed utility control from the local government units and the latter because it was regarded as an obstacle to public ownership. Daniel W. Hoan, famous and long-time Socialist mayor of Milwaukee, struck out vigorously against it with these words:

> The indeterminate permit and grant laws and the law covering certificates of necessity and convenience were the greatest frauds ever perpetrated on the people of this state.... Under these laws, Wisconsin has granted perpetual monopolies to privately owned utilities. It is the only state in the union which has done so.
> The law said that the municipalities should have the right to take over these utilities at any time. But the cities are tied in this respect by another law which forbids them to bond themselves for over 5% of their assessed valuation.
> There is scarcely a city in this state that has not used up this 5% bonded

indebtedness limit in financing school projects or other developments that are real necessities.[34]

Mr. Hoan's statement is emphatic, but it hardly matches an editorial in the *Chicago Daily News* of May 23, 1925 in vigor of expression. Said this newspaper of an indeterminate permit bill introduced into the Illinois legislature:

> Consider the ... public utility bill in all its iniquitous entirety. It is a piece of legislative brigandage incomparably evil in its special field of predatory outrage ... its proponents must think the people of Illinois are half-wits to tolerate such a gigantic robbery of rights, such an unprecedented grab of privileges.

It was commonly said that the Wisconsin utilities threatened to defeat the 1907 law if provisions for the indeterminate permit were not included. Utilities were authorized to exchange existing franchises for permits. Some utilities with generous franchises refused to do so and successfully sought the protection of the courts.[35] Other utilities were more than willing to surrender their old franchises because of burdensome provisions, because the franchises were about to expire or because they wanted protection from possible competition.

The Right to Purchase. The right to purchase may be an empty one. A common constitutional or statutory provision restraining municipalities from bonding themselves for more than five per cent (or some other proportion) of the assessed property values will preclude acquisition without further ado unless the statutes permit the issuance of revenue bonds against the earnings of the utility alone. Revenue bonds do not always present a desirable means of financing. Since the entire cost of the plant will have to be met from the proceeds, there is no margin of security for the bondholders, and the interest rates are likely to be somewhat higher than on general obligations.

The Fight Against Municipal Purchase. These financial obstacles are the least of the troubles the proponents of public ownership will meet. A referendum will have to be taken and the necessary political machinery will have to be set in motion. A "Taxpayers' Committee" will appear as if by magic to fight municipal acquisition. The committee will be made up of the "solid citizens" of the town. It will be backed by bankers, industrialists, large property owners, and by the utility itself. These groups will be motivated by a righteous fear of an increase in taxes and of the loss of utility business. They are well indoctrinated with the belief in inefficiency of public ownership which is identified with political ownership. Isn't it perfectly plain that this movement was started by politicians? Besides, the whole thing is a step towards Communism.

[34] As quoted in the *Madison Capital Times*, Jan. 31, 1929.
[35] *Superior Water L. & P. Co.* v. *Superior*, 263 U.S. 125 (1923).

There will be no lack of funds to get publicity for all the arguments against public ownership. Nor will its opponents be content with the mere dissemination of arguments. Somewhere along the line taxpayers' suits will be started. No law is so clear, no procedure so perfect that points of law cannot be raised. The wording of the referendum question may have been imperfect. The city's powers under its charter may be uncertain. There is a doubt (not a reasonable doubt, it is true, but a doubt nevertheless) about the legal capacity of a certain official to act. Every lawyer must have his day in court. In some instances acquisition may have to wait special legislation. The legal points, however, are immaterial, for it is only necessary to delay proceedings until political control changes or until the whole movement collapses from sheer inertia. The suits will also serve the specific purposes of clouding the legality of any bond issue and hampering the flotation of securities.

If the city can get by these pitfalls and hurdles, deeper and higher ones await it once proceedings are started to actually acquire the property. The fair value will have to be determined. The state commission will probably act as arbitrator; it may or may not be well equipped with funds and personnel for the job. The nettlesome problem of "fair value" will have to be thrashed out in its entirety, as it has been so many times before in courts and commissions. The amount of depreciation, the value of intangibles, each raise their own peculiar problems. The property to be included in the purchase will create a host of arguments. The utility will claim "severance" damages, for it will become a less efficient operating unit once compact urban properties have been divorced from an integrated system and from the scattered and less profitable suburban and rural properties. It is not at all unlikely that the litigation of these matters will tie up proceedings for years.

Other Legal Hurdles. Some indeterminate permit laws are weak in that they provide only for municipal acquisition and operation and do not authorize the resale of the property to another utility company that could presumably supply better service. In some instances a municipality may be bound to purchase before condemnation value is determined and may be thus stuck with a bad bargain.

For these reasons the indeterminate permit system offers little assurance that a municipality will be able to take over its utilities when it desires. In certain respects the municipality is worse off than if it had granted a term franchise. At the expiration of the franchise its rights become relatively clear and unequivocal. However, if the utility is operating under a series of franchises issued at various and sundry times to a multitude of predecessor companies, acquisition becomes virtually impossible because of the impossibility of taking over part of a property. The total effect of all these conditions, whether arising from a term franchise or from the indeterminate permit, is to make for uncertainty and delay. Uncertainty makes financing difficult, while delay defeats the whole movement. Many of the acquisition proceedings started under the Wisconsin law have continued over the course of five or ten years only to end in abandonment. There have been only two instances where certificates of convenience and necessity have been issued to a competing utility. The private electric utilities involved were small, isolated, and, on the basis of the evidence, extremely poorly managed. In the city of Menasha, a large successor company continues to render service to large power customers, maintaining a certain amount of competition with the municipal utility.[36]

Despite these weaknesses in the indeterminate permit, Wisconsin can be said to have handled its utility problem well. Public ownership of electric utilities is well enough established to be a material factor in the regulation of privately owned utilities. Even the limited right of public ownership or competition, if coupled with a good commission, can bring good regulation.

6. THE CONTROL OF COMPETITION

So necessary is the service of some of the utility industries, and notably of the electric utility industry, that a profitable return can be earned upon almost any capital commitment, however grossly excessive or unwise, by merely raising rates. In one way or another excessive capital, drawn into the industry by a single monopolistic firm or by competing utilities, becomes the cause of exorbitant costs and rates.

Before the passage of the public utility laws competition was looked upon with favor and the resulting rate wars were seen as the only means of escaping from outrageous monopoly prices. Any advantages were purely of short duration, for sooner or later combination or elimination resulted, and the surviving utility had not only the opportunity but the necessity of recovering past losses and fixed charges on an over-expanded plant from the hapless and disillusioned public.

A Case Study. Laurence R. Gray presents an interesting case study. Sometime before 1913 a certain Arizona community of 10,000 population was served unsatisfactorily by a local electric plant. Rates were high, service was poor, and the plant was obsolete. The utility's credit was bad. The Arizona Commission somewhat reluctantly issued a certificate of convenience and necessity to a new utility. The older company threatened to abandon service before the new company completed its plant, but instead chose to engage in a thoroughgoing price cutting war with the

[36] For cases see *Re Village of Hustisford,* 5 P.S.C.W. 415 (1934) and 10 P.S.C.W. 817 (1935); *Re City of Menasha,* 17 P.S.C.W. 79 (1937).

newcomer. A typical bill dropped from $10.00 to $6.60. There was other surreptitious price cutting. Domestic consumers received service on lower commercial rates. Two distribution systems clogged up the streets. Both companies operated at a deficit. After six years both companies asked for a 20 per cent rate increase, which was given them. Two years later, in 1922, the companies consolidated. Securities aggregating more than 150 per cent of the value of the property were issued by the new company. Service was improved, but most of the rates remained unchanged and deficits increased. In 1928 the local companies were absorbed by a holding company. In 1930 the holding company, which was grossly overcapitalized, went into receivership. Rate reductions had to wait reorganization.[37]

Regulation and the Level of Rates. Regulation has not always been successful in obtaining the lowest possible rates consistent with a fair return to the utility. This is particularly true of the electric utility industry. So elastic is demand for electric service and so significant are the economies of decreasing costs, that there is ample reason to believe that an electric utility could operate just as profitably after drastic rate reductions have had an opportunity to increase consumption as before. Under regulation, however, there is no compulsion to reduce rates as long as utility profits are not excessive.

Reducing the Cost of Capital. It is conceivable that the high degree of security afforded the utility by an indeterminate permit considerably reduces the cost of capital. The elimination of uncertainty is always an economic advantage. Benefits can be passed on to the ratepayers. On the other hand, even with the assurance afforded by the indeterminate permit, the risks of private enterprise may remain so great that the cost of capital will not be reduced in any way to the level common to public financing. Thus ratepayers, in accepting the conditions of the indeterminate permit, contract away the right to utilize cheap public credit to supply themselves with utility service, while the private utility is still unable to profit commensurably from lower costs of capital.

Standards for the Control of Competition. Typical regulatory policy is one in which monopoly is taken for granted, but competition will be permitted under some circumstances. Under what conditions will a commission issue a certificate of convenience and necessity to a utility company seeking to compete with one already established? The following principles furnish some guidance:

(1) The applicant must show that the proposed service will be of material benefit to the public. Does a high-speed, de luxe, express bus-service duplicate low-fare local service over the same route? The Illinois Commerce Commission held that it did not, but its order granting a

[37] Laurence R. Gray, "Public Utility Competition: A Case Study," 15 *Jnl. Land & Pub. Util. Econ.* 195 (May, 1939).

certificate to the newcomer was reversed by the state supreme court.[38]

(2) The applicant must show that existing utilities are unwilling or unable to render satisfactory service. If the existing utility is unable to render service because of lack of finances or for other reasons, the position of the applicant is made easier. The existing utility may be merely unwilling to give service. A common situation is one in which a small utility applies for a permit to extend service to new customers on the fringe of its territory. A large and well financed utility may be able but unwilling to serve the same customers. There may be an agreement between the two companies whereby that particular area is reserved for the applicant. Nevertheless, a commission may deny the application and order the larger utility to extend service. It is a cardinal principle of regulation that the public interest and not the interest of the utilities must be controlling in such instances. The desires of the customers will have great weight, but even here their desires might not prevail if the extension of service is unsound.

Another common situation is where a utility will rush in to serve customers which it previously ignored after the appearance of potential competition. Here commissions have the tendency to permit the delinquent utility to improve itself before allowing a rival to enter the field.[39]

The problem sometimes presents itself in which a new bus company seeks to compete with an old street-railway rendering service at high rates and bound to old and unprofitable routes. In much more frequent situations the street-railway has already headed off competition by gradually switching to bus service. Here the advantages of competition are usually lost for the street-railway will invariably aim to consolidate its services in such a manner as to earn a return upon both the obsolete street-railway property and upon the more profitable bus service.

(3) The applicant must show that the proposed construction or duplication of facilities will not be a nuisance to the public. Two pole lines on a narrow, congested road may be a nuisance; two telephone companies in the same area would not only render worse service than one, but their poles would overcrowd the highways.

(4) The applicant must show that it has the financial capacity and experience to render the proposed service. A well-financed company will be preferred over a weaker one; an old and established company over a new one.

[38] *Chicago & West Towns Railway* v. *Illinois Commerce Commission,* 48 N.E. (2d) 320 (Ill., 1943).

[39] For examples see *Union Coöperative Telephone Co.* v. *Pub. Serv. Comm.,* 239 N.W. 409 (Wis., 1931); *Re West Milford Electric Co.,* P.U.R. 1926A, 291 (N.J. Comm.); *Town Line Farmers Independent Telephone Co.* v. *Red River Tel. Co.,* P.U.R. 1916F, 211 (Wis. Comm.).

In Pennsylvania, a group of promoters proposed to serve industrial consumers with natural gas at lower rates than those at which they were already being served. In this instance the promoters owned several wells in a pool which was rapidly being exhausted by other wells. The financial success of the venture depended upon the promoters' success in marketing as much gas as possible in as short a period of time as possible. To do this the promoters proposed to sell gas only to large customers. In the interest of continuity of service and long time stability the Pennsylvania Commission refused to grant them a certificate.[40]

Policy Towards Public Ownership. A state policy of regulated monopoly achieved through the franchise and certificate may have to yield to a dominant policy of fostering public ownership. In some instances franchises and certificates are exclusive against other privately owned utilities but not against publicly owned utilities. In Iowa, municipalities are permitted virtually unlimited freedom to establish competing utility service irrespective of the quality of the existing service. By utilizing tax resources a city can engage in cutthroat competition and drive a privately owned utility out of business. Severe competition of this kind is particularly prevalent in the Pacific Northwest and in the Tennessee Valley.

The active search of the Tennessee Valley Authority for power markets made it necessary for the states of the area to delineate their policy toward public competition and public ownership. The Tennessee Commission pointed out that it was not the policy of the state to promote competition, but that the state did seek to promote public ownership. Hence where a utility did not have an exclusive franchise, the commission refused to allow a private utility to cut rates to meet the competition of a municipally owned plant.[41]

Policy Towards Rural Coöperatives. The rural electrification program financed by the Federal Government presented the problem of regulated monopoly versus competitive rural coöperatives. The Rural Electrification Administration made it a policy not to make loans for the duplication of facilities. The question can be raised as to what constituted duplication. In any event, there was a great deal of competition between the newly organized coöperatives and the private power companies to serve particular areas. Commission control of this type of competition depended upon the specific powers granted them by the states. In many instances they had no jurisdiction over coöperatives.

The more conservative states clung to a policy of regulated monopoly and refused certificates to rural coöperatives seeking to render service in areas already partially served by private utilities. In Maryland, the com-

---

[40] *Incorporators of Service Gas Co.* v. *Pub. Serv. Comm.*, 18 P.U.R. (N.S.) 256 (1937).
[41] *Re Kentucky-Tennessee Light & Power Co.*, 41 P.U.R. (N.S.) 65 (1941).

mission denied a certificate to a Pennsylvania coöperative to extend service into Maryland in an area in which a private power company was belatedly building lines as a result of the competitive threat. The commission thought that the wasteful duplication of lines was sufficient reason to deny a certificate to the coöperative. A further ground was found by the commission in that the coöperative was not a Maryland corporation. The state had made it a policy to favor domestic to foreign corporations in such instances.[42]

Other states whose governments were generally characterized as "liberal" or "progressive" made it easy for coöperatives to establish and extend their lines more or less at will by law or by commission policy.

Where this type of competition was permitted, the immediate result was the hurried and frantic construction of lines by both coöperatives and private companies. In the long run there will probably be some kind of regional integration of service and the elimination of competition. There can be little doubt that competition brought sharp and sudden reductions in rates.

7. AN EVALUATION OF LOCAL REGULATION

Municipalities have only reluctantly surrendered their rights of regulation to the state commissions. In an early and comprehensive report, Delos F. Wilcox said of a large number of communities studied, "Nowhere do we find that business-like and friendly, even eager, coöperation between state and local authorities which should be contemplated by the law and should mark all practical efforts of administration."[43]

The concept of a judicially-minded commission charged with maintaining the balance between public and private rights has not always been accepted by many local authorities and politicians, and many more have probably not even heard of it. Eager for rate reductions, or for public ownership, they have regarded commissions as helpless or willing pawns of the utilities. The jovial familiarity that grows from frequent contacts between utility men and commissioners is disquieting to representatives of the people and is taken as easy evidence that their rights are not being protected. Nor is their confidence and faith increased when they are confronted by the fine-spun niceties of utility law or administrative procedure which in the eyes of the layman serve only to obscure a situation in which justice is perfectly clear.

Again it is said that utility commissions lack familiarity with local

[42] *Re Adams Electric Coöp. Inc.*, 38 P.U.R. (N.S.) 193. For leading case see *Littleton* v. *Hagerstown*, 132 Atl. 773 (1926).
[43] Delos F. Wilcox, *General Report to the National Civic Federation on the Regulation of Public Utilities on the Pacific Coast and in Minneapolis*, (1913) p. 117.

problems, and that local representatives cannot easily attend hearings to present their complaints in a distant state capitol. A partial solution to the problem is that of holding hearings in the localities concerned.

Advantages of Commission Regulation. Municipalities seldom have the personnel, the experience, or the data to regulate their utilities. They are at a bargaining disadvantage. Matters that are new and difficult problems to municipal attorneys and officials are handled with a sureness of touch born of repeated contact by officials of large utility corporations. Even an inept and moderately financed commission will develop a degree of proficiency in handling rate litigation—from experience if from nowhere else. Statistical material will be acquired to permit commissions to judge operating costs, rates, capitalization, and other related matters.

Negotiation on the basis of cost is virtually impossible for local authorities. Where a utility serves many communities through a state or regional network of facilities it is impossible to allocate the costs of serving a particular community. It is difficult to determine even local costs. At the best, local authorities can only carry on negotiations on the imperfect basis afforded by a comparison of local rates with those of neighboring communities—which in turn were set by similar comparisons.

Without these instruments of control regulation may become nothing more than control by altercation and agreement. It has been said about municipal regulation in one state that "Regulation as in Iowa may be said to be regulation by lawsuit or by threat of municipal competition." The Iowa system is further described as "an effort to control or to coerce utilities into acceptance of municipal regulation through the antiquated media of competition, threat of competition, or fear of being ousted in favor of a municipally owned plant." [44]

Local regulation is a piecemeal process, both geographically and functionally. Rates and service in rural areas or in small unincorporated communities are left unregulated or must be regulated by another body. There are no means of coördinating the two. Local authorities cannot regulate security issues or exercise any control over the construction or acquisition of facilities to be used for the system in general. Experience has shown that many utility abuses have grown from precisely these unregulated activities.

The varying temper and qualifications of city councilmen may result in rates that are sometimes grossly extortionate and at other times unduly oppressive to the utility. An anti-utility council may demand confiscatory rates, while more conservative councilmen would seek to dissipate the city's bargaining advantages. Local regulation may tempt the utility into local politics. A commanding argument for commission control has been

[44] C. M. Updegraff and R. F. Mark, "Needed Reform in Iowa Public Utility Regulation," 26 *Iowa Law Review.* 21, 25, 26 (1940).

that appointed commissions are removed from political pressure. This assumption is not always valid, but it is probably true that state commissions are under less political pressure than local officials.

The Right to Withhold a Franchise. From what has been said so far there is little doubt that the weight of advantage rests with centralized commission regulation. The answer, however, can not yet be regarded as conclusive. Regulation by state commission is carried on under the police power and is subject to all the hampering restrictions of judicial review.

On the other hand, a municipality may regulate its utilities by contract and demand certain rates and services in exchange for the privilege of the franchise. It has been pointed out that even confiscatory rates will stand if they are based on a valid contract executed in accordance with the state's laws. Under centralized regulation and particularly under certain indeterminate permit laws the states have thus surrendered their most important instrument of control. If the right to contract for service is abrogated and if regulatory commissions are given inadequate powers and finances, the last situation may be worse than the first. It is just this that many municipalities fear.

Even here it is questionable whether local control is superior to centralized regulation. The infirmities of contractual regulation have already been dwelt upon. Actual abuse of municipal powers may result in gross injustice to the utility. Even the possibility of abuse will unduly raise the cost of capital.

A combination of state and local regulation does not necessarily carry with it the advantages of both, for contractual local regulation is inconsistent with the exercise of commission powers. Ohio has attempted to blend both types of regulation with no particularly happy results in the opinion of Ben W. Lewis and E. T. Hellebrandt.[45]

Regulation by Contract. Nevertheless, if the police powers of the state continue to prove insufficient to achieve a fair degree of control over utility rates, it may be necessary to buttress them with a certain amount of contract regulation. Property values could be fixed by contractual provisions in the franchise subject to the approval of the commission. The commission would retain rate-making powers, but local rates would be fixed in accordance with a contractual rate base that would presumably be unassailable in the courts. As most state utility statutes now exist, valuation is entirely in the hands of the commissions and subject to judicial review. Admittedly this plan would only work where utility property is localized. It could not be applied to transmission lines, to isolated generating facilities, and to intercity networks. But the value of

---

[45] Ben W. Lewis, "Commission Regulation and Home Rule in Ohio," 9 *Jnl. Land & Pub. Util. Econ.* 207 (1933); Edwin T. Hellebrandt, "The Development of Commission Regulation of Utilities in Ohio," 9 *Ibid.* 395 (1933), 10 *Ibid.* 78 (1934).

local properties could be brought within the scope of the franchise control, while the other properties would be subject to the normal chaotic processes of valuation.

It would be almost impossible to fit such provisions into existing franchises, but new franchises could contain such controls. Contractual valuations could be made a condition of sale of municipal plants to private utilities.[46] Service-at-cost franchises, which embrace the entire scope of regulation within their provisions, represent a further and successful refinement of the same plan.

8. CONCLUSION

In conclusion it is desirable to draw together certain threads of discussion for the lessons they can give us.

The Problems of Constitutional Law. In the field of constitutional law further light has been thrown upon the police power of the state by a consideration of the limitations placed upon it by the Obligation of Contracts clause of the Constitution. Essential as the institution of contract might be to the preservation of our economic order, it can well be doubted whether Chief Justice Marshall best served the interests of a dynamic and evolving society when he handed down the *Dartmouth College* decision. Certainly since that time the court has done much to negate the principle of that decision. Gradually, and by tortuous reasoning, the police powers of the state have been unshackled. But this process of legal obscurantism has left in its wake a complex web of judicial principles which serve to confuse and emasculate rather than define and strengthen powers that the state should use for the public welfare.

The Problem of Control of Competition. Franchises are usually non-exclusive and leave the way open for competition. Competition may be controlled by certificates of convenience and necessity, issued by state commissions, upon a showing of a public need for service. While competition is theoretically possible, the belief is universally established and incorporated into state statutes that utility service should be rendered by regulated monopolies. The certificate becomes the instrument by which existing utilities are protected from competition and prevented from extending service into territory already occupied by other utilities. On the other hand, even the latent threat of competition contained within the indeterminate permit and the non-exclusive franchise contributes something to the efficacy of regulation.

The Problem of Local versus Centralized Government. The discussion of the franchise has been set against the background of the conflicts

[46] John Bauer, *Standards for Modern Public Utility Franchises* (Chicago, Municipal Administration Service, 1930), p. 19.

between decentralized and centralized governmental units. The many deficiencies and infirmities of franchise regulation have been dwelt upon. While the more dramatic and malodorous incidents of municipal corruption were largely confined to the more important cities, there has been some pettyfogging and hornswoggling in the smaller towns. In neither city nor town did the franchise prove the complete instrument of regulation. The movement has proceeded with abrupt steps away from local regulation. First, in the years following 1907, regulation passed from the hands of local governmental units to the state. In the 1930's the Federal Government expanded its jurisdiction over the utility industries at the expense of the state agencies. The malpractices of the 1890's growing out of the shortcomings of the franchise were at least matched when state commission regulation broke open at the seams and made possible the variegated series of abuses of the 1920's.

Historically both franchise and commission regulation have failed in part to meet the needs of their times. In each instance centralization has brought improvements. State commissions came to their jobs with much better equipment than was ever possessed by local government units. Federal agencies have proven themselves somewhat more aggressive in pursuing their regulatory goals than state commissions. Since many regulatory duties will have to be localized and since the advocates of state and local rights are politically vocal, it may be concluded that the center of gravity of regulation will become more or less stabilized somewhere between the state and Federal agencies. Regulation will be more complex, but it is hoped that the utility industries will not be unduly burdened or harmfully circumscribed. No group can be more interested in the success of the present system, for the only alternative is public ownership.

5. Public Utility Finance

1. THE SIGNIFICANCE OF PUBLIC UTILITY FINANCING

The history of public utility financing offers a valuable case study in almost all aspects of corporation finance. There are few important financial problems or abuses which are not found somewhere in the course of its modern history from around 1880 down to the present time.

Because of the gigantic capital requirements of the industry and because of the rapidity with which it has expanded, public utility financing has represented by far the largest single segment of all corporate financing. From 1920 to 1947 the percentage of all corporate financing attributable to the public utility industries has ranged from 17 per cent to 99 per cent and has averaged around 40 per cent.

2. THE EARLY PERIOD OF MODERN UTILITY FINANCING

The period from 1880 down to the beginning of the First World War was the period of development of the electric, telephone, and electric street-railway industries. The gas industry, a much older utility industry, also expanded during this period. The water utility industry, a still older utility, gradually changed from a privately owned to a publicly owned industry. Thus its problems were somewhat different from those of the other industries.

The outstanding characteristics of this formative period were the extensive and unwise use of debt financing by local utilities; the financing by large utility-equipment manufacturing companies, and, somewhat later, the financing by holding companies who performed functions of management and control and brought about the physical and financial integration of the local utilities.

The first steam-generating electric central station and the first hydro-generating station were both placed in operation in 1882, the former in New York City and the latter in Appleton, Wisconsin. With growing rapidity, new stations were placed in operation throughout the country as one technical improvement followed another. During the development period, a great deal of difficulty was experienced by the early promoters in securing the necessary capital from a general public that was as yet unacquainted with the significance and potentialities of the stream of inventions and improvements emanating from the workshops and laboratories of inventors and equipment manufacturers.

TABLE 4

COMPARATIVE CAPITAL STRUCTURES *

(Percentages of Total Capital and Surplus)

	Gas and Electric Utilities Class A and B	Telephone Companies Class A	Natural Gas Companies	Western Union Telegraph Company	Four Ocean Cable Companies
Funded Debt	46.8	40.8	41.2	37.3	....
Preferred Stock	15.0	} 51.2	9.7	....	....
Common Stock	28.0		35.5	43.0	79.9
Surplus	10.2	8.0	13.6	19.7	20.1
TOTALS	100.0	100.0	100.0	100.0	100.0
Total capital and surplus in millions of dollars.	$14,117	$4,495	$2,154	$244	$31

* Figures for gas and electric and natural gas companies are computed from Federal Power Commission figures for 1947 and 1946 respectively. Figures for telephone companies are for all companies reporting to the Federal Communications Commission for 1947. Figures for the Western Union Company are computed from *Moody's* figures for 1947. Figures for ocean cable companies are from the Federal Communications Commission for 1945.

The general reluctance of the public to participate in the risks of a new and untried industry forced the local electric utilities to resort to debt financing to purchase the new equipment constantly being urged upon them by the electric manufacturing companies. Financing through the sale of stock was difficult, and only debt securities could be conveniently marketed. Some of the bond and note issues of the local companies were taken by the manufacturing companies in their entirety in exchange for equipment, while other issues found their way more generally into the hands of the public. Many of the bond issues were based on closed end mortgages that made further borrowing difficult or impossible and thus raised serious financial problems for the future.

As the credit of the utilities grew better, they were able, except for the restrictions previously created, to finance on more desirable terms. After 1900 there was greater resort to open end mortgage bonds. Bonds were made callable at premiums ranging from 1 to 5 per cent above par with provisions for the reduction of these premiums as maturity approached. Conversion privileges, and sinking fund and depreciation provisions increased their marketability.

However, the existence of these restrictions in many cases now forced the local utilities to resort to stock issues to raise capital. Financing through equity securities remained almost as difficult as it was at the inception of industry. So the stocks of the local companies, rather than their bonds and notes, were absorbed by the manufacturing companies and by the first holding companies which had begun to appear on the scene in the eighties.

After 1898, holding and manufacturing company financing was characterized by the use of collateral trust bonds to an appreciable extent to effect consolidations. Refunding issues were used to simplify corporate structures and to take advantage of lower interest rates. The credit of a holding company was considerably better than that of the small and unknown operating companies, and the cost of financing was considerably reduced. The holding company could also escape legal liability for the debts of the operating companies. At other times it was thought desirable to leave the financial structure of the operating utilities undisturbed and control was effected by the mere purchase of their securities.

Much the same situation existed in connection with the financing of gas utilities. As in the electric utility industry, there was a great deal of competition between rival gas companies serving the same communities, which made financing difficult in many instances. The predecessor of the United Gas Improvement Company was likewise organized to finance the purchase of new and improved equipment by local gas utilities.

Telephone securities enjoyed much more popular favor than those of the other utilities, particularly after 1879 when the long-standing period of competition with the telegraph industry was brought to a close. Securities of the American Bell Telephone Company and its successor, the present American Telephone and Telegraph Company, were marketed with relative ease. These companies in turn invested in the common stocks of the various operating companies.

3. PUBLIC UTILITY FINANCING, 1920-1930

America's entry into the First World War brought an end to the expansion of the public utility industries. The shortages of labor, material, and capital all played their part. After the cessation of hostilities, expansion was resumed at an even more rapid pace.

The Economic Significance of Utility Expansion. Public utility financing during this period must be considered against the general background of the trend of social and economic conditions. National income increased from 53 billion dollars in 1921 to 83 billion dollars in 1929. The public utilities contributed an amazing and prodigious share to the unrivaled prosperity and industrial expansion. Utility financing, exclusive of that of the railroads, accounted for more than a third of all corporate financing. The problem escaped the bounds of the industry itself, for the expansion of the industry must be considered not only as an effect of the expanding economy but as one of its most significant causes.

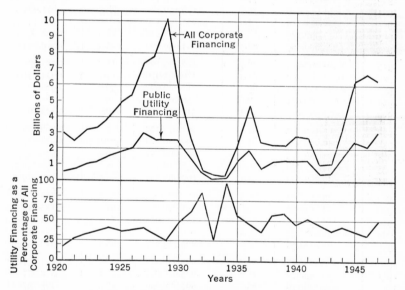

FIG. 1. PUBLIC UTILITY FINANCING COMPARED WITH ALL
CORPORATE FINANCING.

(1920-1947)

Data compiled from the *Commercial and Financial Chronicle.*

The high level of national income created an ever-increasing store of savings to be drawn upon to finance still greater capital expansion, which in turn created and maintained the national income. Not only did the high level of income produce the necessary savings to finance the industrial expansion of the period, but the expansion was necessary to create a field of capital investment to keep the nation's savings in circulation. As previously pointed out, the utility industry requires an unusually large capital investment to produce a given amount of income. This factor, coupled with the expanding demand for utility services which had been dammed up during the war years, produced a tremendous demand for the nation's savings, to which Figure 1 so eloquently testifies. It was this demand for savings which contributed so materially to keeping the capitalistic society agoing.[1]

TABLE 5

PUBLIC UTILITY FINANCING, 1920-1948

ACCORDING TO PURPOSE *

Year	New Capital		Refunding		Total
	Amount	Per Cent	Amount	Per Cent	Amount
1920	$ 382,339,052	77.0	$ 114,483,498	23.0	$ 496,822,550
1921	491,934,940	73.3	179,150,280	26.7	671,085,220
1922	726,241,509	74.0	254,192,286	26.0	980,433,795
1923	887,990,729	78.0	250,405,429	22.0	1,138,396,158
1924	1,325,600,827	86.7	204,039,000	13.3	1,529,639,827
1925	1,496,098,404	86.7	228,935,100	13.3	1,725,033,504
1926	1,604,385,376	81.3	370,065,970	18.7	1,974,451,346
1927	2,074,474,488	69.4	912,029,690	30.6	2,986,504,178
1928	1,811,480,934	70.6	750,807,398	29.4	2,562,288,332
1929	1,931,972,228	79.1	510,796,307	20.9	2,442,768,535
1930	2,365,140,852	92.2	201,075,722	7.8	2,566,216,574
1931	948,636,561	61.7	590,250,500	38.3	1,538,887,061
1932	274,350,175	50.8	265,906,720	49.2	540,256,895
1933	34,221,000	36.9	58,510,478	63.1	92,731,478
1934	49,359,500	31.1	109,085,500	68.9	158,445,000
1935	83,550,882	6.5	1,200,201,064	93.5	1,283,751,946
1936	123,684,098	5.8	2,001,659,865	94.2	2,125,343,963
1937	149,398,889	18.6	653,867,985	81.4	803,266,874
1938	272,907,472	22.4	949,730,815	77.6	1,222,638,287
1939	61,244,676	4.6	1,265,712,857	95.4	1,326,957,533
1940	268,429,038	21.1	1,005,648,272	78.9	1,274,077,310
1941	399,049,070	28.8	983,928,075	71.2	1,382,977,145
1942	156,196,176	33.7	307,600,890	66.3	463,797,066
1943	18,191,380	4.6	380,957,220	95.4	399,148,600
1944	48,186,030	3.5	1,336,146,552	96.5	1,384,332,582
1945	111,775,337	4.7	2,285,645,447	95.3	2,397,420,784
1946	817,804,253	38.7	1,296,747,105	61.3	2,114,551,358
1947	2,035,202,103	65.2	1,087,584,962	34.8	3,122,787,065
1948	2,836,078,511	95.7	129,191,346	4.3	2,965,269,857

* Compiled from the *Commercial and Financial Chronicle*.

[1] Among other industries which drew upon significant portions of the savings made from our national income during the period were the automobile, petroleum, rubber, moving picture, radio, and state and private construction industries.

It is not our purpose to speculate as to whether the general expansion of industry could have been carried on into the 1930's or whether or not the subsequent crash was inevitable. It is sufficient to say that the boom and later stagnation of the utilities industries was a significant and causal factor in prosperity and depression.

Increasing Investor Confidence. The movement of the nation's savings into the utility industry was accelerated by growing investor confidence as reflected in a decline in interest rates. Figure 3 indicates a steady decline in the cost of utility bond financing from 7½ per cent in 1921 to less than 6 per cent in 1922, with a gradual and continuous decline thereafter to less than 5 per cent as late as 1931. From 1921 to 1924, the simple average yield of new public utility interest-bearing securities dropped below that of other industries (excluding railroads) by one-half of one per cent or more. The demand for utility securities was further increased by the adoption of laws permitting savings banks to invest in utility securities. This not only represented a new source of capital but created an aura of safety and security around utility stocks and bonds in general.[2] In short, the industry came to be regarded not only as one in which it was impossible to lose one's money, but one in which an increase in security values was to be regarded as the normal and natural course of affairs.

Characteristics of Utility Financing During the Period. Most of the capital flowing into the industry was new capital and by and large went to finance new construction. Between 1921 and 1929, new capital financing for the industry ranged from 69 per cent to 87 per cent of all the financing, and reached a new high both in respect to volume and proportion of new financing in 1930. New utility capital issues amounted to over $2,365,-000,000 in this year and constituted 92.2 per cent of all utility financing. Refunding issues were correspondingly low. The high for the decade was reached in 1927 when almost $3,000,000,000 of security issues were floated.

The financing of 1928 and 1929 was the product of the stock market inflation that carried our economy upward to the brink of the precipice of 1929. Interest rates ceased to fall and in fact showed a slight upward trend as investors turned from security to the vicarious and bizarre profits to be obtained in the soaring stock market. Stock yields went down as prices went up, and utilities found it easy to get whatever price they asked for whatever kind of security they pushed out on the market. New and wondrous stock issues were devised to separate the investor

---

[2] In 1922, there were only twelve states that permitted the investment of savings banks funds in utility security issues of some form. There was an absence of statutory authorization in at least thirty-one states. The problem was a matter for considerable concern on the part of utility management. See W. E. Lagerquist, *Public Utility Finance* (New York, McGraw-Hill Book Company, 1927), pp. 276-278.

from his money without either shouldering the responsibilities for interest payments or the disadvantages of surrendering control. In 1927, stock financing amounted to 28.6 per cent of the total, in 1928 to 35.8 per cent, and in 1929 to a wacking 58.6 per cent.

TABLE 6

Public Utility Financing, 1920-1948

By Types *

Year	Long Term Bonds and Notes		Short Term Bonds and Notes		Stocks		Total
	Amount	Per Cent	Amount	Per Cent	Amount	Per Cent	Amount
1920	$ 218,048,100	43.9	$ 218,065,500	43.9	$ 60,708,950	12.2	$ 496,882,550
1921	473,205,000	70.5	72,235,000	10.8	125,645,220	18.7	671,085,220
1922	632,406,000	64.5	45,756,000	4.7	302,271,795	30.8	980,433,795
1923	812,188,100	71.4	64,675,000	5.7	261,533,058	22.9	1,138,396,158
1924	880,110,900	57.5	128,073,000	8.4	521,455,927	34.1	1,529,639,827
1925	1,027,080,000	59.6	148,820,000	8.6	549,133,504	31.8	1,725,033,504
1926	1,380,317,500	69.9	105,980,000	5.4	488,153,846	24.7	1,974,451,346
1927	1,995,955,500	66.8	139,622,000	4.7	850,926,678	28.6	2,986,504,178
1928	1,508,661,900	58.9	135,682,000	5.3	917,944,432	35.8	2,562,288,332
1929	918,072,500	37.7	90,240,000	3.7	1,434,456,035	58.6	2,442,768,535
1930	1,460,886,600	56.9	330,448,500	12.9	774,881,474	30.2	2,566,216,574
1931	1,012,481,500	65.8	242,487,000	15.8	283,918,561	18.4	1,538,887,061
1932	385,022,800	71.3	146,429,000	27.1	8,805,095	1.6	540,256,895
1933	43,239,000	46.7	40,344,700	43.4	9,147,778	9.9	92,731,478
1934	82,945,000	52.4	75,500,000	47.6	. . . .	. . .	158,445,000
1935	1,228,921,400	95.7	20,000,000	1.6	34,830,546	2.7	1,283,751,946
1936	2,075,606,200	97.7	1,850,000	0.1	47,887,763	2.2	2,125,343,963
1937	663,453,000	82.6	47,700,000	5.9	92,113,874	11.5	803,266,874
1938	1,194,279,795	97.7	6,000,000	0.5	22,358,492	1.8	1,222,638,287
1939	1,181,523,800	89.0	7,726,000	0.6	138,173,733	10.4	1,326,957,533
1940	1,119,298,300	87.8	910,000	0.1	153,869,010	12.1	1,274,077,310
1941	1,241,242,900	89.8	7,450,000	0.5	134,384,245	9.7	1,382,977,145
1942	428,834,000	92.5	. . . .	. . .	34,963,066	7.5	463,797,066
1943	378,082,500	94.7	1,000,000	0.3	20,066,100	5.0	399,148,600
1944	1,261,469,000	91.1	750,000	0.1	122,113,582	8.8	1,384,332,582
1945	2,171,589,000	90.6	44,000,000	1.8	181,831,784	7.6	2,397,420,784
1946	1,646,756,700	77.9	2,500,000	1.1	465,294,658	22.0	2,114,551,358
1947	2,621,676,450	84.0	400,000	0.0	500,710,615	16.0	3,122,787,065
1948	2,569,882,800	86.7	850,000	0.0	394,537,057	13.3	2,965,269,857

* Compiled from the *Commercial and Financial Chronicle.*

Table 6 illustrates some significant aspects of corporation finance. The high proportion of short-term financing in 1920 was a reflection of the high interest rates that prevailed for a short while after the end of the

World War. Utility companies resorted to temporary financing in order
to be free to take advantages of the lower interest rates that were expected
in the future.

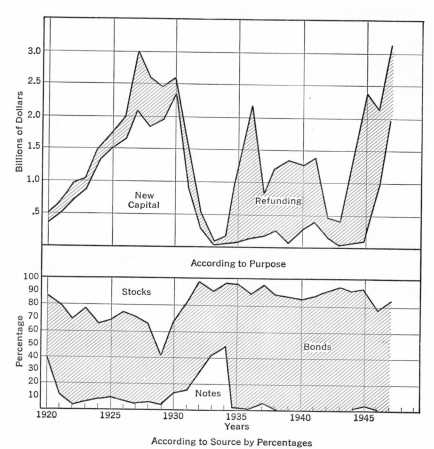

FIG. 2. PUBLIC UTILITY FINANCING BY PURPOSE AND SOURCE.
(1920-1947)

Data compiled from the *Commercial and Financial Chronicle*.

With the exception of the year 1929, the majority of the utility financing
during the period was by means of long-term debt securities. Only in
1929, when utility companies floated a total of $1,434,456,035 of stocks,
did stock financing exceed bond financing. Over the period, bond financing exceeded stock financing in the ratio of 1.8 to 1. However, a large
percentage of the bond financing was for refunding purposes. If only new
capital financing is considered, the disparity was not so great. Here the
relationship over the period was approximately 1.4 to 1.

Holding Company Finance. Public utility financing during the period can only be considered in connection with the holding company device. It was a time when utility promoters "threw together" many isolated properties into more or less integrated systems. The term "threw together" is used advisedly. Holding companies issued vast amounts of securities either in exchange for the securities of operating companies or for sale to the general public to acquire liquid resources. Table 7 gives a picture of the changing aspect of utility financing as reflected by bond flotations.

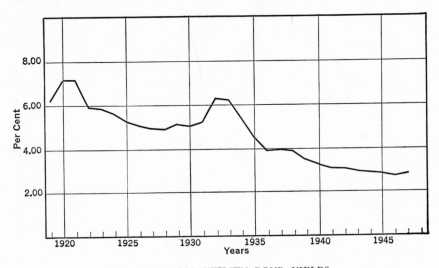

FIG. 3. PUBLIC UTILITY BOND YIELDS.

Data are taken from Moody's *Public Utilities* and represent composite yields for all class of public utility bonds. For a comparison with public utility common stock yields see Figure 9.

The Use of Preferred Stock. Much of the gas, electric, street-railway, and water utility equity financing was effected through the sale of preferred stocks. Since these stocks commonly carried no voting rights, the danger of loss of control of either operating or holding companies by their management was reduced to a minimum. Furthermore, the apparent safety of the issues made them rather desirable to the many small investors whose savings were tapped to finance the expansion of the industry. The telephone and telegraph utilities did not resort to preferred stock financing to any significant extent. Nevertheless, for the period 1919-1925, 46 per cent of all the stock issued by the utility industries was preferred.[3]

3 See H. B. Dorau, in W. E. Lagerquist, *Public Utility Finance, op. cit.*, p. 259.

The Customer Ownership Movement. The customer ownership movement was another phenomenon of utility financing during the twenties.
Prior to the first World War, utility securities, like other securities, were
commonly marketed through investment banking houses. After the war,
the public utilities adopted the policy of selling their securities directly
to the public through professional salesmen and their own employees.
The direct contact which they had with their own customers made the
policy largely one of customer ownership.

TABLE 7

DISTRIBUTION OF PUBLIC UTILITY DEBT SECURITIES *

1919-1928

Year	Percentage Issued	
	By Operating Companies	By Holding Companies
1919	68.54	31.46
1920	90.22	9.78
1921	95.98	4.02
1922	86.02	13.98
1923	89.56	10.44
1924	81.82	18.18
1925	62.29	37.71
1926	73.33	26.69
1927	63.24	36.66
1928	44.70	55.30
1919-1928	71.09	28.91

* R. L. Reierson, "Utilities in Recent Financial Markets," 6 *Jnl. of Land & Pub. Util. Econ.* 18
(Feb., 1930).

The Southern California Edison Company and the Pacific Gas and
Electric Company were pioneers in the movement, and the plan was
adopted by the Byllesby system in 1915 and by Stone and Webster in
1919 among the holding companies. By 1923, utilities representing more
than half of the light and power industry on the basis of gross revenues
were marketing their securities in this manner.

Many factors contributed to the widespread adoption of customer
ownership plans. Among the more significant were the following:

(*1*) *The Enormous Need for New Capital.* The utilities industries out-
ranked all others in the volume of capital required to produce a given
amount of annual revenue. Urgent demands for utility service made it
desirable, if not necessary, that utility promoters tap every available
source of funds.

(2) *A Growing Security Consciousness on the Part of the Public.*

Countrywide participation in Liberty Loans had made the public security-conscious. Prosperity produced the necessary savings. The gradual and sometimes startling increase in the value and earnings of securities attracted still more "investors." Success fed on itself as the decade moved on, and larger and larger proportions of the public avidly bought more and more securities at higher and higher prices.

(3) *Organized Sales Methods.* The large number of utility employees with frequent contacts with company customers and with other members of the community made an ideal, if untrained, sales force. It was easy to organize and train this force by mass-production methods. Professional salesmen sometimes constituted the backbone of the selling organization. Sales managers were not too reluctant to resort to high-pressure sales methods, and employee sales meetings had some of the aspects of an old-time revival in a country church. Efforts were also made to maintain a market for the securities sold both in respect to the ease of selling or trading and in respect to price. The practice of supporting prices during sales campaigns came in for vitriolic condemnation in later years.

(4) *The Reduction in Financing Costs.* The utilization of employees to sell securities in their spare time, or during "company" time, during which their wages and salaries were charged to operating expenses (and eventually to the ratepayer), materially reduced financing costs. Professor Heilman points out that selling costs ranged from $3 to $5 a share, and the National Electric Light Association reported average selling costs to be $4.60 a share for 185 companies in 1924. This compared with a cost of from $6 to $8 or more for securities sold through the regular channels.[4]

(5) *Customer Familiarity with the Company.* The utility company had its plant in the local community, where the customer felt that he could keep his eyes upon it. Even if he bought the securities of the holding company with properties scattered over half the country, the customer nevertheless identified his securities with his little local plant. Such a feeling could contribute very materially to breaking down the sales resistance of the typical uninformed investor whose dollars were sought by the utility companies.

(6) *The Desire of Utility Management to Retain Control.* The sale of securities through an investment banking house would have carried with it the surrender of a great deal of control. In no event were the Insulls, Dohertys, Hopsons, Foshays, or any of the other empire builders of the period willing to surrender a voice in the management in return for capital when such capital could be obtained from an army of scattered small investors with neither the knowledge nor the ability to exercise any concerted power. Even worse, experienced bankers could have been ex-

---

[4] R. E. Heilman, in W. E. Lagerquist, *Public Utility Finance, op. cit.,* p. 294.

pected to have a keen and suspicious nose for the sharp odors that frequently arose from utility-security flotations.

(7) *As a Means of Improving Public Relations.* There was a widespread belief and fervent hope among utility executives that the common participation in the earnings and the speculative profit incident to ownership of utility securities would forestall agitation for rate reductions or public ownership. Many committees of taxpayers and investors made their appearance in commission proceedings and political forums. After the stock market crash of 1929, the hoped-for good-will of clerks, teachers, small businessmen, and others who purchased utility stocks (sometimes under pressure) became the most violent kind of ill will.

4. PUBLIC UTILITY FINANCING, 1930-1935

It is a matter of opinion whether the year 1929 or the year 1930 should be taken as the point of watershed in the story of utility financing. The stock market crash of "Black Thursday," of October, 1929, marked the end of an era and, in the belief of many economists, the end of America's great period of expansion. America had attained the status of a mature economy. Henceforth, in their belief, the prospects of internal expansion were to be limited and society was to be forced to adjust itself to new ways of thinking, living, and being. However that might be, the public utility industry was not excepted from all the malignant features of a prolonged and perhaps the most severe depression in American history.

However, the utility industry carried its expansion program over into 1930, and, in contrast with industry in general, floated a larger amount of new capital issues than in 1929 or in any other year in history. New capital construction fell off sharply in 1931 and declined almost to the vanishing point in 1934. Other characteristics of the period included the growth of refunding issues to take advantage of declining interest rates; the disappearance of equity, and particularly preferred, stock financing; and a decline in holding company financing.

Capital Costs. The disorganized state of the securities markets and the almost complete lack of investor confidence is indicated by the unusually high utility bond yields during 1932, 1933, and 1934. Short-term financing was expensive, while the values of preferred and common stocks tumbled downward with a corresponding increase in their yields and in the costs of new equity financing.

Decline in New Construction. After the onset of the depression in 1929, President Hoover asked American industry to continue its construction program in an attempt to halt the onrushing depression. During the year 1930, the utility industry coöperated to the fullest extent and far beyond industry in general. New utility capital issues reached a new high in 1930. But the program was foreordained to failure and as business activity continued to decline and a new demand for goods and services failed to materialize, the utility industries, with new and excess capacity, were forced to curtail construction as other industries already had done. During the years 1930, 1931, and 1932, however, utility financing was the most significant segment of all financing, and in the two later years actually constituted its major part. The decline in construction continued until 1935, in which year new capital issues showed an increase over the preceding year.

Refunding Operations. Investors seeking security in economic adversity turned their attention to the bond markets after 1931. A few years later, the government's policy of deficit financing began to build up a plethora of idle funds. As the 1930's moved on, a measure of prosperity returned, but not to the extent necessary to create pressure on industry's capacity to produce. New capital financing lagged. There was more than enough money for everybody. The demand was lacking. Consequently, interest rates weakened and declined. Those companies that could, refinanced high interest bearing bond issues with new issues bearing lower rates.

Less than 8 per cent of the total utility security issues in 1930 were for refunding purposes. Thereafter, the proportion of refunding issues (although not the absolute amount) increased each year until in 1936 it amounted to 94.2 per cent. According to Moody's, the cost of utility bond financing declined from a high of approximately $6\frac{1}{2}$ per cent early in 1932 to less than $3\frac{1}{2}$ per cent late in 1936.

This resulted in enormous savings to the utilities. Professor Waterman estimates that during 1935 the utilities called in $1,064,250,725 of securities, saved a total of $10,918,050 per annum in capital costs, incurred approximately $58,000,000 of expenses in call premiums and other items, and reduced the average rate of interest on the affected issues from 5.14 to 3.93 per cent.[5] The Southern California Edison Company, for example, replaced a 7 per cent preferred stock with serial debenture bonds yielding 3.28 per cent.

Absence of Equity Financing. Equity financing virtually disappeared as the depression dragged on. Utility stocks declined in value along with all other stocks. Lack of profits, the government attitude toward the utilities, and the ill-repute of the holding companies occasioned by the excesses of the twenties did not encourage investors to commit their funds to this type of securities. Nor was there any great demand for venture capital from the utility industry itself. The decline in the demand for

[5] M. H. Waterman, *Public Utility Financing, 1930-1935,* (University of Michigan, 1936) p. 26.

utility services converted most of the new construction of 1930 and the twenties into excess capacity.

The once-popular preferred stock issues were no longer offered or wanted. Lack of investor confidence extended to debt financing. There was little long-term debenture financing by utility operating companies from 1932 to 1935. Mortgage bonds were the prime favorites. There was an increasing tendency to provide some sort of a retirement plan in bond indentures. President Roosevelt recommended that utilities provide for systematic retirement of their debt through sinking funds.

Holding Company Financing. Holding company flotations accounted for a smaller and smaller proportion of the total utility financing during the thirties. Their securities were considerably more risky than those of the underlying operating companies and were made more so by the considerable leverage employed in system financing. Several bad smash-ups, of which the Insull crash was the most spectacular, further decreased investor confidence in their issues, and their uncertain status under the New Deal did not add to investor equanimity. After 1935, the Public Utility Holding Company Act and particularly the "death sentence" clause was a very disquieting factor.

A significant and interesting phase of utility financing during the period was the holding company practice of drawing dividend and interest payments from subsidiary companies on one hand while they reloaned them funds on open account on the other. This did provide some operating companies with the necessary funds to make whatever additions to their plant were necessary, but it was hardly sound finance for them. The practice improved the appearance of the holding companies' income statements and strengthened their position for the financial and legal storms to come.

Professor Waterman cites the instance of one large holding company that took dividends amounting to $1,140,500 from four subsidiaries while making them loans of $1,074,000. A fifth subsidiary simultaneously ran deficits, paid dividends on its preferred stock to the holding company, and borrowed money from it to retire its debts. Many other examples were cited.[6]

Private Sale of Security Issues. After 1932, there was an increasing tendency to sell securities at private sale, usually to insurance companies. The scarcity of sound investments made such sales easy and they were also exempted from certain provisions of the Securities Act. Professor Waterman's study indicates that such sales increased from less than 1 per cent of the total sales in 1932 to 19.5 per cent in 1934.[7]

[6] M. H. Waterman, *ibid.*, pp. 80-81.
[7] M. H. Waterman, *ibid.*, p. 52.

5. PUBLIC UTILITY FINANCING, 1936-1941

This period was characterized by continued refunding to take advantage of the declining cost of capital. Debt and operating company securities were favored over equity and holding company issues. There were significant changes in the manner of floating security issues which can be expected to have some material effect upon the financial organization of our economy and upon our economy itself. Even more significant was the growing utilization of internal financial resources.

Capital Costs. The scarcity of alternative investment opportunities, the high level of national income, and the abundance of investment funds available as a result of the government deficit financing served to force the price of utility securities upward and the yield downward from 1937 on. Figure 3 (p. 108) indicates the yield on utility bonds declined from a little less than 4 per cent late in 1937 to a little over 3 per cent at the outbreak of the war. Such a decline was not as precipitous as that which took place after 1931, but it encouraged still further refunding.

Continued Refunding. Refunding operations which began in substantial volume in 1935 continued at a high level through 1941 in spite of uncertainty as to the effects of the "death sentence" clause. Refunding operations amounted to from 71 to over 95 per cent of the total utility financing during the period. New capital issues increased in volume over the worst of the depression years, but the total volume was hardly comparable with that of the golden days of the twenties.[8]

Types of Security Issues. Table 8 indicates that mortgage bonds constituted by far the largest share of utility security issues. The depressed price of utility stocks and the low cost of debt capital left utility management with but little choice as to the type of financing they would adopt. Common stock issues almost completely disappeared. There was more financing by preferred stocks, notes, and debentures; but the total of all these was small in comparison with that of bond issues. The burden of Federal income taxes also led some utilities to resort to debt financing.

Operating Company Financing. As in the preceding period, securities of the operating companies continued in much greater public favor than those of the holding companies. Holding company financing remained at a low level.

Private Utility Financing. Security issues can be placed on the market in three ways, namely (1) by a negotiated sale through one or more investment banking houses, (2) after competitive bidding, and (3) by private sale.

For years, many utility companies, like almost all other companies, sold their securities through investment banking houses without competitive

[8] See Table 5.

bidding. Characteristically, some utility systems maintained close relations with, if they were not actually dominated by, particular investment banking groups. These banking houses also acted as financial advisors. The relationship was a professional one, and the frequently cited analogous relationship of doctor and patient might well be significant in several respects. The relationship was also an extremely profitable one, as financing costs would generally average around 2½ per cent of the issuing price.

TABLE 8

GAS AND ELECTRIC UTILITY SECURITY ISSUES, 1935-1946 *

(Thousands of Dollars)

Year	Bond Issues	Debentures	Notes	Preferred Stock	Common Stock	Total
1935	964,158	45,500	. . . .	26,800	12,420	1,052,877
1936	1,236,392	116,750	13,890	43,170	550	1,410,752
1937	532,544	6,920	35,650	87,279	130	662,523
1938	681,457	239,730	53,425	8,891	. . . .	983,503
1939	622,482	155,750	56,556	55,666	. . . .	890,454
1940	759,336	40,750	24,205	51,441	5,973	881,705
1941	642,874	13,400	114,826	68,563	4,265	843,920
1942	240,264	16,250	75,734	43,423	954	376,625
1943	344,000	11,000	55,532	16,814	3,109	430,454
1944	1,089,923	27,450	82,750	94,596	1,471	1,296,190
1945	1,221,767	56,000	232,170	87,759	9,930	1,607,626
1946	561,838	118,450	94,786	217,239	51,976	1,044,290
TOTAL	8,897,035	851,950	839,524	801,640	90,769	11,480,918

* Securities and Exchange Commission, *Security Issues of Electric and Gas Utilities, 1935-1946*. Bond issues, debentures, and notes stated as principal amount; preferred stock at stated or liquidating value; common stock at par or book value. Table includes securities offered publicly for all utilities and sold privately for registered utilities.

The scarcity of good-investment opportunities and the overabundance of investment funds in the latter part of the decade made it more and more easy for many utilities to sell their securities directly to insurance companies without the services of banking intermediaries. Furthermore, direct sales to insurance companies did not have to be registered with the Securities and Exchange Commission under the Securities Act of 1933. This resulted in material advantages to the issuing company. Thus, there was an increasing tendency to sell bond issues directly to insurance companies. Table 9 indicates the increasing importance of this type of sales.

Competitive Bidding. A second significant change in the manner of financing took place in 1940 when the Securities and Exchange Commission adopted Rule U-50 requiring, with some exemptions, the competitive bidding for securities to be issued by registered public utility holding companies and their electric and gas subsidiaries. It had been established practice among investment bankers not to compete for security offerings, nor did the companies themselves shop around for the best possible market. Thus, particular investment banking houses stood virtually in the position of monopolies (or monopsonies) in respect to their customers' business. Although both the utilities and their established banking affiliates advanced strong arguments for the continuance of the old system, competitive bidding apparently resulted in a substantial decrease in the cost of financing. Interestingly enough, competitive bidding was favored by a number of investment banking houses which were seeking to establish themselves in the market. The problems are discussed in more detail in the chapter on Regulation of Securities and Finance.

TABLE 9

GAS AND ELECTRIC UTILITY BOND ISSUES
PERCENTAGE SOLD AT PRIVATE SALES *

Year	Per Cent
1935	5.5
1936	3.5
1937	2.4
1938	14.2
1939	19.5
1940	15.4
1941	31.5
1942	10.5
1943	2.1
1944	15.2
1945	0.2
1946	1.3

* Computed from data presented by the Securities and Exchange Commission, *Security Issues of Electric and Gas Utilities, 1935-1946.*

Institutional Buyers of Utility Securities. The financial policies of the utility industries are closely entwined with those of the country's insurance companies, banks, trusts, and foundations. One writer on public utility finance estimated that on the basis of incomplete figures these institutions owned from 85 to 90 per cent of all utility bonds in 1946.[9] In addition they owned possibly a quarter of the utilities' preferred stock and something less than a tenth of their common stock. Table 10 furnishes an approximate picture of the size of these holdings. On the basis of 1947 figures, public utility securities constituted 14.4 per cent of the assets of life insurance companies. This figure represents a continued increase in their holdings.

[9] Owen Ely, "Institutional Holdings of Utility Securities," 40 *Pub. Util. Fort.* 556, 563 (Oct. 23, 1947).

TABLE 10

ESTIMATED HOLDINGS OF PUBLIC UTILITY SECURITIES

BY INSTITUTIONAL BUYERS, 1946 *

(Billions of Dollars)

Institutions	Bonds	Preferred Stocks	Common Stocks	Total
Life insurance companies	4.7	.2	.1	5.0
Other insurance companies	.1	.2	.1	.4
Banks	3.5	•	•	3.5
Fiduciary trusts	2.5	.3	.7	3.5
Foundations and colleges	.5	.2	.3	1.0
TOTALS	11.3	.9	1.2	13.4
Other corporations and individuals	1.7	3.1	11.8	16.6
COMBINED TOTALS	13.0	4.0	13.0	30.0

* Owen Ely, "Institutional Holdings of Utility Securities," 40 *Pub. Util. Fort.* 556, 561 (Oct. 23, 1947). These figures are estimates and in some instances are based only on the general knowledge of institutional portfolios.

TABLE 11

DISTRIBUTION OF ASSETS OF UNITED STATES

LIFE INSURANCE COMPANIES, 1947 *

Type of Holding	Amount in Billions of Dollars	Percentage
Public utility bonds	7.0	13.6
Public utility stocks	.4	.8
Railroad bonds	2.9	5.6
Railroad stocks	.1	.2
Other corporate bonds	4.9	9.4
Other corporate stocks	.9	1.7
United States government bonds	20.0	38.7
Domestic and foreign government bonds	1.9	3.7
Mortgages	8.7	16.8
Real estate	.9	1.7
Policy loans	1.9	3.7
Miscellaneous assets	2.1	4.1
TOTALS	51.7	100.0

* Adapted from Owen Ely, in 42 *Pub. Util. Fort.* 673 (Nov. 4, 1948) citing figures from *Life Insurance Fact Book of 1948* (Institute of Life Insurance).

These facts are significant in at least two important respects. First, it is evident that the insurance companies (and other institutional buyers) have a tremendous direct interest in the well-being of the utility industries. Their policy holders have an equally significant indirect interest. Insurance companies are directly interested in government ownership, rate and security regulation, and in any public policies which affect the value of utility securities.

Second, insurance companies represent an institutional device by which a large portion of the national income is automatically converted into savings. In a sense this saving is involuntary and is in no way related to the needs of industry for new capital. In the past the railroad and utility companies have constituted an important field of investment for these funds. Maintenance of the national income requires that public utility, or other investment fields, be maintained to keep these savings in circulation.

6. WAR-TIME UTILITY FINANCING

1. The Trend of Financing During the War

The war period saw new factors establishing the nature of utility financing.

(1) The government's war financing took most of the free capital. Financing by private industry was difficult. In the early days of the war, the value of both stocks and high grade bonds declined.

(2) Material shortages kept new construction to an absolute minimum. The utility industry found ways of making old equipment do. Round-the-clock operation of many war industries permitted the electric power and other utility industries to increase their output without adding new facilities.

(3) There were few new stock issues. Stock prices gradually rose. Since utility companies had a great deal of preferred stock, income and excess-profits taxes rested heavily upon the common stock and decreased its desirability.

(4) Bond financing was for refunding purposes and in large measure was incident to the reorganization of the utility systems under the Holding Company Act. Even this type of financing was somewhat limited by the Securities and Exchange Commission's policy of reducing debt capital to fifty per cent of the capitalization wherever possible.

2. Internal Financing

The degree to which industries are resorting to internal financing has been given increasing attention in recent years by economists interested in the business cycle and in the functioning of our national economy. During the first and growing years of an industry, outside sources of capital must be used to finance an ever-expanding construction program. Once an industry reaches maturity, it can commonly meet its financial needs from within itself owing to its large annual reserve and surplus accumulations and, in many instances, to its declining need for new plant and property. While it is questionable whether the electric, gas, and telephone industries can be classed as mature industries, it is true that in the decade of the thirties they passed through a period in which their growth leveled off. This might be called a period of temporary maturity or arrested growth. Such periods will be characterized by new methods of finance considerably different from those of periods of expansion.

An analysis of approximately three billion dollars raised by about two thirds of the electric utility industry from 1925 to 1930 indicated that about 26 per cent of the capital came from reserves and undistributed earnings and 74 per cent from the sale of securities. In contrast, during the eight years ending 1942, the entire electric utility industry raised $3,250,000,000, of which 82 per cent came from current funds and only 18 per cent from the sale of securities. President Kellogg of the Edison Electric Institute pointed out that electric construction budgets for 1943 amounting to $283,000,000 (or about 10 per cent of the industry's gross revenue) would require no security financing whatever for the industry as a whole.[10] Figure 4 and Table 12 indicate the striking change from security to internal financing that took place in the thirties.

The utility industry is financed internally from four significant sources:

(1) *The Use of Depreciation Accruals.* The adoption of new systems of accounts for electric and gas utilities which required depreciation rather than retirement accounting increased the funds available for capital expenditures. Under the retirement accounting procedure followed by most utility companies in previous years, annual charges were little more than sufficient to take care of current retirements. Reserves were small and were kept so. In contrast, during the years 1939-1941, depreciation accruals financed more than 50 per cent of the private electric utility industry's gross capital expenditures.[11]

(2) *Undistributed Net Income.* In varying degrees, many utility companies financed new construction out of earnings. For example, the Metropolitan Edison Company retained over 60 per cent of its net income and paid no common dividends in 1941. During the period 1938-1942, electric utilities retained between 14 and 19 per cent of their net income.[12]

Among the factors leading to a more conservative dividend policy on the part of some companies might be included the restrictions of regulatory authorities, the reduction of the pressure from holding companies for more liberal dividend payments, and the plain desire to rehabilitate

[10] *Edison Electric Institute Bulletin* (October, 1943), p. 293.

[11] National Association of Railroad and Utilities Commissioners, *Proceedings,* 1942, pp. 274 ff.

[12] Federal Power Commission, *Statistics of Electric Utilities in United States,* 1942, p. IX.

weakened financial structures. On the other hand, liberal dividend policies were adopted in many instances where it was thought desirable to maintain the market value of the stocks or where the holding companies were in the need of cash.

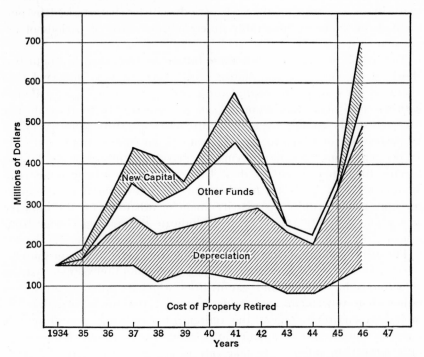

FIG. 4. SOURCES OF FUNDS FOR CONSTRUCTION EXPENDITURES AND POWER COMPANIES.

(1934-1946)

Adapted by permission from *Public Utilities Fortnightly* (December 4, 1947), p. 784. Material from the Edison Electric Institute.

(3) *Amortization of Bond Discount and Expense.* A relatively minor source of new funds is the reservation of earnings for the amortization of bond discount and expense. In the aggregate, such amounts are small, but for particular companies the item will be of considerable significance.

(4) *Tax Accruals.* The time lag between the accrual and payment of taxes results in the accumulation of funds which may be used as a means of temporary financing. It may even provide some permanent capital. An increasing tax rate increases the amount that must be accrued over current payments, while a decreasing rate will draw down the company's liquid resources.

7. POST-WAR UTILITY FINANCING

The New Boom. Following World War II the nation entered upon a period of unprecedented prosperity, based in some part upon the release of the pent-up demand for consumer goods but in greater part upon the boom in the construction industry. Expansion in certain other industries such as the chemical industry was also a primary source of economic activity. The demand derived from the activity in these industries and from the need of replacing worn out equipment was diffused throughout the entire economic system. Industrial expansion and residential building brought an increase in the demand for utility services. All demands were pressing; none could be delayed for more favorable price conditions. The period presents considerable proof of the cumulative nature of prosperity and the virtual impossibility of staggering activity in the capital goods industries so as to smooth out the business cycle. Even expenditures on public works, presumably the most amenable to cyclical control, increased.

Plant capacity, already taxed by wartime construction restrictions, was further burdened by new demands. The utility industries launched themselves upon a building program that threatened to surpass that of the 1920's. Financing became the critical function of public utility management. Internal financing was no longer sufficient for the new demands. Security flotations of 1947 were above those of 1946 and were in turn exceeded by those of 1948. Moreover, after 1947 and for the first time since 1932, new capital issues exceeded refunding issues and moved towards an all-time high.

Financial Markets. The stock market did not completely reflect the nation's economic prosperity. The lessons of the 1920's had been learned too well and in the midst of a boom all thoughts were on the depression, which, if it did not follow the war, must inevitably follow the boom. The foreign situation gave no reason for confidence. Venture capital was scarce. In the midst of rising prices, investors, somewhat illogically perhaps, sought security in fixed income bearing evidences of debt.

Utility Financing. Stock yields were high and interest rates were low. Hence utilities, like other industries, sought their funds in the sale of bonds. For a while they were able to do their financing on their own terms. Insurance companies and other institutional buyers were eager takers. But by 1947 the situation changed. Capital markets began to tighten as the construction boom drained off the available supply of capital. With the alternative real estate market open to them, institutional investors became less and less eager to take over utility security issues. The weight of bargaining power shifted to the insurance companies. Only the Treasury's support of government bonds kept interest rates low.

Interest rates began to rise, but they were still far from comparable with equity yields. Debt financing continued. Neither management nor regulatory authorities were happy about the situation. Some of their fears were allayed by resort to convertible debentures, a type of security that had fallen into disuse since the early 1930's. It was hoped and expected that these debentures would be turned into stock. Preferred stock was also made more acceptable to investors by a new device, the provision for a sinking fund. Without a developed market for common stocks utility companies turned to their own stockholders for more funds and secured some new equity capital through the issuance of warrants entitling stock-holders to subscribe for new stock.

The real financing problems were those of the weaker utilities. Un-balanced capital structures, poor operating territories, and even poorer financial histories made financing difficult. A heavy debt burden pre-cluded further bond financing, while their smallness of size kept them from easy access to the stock markets. Two sources of capital were avail-able—internal sources and the sale of additional stock to existing stock-holders through warrants. But the former course made the latter more difficult, as the retention of earnings reduced the saleability of the stock. Truly their lot was not a happy one.

The capital structures of many gas and electric utilities had been thoroughly overhauled by the Securities and Exchange Commission inci-dent to disintegration and simplification proceedings under the Holding Company Act. Other commissions also played a part in the general "clean-up." Hence heavy debt financing did not unduly weaken the utility industries, although it was not always in accord with the 50-25-25 ratio between bonds, preferred stock, and common stock sought by the SEC. The real test of the soundness of the gas, electric, and telephone indus-tries' financing must come if and when those industries follow the life path of the railroad, telegraph, and transit industries.

8. UTILITY CAPITALIZATION TODAY

Utility financing is unique in several respects. First, the amount of capital required is much greater than in other industries and is several times the annual revenue. Second, an unusually high percentage of utility capital is obtained from bonds. Today the Securities and Exchange Com-mission is attempting to hold down the debt capital of many companies to what it considers a desirable amount of 50 per cent. Third, electric utility capital structures contain more than the usual amount of pre-ferred stock.

Few firms in other industries would willingly burden themselves with such a large percentage of debt and fixed dividend paying securities. The confidence, shared alike by promoters and investors, that utility earnings were shock proof against the forces of depression and economic trends has made this possible. The confidence was not always justified. Similar beliefs held about the earnings of railroad and street-railway companies proved disastrously unfounded. The earnings of many gas and water companies have not held up to a satisfactory level. Even the future of the electric utility industry is clouded by the threat of government competition. Certainly programs of debt reduction instituted by several regulatory commissions appear to be sound.

9. CONCLUSION

All the basic principles by which financiers and economists attempt to analyze the interplay of demand and supply on the financial markets are illustrated somewhere in the history or extent of utility financing. Trading on the equity and the institution of the holding company found a common reason for being in the actual or supposed stability of utility earnings. Somewhere in the realm of utility finance can be found examples of all the rarer and more exotic types of securities, and in addition many which are not met with elsewhere. In justice to many of these securities that have been issued in the past, it may be said that they were printed on an excellent quality of paper.

Among the many controversial issues of economic theory has been that of the effect of interest rates upon capital formation. Since capital costs are such an important element in utility costs and since utility financing is such a significant portion of all financing, the experience of the industry should throw some light upon the question.

The effect of capital costs upon financial policies is everywhere apparent, but there is little evidence that they had any great stimulating or controlling effect upon the expansion of the industry. Changes in capital costs merely changed the type of financing. The high interest rates of 1921, 1931, and 1932 led to the use of short-term notes. The moderately high interest rates of the 1920's led to equity financing. Even the more or less complete lack of confidence of an investing public in the future of the utility industry did little to retard its expanding force. Faced with public suspicion in its early days, the electric and gas utility companies relied upon equipment companies for capital. In a later period, the utilities turned to themselves for the financial means of expansion when the securities market was not propitious. The urban transportation industry has in many instances completely changed the nature of its plant and equipment without resort to a capital market that was distrustful of its securities.

It might have been said that the extremely high price-earnings ratios and the avidity with which the public grabbed up utility stock offerings in the 1920's contributed to the expansion of the industry. It is true that equity capital was cheap, but bond capital was not. The expansion of the period was more to be explained by the demand for more and better utility service than it was by the cheapness of equity capital.

In a broader sense, the lessons of public utility finance lie in the field of business cycle theory. Since 1920, the utility industry has furnished the demand for one third to one half of all the funds going into corporate securities. To the extent that utility companies can finance from internal sources this market for securities and savings disappears.

The important savings made in our national economy may be roughly classed as follows:

(1) Social security payments made by individuals, with which we cannot be concerned here.

(2) Personal savings made more or less voluntarily and going into savings deposits, building and loan societies, and into the purchase of corporate securities.

(3) Personal savings made more or less involuntarily in the form of premiums paid to insurance companies.

(4) Corporate savings resulting in internal financing of corporations.

Our economic society has a relatively high propensity to save. Normal human instincts are sufficient to lead individuals to save for the future. A large percentage of their savings seeks the investment field provided by corporation securities. In the case of insurance premiums, saving becomes even more automatic, for an individual will go to extreme lengths to keep his insurance policy from lapsing. In turn, the insurance companies are faced with the necessity of employing the funds they receive in profitable investments. Idle savings create no new income. The well-being of our economy requires that any savings or income not used in the purchase of consumption goods be returned to the national income stream in the production of capital goods.

Our study of internal financing easily leads us beyond the utility industries. Depreciation accounting and other forms of internal financing are forms of corporate savings by which certain portions of a company's revenues are retained within the corporation and not, in the first instance, paid out to the stockholders. It is necessary that these corporate savings, like individual savings, be regularly returned to the national income stream in the form of expenditures for plant and equipment if our economy is to function properly and we are to avoid deflation and a steady decline in the national income.

The reinvestment of these savings is a financial problem of the first magnitude. It is perfectly possible over a relatively short period of time to have a technological revolution in which every piece of old equipment is scrapped and a complete new physical plant created without resort to the capital markets. Moreover, industries can expand indefinitely at a moderate rate merely by the reinvestment of their depreciation reserves. Thus from 1921 to 1936 the United States Steel Corporation modernized its plant by expending a total of $1,222,000,000. To finance this huge long-range program it retained $192,000,000 from its profits of over a billion dollars, set aside $938,000,000 for depreciation and amortization, and sold only $240,000,000 of new stock.[13]

TABLE 12

SOURCES OF FUNDS FOR THE FINANCING OF NEW PLANT AND EQUIPMENT *
(Millions of Dollars)

Period	Average Annual Outlay for Plant and Equipment	Percentage		
		Financed From Earnings	Financed From Depreciation and Depletion	Financed From Security Issues
1923-1929	8,664	25.1	48.5	20.2
1933-1939	5,005	− 3.7	87.9	5.4

* Computed from Temporary National Economic Committee, *Savings, Investment, and National Income,* Monograph No. 37, p. 57.

More recently, a survey indicated that a nation-wide expansion program designed to increase our industrial capacity by 52 per cent over 1939 by the end of 1948 would be financed to the extent of 84 per cent out of capital, reserves, and surplus.[14] Table 12 compares the sources of corporate funds during two seven-year periods, 1923-1929 and 1933-1939. Table 13 shows the sources of corporate funds in 1947.

This aspect of our national economy may be of greater significance than the questionable assumption that the need for new capital is subject to a secular downward trend. Whatever demands for new capital that might be opened up by atomic energy, by electricity, by chemistry, or by any of the many technical wonders of our age, the financial resources of large-scale enterprise will be able to supply much of the new capital unaided by financial markets. Only immense expansion, similar to that enjoyed by the utility industries in the late 1940's, will draw them into the new capital markets.

It is not only quite true that depreciation reserves supply the resources for expansion; it is also likely that they create the urge, if not the neces-

[13] Stuart Chase, "Capital Not Wanted," *Harpers Magazine* (February, 1940), pp. 225, 229.

[14] *Cf.* a survey made by the McGraw-Hill Publishing Company, *Business Week,* February 2, 1947, pp. 65-72.

sity, to expand. It does not profit management to allow funds to lie idle. Therefore corporate management must constantly seek new fields of investment. The very size of uninvested surplus and reserves is sufficient to make large-scale corporations grasp eagerly for footholds in other industries even loosely related to their existing fields of endeavor.

TABLE 13

SOURCES OF CORPORATE FUNDS, 1947 *

	Amount in Billions of Dollars	Percentage
Retained net income	10.1	37.8
Depreciation	4.3	16.1
Cash and deposits	− 1.0	− 3.7
Sale of U.S. Government securities	1.5	5.6
Payables, etc.	1.7	6.4
Income tax liability	2.3	8.6
Bank loans	3.0	11.2
Mortgage loans	0.7	2.6
New capital stock issues	1.3	4.9
New bond and note issues	2.8	10.5
TOTALS	26.7	100.0

* U.S. Department of Commerce, *Survey of Current Business*, March, 1948.

The history of public utility financing is a significant although not an entirely typical chapter in the history of all corporate financing. The growth of the industries is somewhat similar to that of a number of other giant industries which had their birth around the turn of the century and saw their greatest expansion in the 1920's. Hence they must be set apart from the older and more mature industries. On the other hand, the financial problems of growth are more typical of the general problems of corporate finance, since financial problems are essentially dynamic ones related to the growth—or to the decay—of firms and industries.

6. Operating Expenses and Their Regulation

1. THE PROBLEM OF OPERATING EXPENSES

The financial statements of an electric utility show that it is earning less than a fair return. However, depreciation expense constitutes twenty per cent of its revenues, and general and administrative expense takes up fifteen per cent more. Production costs are high; the company purchases coal from a mining company owned by the president. Service is poor and the equipment is inefficient. Of what significance are these facts to a regulatory commission from whom the utility is seeking a rate increase? Of what significance are they to management?

In this chapter we will concern ourselves with operating expenses in three connections: (1) their place in the rate-making procedure, (2) their regulation by law, and (3) their statistical control as an aid to management and regulation.

The Determination of the General Rate Level. We shall now turn to what has been regarded as the central problem of public utility regulation, namely, the problem of rate making. We have already seen that public utility rates are set so that

$$R = E + (V - D) r$$

where R is the total revenue to be obtained from the rates in question, E is the operating expenses, V is the fair value of the property when new, D is the depreciation in the value of the property, and r is the rate of return to be allowed on the fair, depreciated value. Hence when a utility comes before a commission in a rate case, the utility's operating expenses become a matter for the commission's attention. A commission will determine a reasonable allowance on the basis of the company's past experience modified by expected future conditions.

It can be easily recognized that all regulation could be set at naught if a utility could extravagantly increase its costs and pass them on to the ratepayers with impunity. The United States Supreme Court held as early as 1892 that the power to set fair rates included the right to examine operating expenses; [1] but it has been only in recent years that control has been effective. There were several reasons. It was too loosely assumed that the interests of management in lower expenses were identical with those of the ratepayers. Commissions lacked adequate quantitative standards of reasonableness. Some expenses were beyond their jurisdiction. Finally, any rights of control were offset by a well-established legal principle that a commission sits as a regulatory agency and cannot usurp the functions of management.

With certain exceptions, a commission cannot prevent a utility from incurring improper operating expenses. Only in the event that the utility is required by law to submit a budget for commission approval does a commission even have advance knowledge of them. In general a commission's powers are limited to disallowing such items in the determination of the proper amount of operating expenses to be covered by rates. Capital expenditures are subject to some control in that a utility must obtain a certificate of convenience and necessity before adding new plant units. Control over accounting practices carries with it control over depreciation and some other expense items.

To determine the proper allowance to be made for operating expenses, a utility commission will examine the financial statements of one or more preceding years. On the basis of these a prediction of the future will be attempted. Unusual and non-recurring items will be eliminated as well as improper items. Some items will be reduced if the commission has reason to believe them to be excessive. Standards of reasonableness will be discussed later.

2. THE TREATMENT OF SOME SPECIFIC EXPENSES

An examination of certain items of operating expenses that are most frequently in dispute in rate cases brings out some of the detail of administrative procedure and illustrates several underlying principles.

1. Salaries

As in other kinds of business enterprises, salaries may constitute a form of concealed profits. Because of regulation, utility management in particular might be more interested in high salaries than in high earnings. Hence the salaries of officers and directors are always subject to scrutiny. The Utah Commission found a little water company whose revenues never ran over $17,000 a year paying out as much as $5,100 for officers'

[1] *Chicago & Grand Trunk Ry.* v. *Wellman*, 143 U.S. 339 (1892).

salaries and directors' fees. In one year 39 per cent of the total operating revenues went in this manner. The company could not hire a full-time bookkeeper and did not pay dividends, but its five directors received $520 each in fees. The Commission thought $40 would be a more reasonable estimate of the value of their services.[2]

It must be stated, however, that there is no particular reason for believing that the salaries of operating officials in general are excessive in comparison with those paid in competitive industries. It is probable that exceptional salaries are found most frequently in small utilities that are owned by their management and in the case of top flight executives and promoters of holding company systems.

2. Pensions

Pension system provisions for officers and employees are generally permissible operating expenses provided the plans are handled in a proper manner. Management can hardly be penalized for not pursuing a cold-blooded policy of laying off faithful old employees. Indeed the systematic retirement of elderly employees of declining ability increases efficiency and morale, reduces personnel turnover, and enables the utility company to compete in the market for the services of workers and executives.

On occasion commissions have looked askance at some pension plans. The Wisconsin Commission criticized the plan of one company as being nothing more than a means of building up a segregated surplus. There was no written contract between the company and its employees, and the plan could be cancelled at will by the company. Pension accruals were invested in company properties, the trustee of the plan merely receiving a promissory note.[3]

3. Costs of Regulation

In some states utilities are assessed with the costs of the regulatory commission. In addition companies have to spend money preparing material and hiring lawyers and experts in rate cases. They may spend still more appealing an unsatisfactory order to the courts. Should these expenses be included in determining the allowable operating expenses? More is involved than the mere handling of an item of expense. If the costs of litigation can be passed on to the ratepayers, the temptation to defeat the ends of regulation is increased. In fairness to the utility, some allowance, however, should be made for these expenses.

The usual assessments against a utility to cover commission expenses are allowable expenses. The expenses of preparing a rate case are fre-

[2] 55 P.U.R. (N.S.) 99 (1944).
[3] See 2 P.S.C.W. 106, 128 (1932).

quently amortized over a period of ten years or less. If an order is appealed to the courts and the rates are found to be confiscatory, the expenses will be allowed. But suppose the company loses the case? There is no certain answer to this question, but wisdom would seem to indicate that the right of a utility to recover all of the expenses should be limited. Commissions may even refuse to allow the expenses of presenting a case. The Pennsylvania Superior Court has held that a commission need not allow a company to recover the full expense of litigation arising from an attempt to raise rates unreasonably.[4]

Illustrative of procedure is that of the Wisconsin Commission. A telephone company making an excessive return on the basis of its sworn reports declined to make a voluntary reduction and spent $2,700 in fighting a reduction in formal proceedings. The Commission refused to allow the amount in setting rates.[5]

4. Promotional Expense

Utility companies often sell appliances and engage in other promotional activities to increase the use of service. It is not expected that many of these activities show a profit; the utility gains through the increased use of its service. Eventually the customer may gain through lower costs. Can the customers rightfully be charged with these costs?

Regulatory commissions generally approve expenditures for advertising which seek to increase or improve the use of service. The loss on the sale of merchandise presents another problem. In the past, vigorous sales programs have aroused the antagonism of local merchants who claim that they are a form of unfair competition. In reply the utility companies argue that their own promotional efforts will increase the sales of the merchants. In some instances a vigorous appliance-selling campaign is absolutely necessary to build up the load on rural electric lines if they are to become self-sustaining.

Accounting classifications distinguish between expense (and income) from merchandising, jobbing, and contract work and so-called promotional expense. The former group of accounts includes such items as salaries and commissions of salesmen, which are excluded in the determination of rates. The latter type of expense is included.

5. Donations

In the interest of good public relations, utility officials regard it as desirable that their company be identified with worthy local charities and civic activities. Utility commissions, however, have almost invariably refused to include donations among operating expenses in rate cases. Inclu-

[4] 51 P.U.R. (N.S.) 129, 144 (1943).
[5] 6 P.S.C.W. 407 (1934).

sion would place the ratepayers in a position of becoming involuntary contributors to charity. Moreover there is a belief that donations might be a means of influencing public opinion. On the other hand less charitable contributions to business associations to stimulate business activity are frequently allowed if it can be shown that the consumer will benefit from the larger volume of business done by the company.

6. Payments to Affiliates

Payments to affiliates constitute an extremely important regulatory problem, for it may be assumed that there is little if any real "arms-length" bargaining between, say, a holding company and its subsidiary. Operating companies have paid their parent companies a certain percentage of gross revenues for all sorts of services, both real and imaginary. Of course many management, financial, engineering, and other services were of considerable value. But for a long while the reasonableness of these payments could not be questioned, since the records of the holding companies could not be reached. State public utility laws have now been generally revised to place the burden of proving the reasonableness of these charges on the operating company. In some instances a commission can void such contracts.[6]

7. Losses Due to Inefficiency

A regulatory commission is justified in reducing or eliminating expenses traceable to inefficiency, but this cannot be done without evidence or at least without according the opportunity to be heard. Generally speaking, the actual experienced expenses will be given greater weight by the courts than the testimony of experts as to what expenses should be.[7] Knowing this, commissions have been reluctant to push forward into what has been considered the field of management. For better or worse, the problem of quantitative standards of reasonableness falls more in the field of management than in the field of regulation.

3. QUANTITATIVE STANDARDS OF REASONABLENESS

The Use of Ratios. How can a utility commission—or utility management—decide whether certain expenses are reasonable or whether they arise through lax management or woeful inefficiency? The most effective approach to the problem is through the use of expense ratios in which the expenses of many companies are reduced to a comparable basis. There

---

[6] *Western Distributing Co.* v. *Pub. Serv. Comm. of Kansas,* 285 U.S. 119, 124 (1932).
[7] *Ohio Utilities Co.* v. *Pub. Util. Comm.,* 267 U.S. 359, 363 (1925); *West Ohio Gas Co.* v. *Pub. Util. Comm.,* 294 U.S. 63, 68 (1935).

are many ratios, but the simplest and most commonly used groups include the following:

1. Expenses as a percentage of revenues.
2. Expenses per unit of consumption.
3. Expenses per customer.

Expense ratios must be used with judgment. They are comparable only to a degree. A utility with a large industrial load will not operate under the same cost conditions as one with a large residential load. The costs of one utility may be high because the demand tends to be concentrated at one hour of the day or at a certain day of the year. Expense ratios are merely points of departure for further questioning and analysis.

1. Electric Utilities

Electric utility expenses have probably been subject to more detailed analysis than those of any other utility. The sharpness of the dispute over private and public ownership and research by the Federal Power Commission and several of the better financed state commissions have contributed to the information on the subject. Private utilities have also done a great deal of research for the purpose of making competitive rates.

Typical ratios are shown in Table 14.

Production Expense. A typical electric utility will incur a relatively large proportion of its expenses in producing electricity, although this proportion is not as large as the layman commonly assumes. The proportion varies with the type of utility. A hydro-electric utility will have low production costs, although its fixed costs will be high. Production costs of steam-generating utilities will vary with the cost of fuel and of course with the amount of electricity produced.

Transmission Expense. Transmission expense includes the expense of transmitting power at high voltage (or pressure) from the generating station to the distribution system, which serves a concentrated group of consumers. Power cannot be efficiently transmitted for long distance at the relatively low voltages at which it is generated, nor can it be effectively distributed or used except at low voltages. Hence the voltage is increased or stepped up at the generating station and stepped down again to the distribution system. Transmission expense includes all the maintenance and operating expense incident to the first transformation and transmission.[8]

Transmission expense varies widely between utilities. Some utilities may buy their power and hence have no transmission expense at all. Other

[8] The cost of transforming power to distribution voltage is classed as distribution expense. We shall see that this distinction had a great legal significance in connection with the jurisdiction of an agency of the Federal Government. See the chapter on Federal regulation.

utilities may be able to locate their generating plants within a large city and close to their consumers and therefore have very little transmission expense. On the other hand, water power sites may be located in a wilderness miles from the urban load centers. A utility must then construct costly high-voltage transmission lines. Even steam power plants cannot always be located at will and close to consumers, for they require large supplies of cooling water. Utility engineers designing a power system must often balance the cheaper production costs of an advantageous generating site against transmission costs.

TABLE 14

EXPENSE RATIOS OF WISCONSIN ELECTRIC UTILITIES *

1945

Expense	As a Percentage of Revenues	Per Kilowatt Hour	Per Customer Per Year
Production	28.6%	6.2 mills	$35.37
Transmission	1.2	.3	1.49
Distribution	6.4	1.4	7.91
Customers Accounting and Collecting	2.3	.5	2.93
Sales Promotion	1.3	.3	1.57
Administrative and General	5.8	1.3	7.23
TOTAL OPERATING EXPENSES	45.6	10.0	56.50
Depreciation	9.8	2.1	12.12
Taxes Other than Income	9.1	2.0	11.32
Income Taxes	15.4	3.4	19.08
TOTAL REVENUE DEDUCTIONS	79.9	17.5	99.02
Utility Operating Income	20.1	4.4	24.89
TOTAL OPERATING REVENUES	100.0	21.9	123.91

Total Revenues	$91,168,415
Total Customers	735,784
Total Kilowatt-Hours Sold	4,176,300,000

* Computed from *Statistics of Wisconsin Public Utilities, 1944-1946* (Mimeo.), Bulletin Rates and Research Dept., Wisconsin Public Service Commission, 1947. Total revenues include $10,464,237 from sales to other than ultimate consumers. Municipal utilities account for 7.4% of the total revenues.

Transmission costs are generally low, and they do not show any close relationship to either the amount of electricity consumed or to the number of customers. Investment in transmission equipment varies widely depending upon the nature of the system.

Distribution Expense. A surprisingly high percentage of the cost of electricity can be traced to its distribution and utilization. This expense, including depreciation, taxes, and return upon the investment, may run up to 30 per cent or more of the total cost of electricity. It varies more or less directly with the number of customers and is influenced to only a small extent by the amount of the electricity consumed.

Expense Ratios as an Instrument of Management. The simple ratios suggest an extremely important technique of management. Ratio analysis is used not only by public utility management and by regulators but by

TABLE 15

EXPENSE RATIOS OF WISCONSIN MANUFACTURED GAS UTILITIES *

Classes A and B, Privately Owned

1946

Expense	As a Percentage of Revenues	Per MCF Sold	Per Customer Per Year
Production	40.8%	35.0¢	$16.78
Transmission and Distribution	13.3	11.4	5.47
Customers' Accounting and Collecting	5.4	4.6	2.22
Sales Promotion	2.8	2.5	1.17
Administrative and General	7.6	6.5	3.12
TOTAL OPERATING EXPENSES	69.9	60.0	28.76
Depreciation	8.7	7.4	3.56
Taxes other than Income	7.2	6.2	2.97
Income Taxes	3.5	3.0	1.43
TOTAL REVENUE DEDUCTIONS	89.3	76.6	36.72
Utility Operating Income	10.7	9.2	4.40
TOTAL OPERATING REVENUES	100.0	85.8	41.12

Total Revenues	$16,900,995
Average Number of Customers	411,004
MCF Sold	19,694,576

* Computed from *Gas Utilities Expense Ratios, 1944-1946* (Typewritten), Bulletin of Rates and Research Dept., Wisconsin Public Service Commission (January, 1948).

business management in general. Expenses are broken down on a percentage basis, or they are expressed in per-unit-of-output terms. They may be compared with similar ratios of other companies or with the company's own ratios in times past. Such comparisons may turn up valuable information on trends and weaknesses that would otherwise go unnoticed. A rise in the production cost of electricity from 6.0 to 6.2 mills per kilowatt-hour may indicate increased coal costs or it may mean inefficient boiler room operation in which heat is wasted. In any event, those re-

sponsible—the general manager, the plant manager, the boiler-plant super-
intendent—may be called to account by their superiors.[9]

2. Manufactured Gas Utilities

Typical expense ratios for manufactured gas utilities are shown in
Table 15.

Transmission expenses are very low, since there is practically no intercity transmission of artificial gas. On a per customer basis administrative
and general expenses are lower than for electric utilities, since a gas utility
business is generally somewhat more simple. Taxes are high, although
not as high as those of an electric utility.

TABLE 16

EXPENSE RATIOS OF WISCONSIN WATER UTILITIES *

1945

Expense	As a Percentage of Revenues	Per 1000 Gallons Pumped	Per Customer Per Year
Source of Water Supply	3.4%	.4¢	$ .99
Pumping	18.4	2.4	5.44
Purification	5.4	.7	1.59
TOTAL PRODUCTION EXPENSE	27.2	3.5	8.02
Transmission and Distribution	8.7	1.2	2.58
Customers' Accounting and Collection	4.3	.6	1.27
Sales Promotion	. . .	. . .	.01
Administrative and General	6.4	.8	1.88
TOTAL OPERATING EXPENSES	46.6	6.1	13.76
Depreciation	11.3	1.5	3.33
Taxes Other than Income	16.0	2.0	4.73
Income Taxes	.5	.1	.13
TOTAL REVENUE DEDUCTIONS	74.4	9.7	21.95
Utility Operating Income	25.6	3.3	7.56
TOTAL OPERATING REVENUES	100.0	13.0	29.51

Total Revenues	$11,502,850
Average Number of Customers	373,637
1000 Gallons Pumped	73,650,067

* Computed from *Statistics of Wisconsin Public Utilities, 1944-1946* (Mimeographed), Bulletin of Rates
and Research Department, Wisconsin Public Service Commission, 1947.

[9] For practical purposes expenses must be much more finely subdivided than those
presented here. A somewhat more detailed breakdown of the expenses of private and
municipal electric utilities in Wisconsin in 1946 is presented in Chapter 23.

3. Water Utilities

The expenses of water utilities may be compared and analyzed as percentages of revenues, as costs per unit produced, or as costs per customer. Because fire protection service is unmetered and because many utilities furnish water to general customers at a flat rate without metering, water consumption figures are lacking. Pumping figures are used instead. Table 16 presents representative figures for Wisconsin water utilities. What do these figures tell us about the water industry?

Total operating expenses of 46.6% of revenues are low in comparison with every other utility industry. On a per customer basis they amount to $13.76 a year in comparison with $28.76 for gas, $32.98 for telephone, and $56.50 for electricity. It is apparent that production problems are simple. Pumping expense constitutes the greatest element of cost. Commercial expenses (customers' accounting and collections) of only $1.27 a year are extremely low and reflect the usual practice of billing on a quarterly or semi-annual basis. New business (sales promotion) expense is practically non-existent, as water utilities do little to increase the use of service.

The cost of a water system is very high and the traditional 5 to 1 ratio between capital investment and operating revenues of utility companies is often exceeded. A 10 to 1 ratio is usual. Both depreciation and operating income, expressed as percentages of revenues, are correspondingly high. The return must come from operating income. Depreciation is not as high as might be expected because of the long life of a great deal of water utility equipment, such as dams and pipe.

4. Telephone Utilities

Telephone utilities sell service rather than a commodity and so their expense classification falls in a somewhat different pattern from those of the preceding utilities. The delicate nature of a large part of the plant investment, which includes the instruments in subscribers' homes, is reflected by high maintenance expense.

The service supplied by a telephone company is largely the personal service rendered by its operators. Traffic expense, that is, the expense of handling calls, takes up about 30 per cent of a company's revenues. Two thirds of the traffic expense consists of operators' wages. Superintendence and the cost of power are also included. The gradual introduction of the faster and more accurate dial-operated central office [10] is reducing the

10 A central office includes a switchboard and other associated apparatus. One or more central offices may be included in an exchange. An exchange includes all the lines and facilities by which the telephones, or stations, of a community are given service. Central offices are connected by trunk lines; exchanges are connected by toll lines. In

number of operators. This brings with it an increase in maintenance expense and in the number of maintenance employees.

5. Urban Transportation Utilities

Cost analysis does not have quite the significance in the urban transportation industry that it does in other utilities. Here the problem of balancing the costs and revenues of various classes of service gives way to

TABLE 17

EXPENSE RATIOS OF WISCONSIN TELEPHONE UTILITIES *

1945

Expense	As a Percentage of Revenues	Per Revenue Station Per Year
Maintenance	18.7%	$ 9.34
Traffic	30.5	15.21
Commercial	5.8	2.90
General and Miscellaneous	9.9	4.94
General Service and License Fees	1.2	.59
TOTAL OPERATING EXPENSES	66.1	32.98
Uncollectible Bills	.1	.04
Depreciation	10.5	5.23
Taxes Other than Income	7.2	3.61
Income Taxes	5.9	2.94
Rent Deductions	1.1	.55
TOTAL REVENUE DEDUCTIONS	90.9	45.35
Utility Operating Income	9.1	4.55
TOTAL OPERATING REVENUES	100.0	49.90

Total Operating Revenues	$34,305,901
Total Revenue Stations	687,485

* Computed from *Statistics of Wisconsin Public Utilities, 1944-1946* (Mimeo.), Bulletin of Rates and Research Dept., Wisconsin Public Service Commission, 1947.

the problem of finding sufficient revenues to cover costs. Moreover, under the pressure of inadequate earnings street-railway management must be on the alert constantly to cut expenses without prompting from any regulatory commission. No industry, except perhaps the bankrupt railways, can surpass the street-railway industry in attempting to win public

---

the larger systems power is supplied from a central point. Small rural systems still have a large number of magneto-operated switchboards, in which power is supplied from batteries and a crank-operated magneto generator on the customer's premises.

favor. On the other hand, in all too many instances street-railways have been prevented from installing new, desirable, and possibly profitable equipment by the mere lack of capital.

A large percentage of the cost of operating an urban transportation system is incidental to supplying transportation itself. Employee compensation may take half of a transit company's revenues. Rising labor costs, coupled with the inability of most companies to pass wage increases on to consumers, have contributed in part to the ills of the industry. Many companies have gone far in reducing labor costs by using larger cars and one-man streetcars.

TABLE 18

EXPENSE RATIOS OF WISCONSIN URBAN ELECTRIC RAILWAYS *

1946

Expense	As a Percentage of Revenues	Per Vehicle Mile	Per Revenue Passenger
Maintenance of Ways and Structures	4.4%	1.99¢	.25¢
Maintenance of Equipment	10.4	4.71	.58
Conducting Transportation including Power	46.5	20.92	2.60
Traffic	.4	.18	.02
General and Miscellaneous	6.2	2.79	.35
TOTAL OPERATING EXPENSES	67.9	30.59	3.80
Depreciation	8.0	3.60	.45
Taxes	14.7	6.63	.82
Rent	.3	.12	.02
TOTAL REVENUE DEDUCTIONS	90.9	40.94	5.09
Utility Operating Income	9.1	4.09	.51
TOTAL OPERATING REVENUES	100.0	45.03	5.60

Total Revenues	$15,375,710
Total Vehicle Miles	34,149,574
Total Revenue Passengers	274,752,938

* Computed from *Statistics of Wisconsin Public Utilities, 1944-1946* (Mimeo.), Bulletin of the Rates and Research Dept., Wisconsin Public Service Commission, 1947.

Taxes do not rest quite as heavily upon transit companies as upon other utilities. This is partly due to their lack of income. On the other hand, they are frequently burdened by onerous franchise taxes and paving assessments, which were placed upon them by the city fathers in more prosperous days. In some instances companies have been relieved of them in order to induce them to continue service.

4. SUMMARY

This chapter deals with the techniques of regulating and controlling operating expenses. This particular field of regulation has been little developed except where abuses have been flagrant and apparent. Regulation has been based upon the standard of reasonableness rather than efficiency. Commissions have been restrained by a somewhat passive acceptance of the doctrine that expenditures are within the field of management rather than regulation. Much more attention has been given to the problems of value and depreciation than to operating expenses in the rate-making process.

An attempt has been made to outline the use of cost comparisons as a tool of regulatory and management control. A few commissions are using this technique in a limited manner to subject public utilities to a measure of "competitive" control but its primary use is found in the hands of utility management. In other than the utility industries the techniques illustrated here have gained widespread acceptance as devices for management control.

Limitations on the Use of Ratios. Words of warning are called for here. Ratio analysis does not represent the touchstone of managerial efficiency. Accountants and statisticians are frequently and justifiably criticized because they use comparative statistics without regard for or comprehension of the different operating circumstances. Ratios serve merely as a point of departure for managerial analysis.

Statistical standards of performance do not always act as a spur to efficiency. It is true that operating heads will attempt to meet standards of comparison. They are cautious, however, and frequently avoid improving upon what has come to be the standard, in the fear that even more might be expected of them in the future. "Let well enough alone" is an old adage of practical men.

Operating standards are no better than the basic data from which they are compiled. Workmen in the field, foremen, and managers will often spread expenses between various accounts by broad rule of thumb, by guess, or by sheer imagination. Operating men are seldom good bookkeepers, they are inclined to be utterly impatient with the refinements of the "pencil-pushers" in the office. Daily cost reports may be prepared a week in advance. Or figures may be completely fabricated to conform as closely to standards as possible, so as to cause the least possible comment in the main office. In that way trouble is avoided. Poor figures invite criticism; good figures set too high a standard. Respect for statistical methods of control is not increased when these men see their completely fabricated figures used to establish standards of performance—carried to the fourth decimal place.

7. The Valuation Problem

Chapter 3 set forth the framework of commission regulation and sketched in the rate-making process. Once an industry is removed from the orbit of competitive economics and its pricing policies made subject to public authority, questions of standards of justice immediately arise. The "just price" rather than the market price becomes the goal of inquiry.

What is a just price? Obviously it must cover operating expenses, taxes, and depreciation, plus a fair return upon the fair value of capital committed to the enterprise by investors. The criterion of fairness is delusive. How is the fair value of the property to be measured? Is it the original cost of the property with or without improvements or extensions? Is it the present value of the property on the open market, if an open market exists? Should depreciation be deducted? These and other questions lie at the threshold of our discussion. The problem has been considered to be the root of all evils in public utility regulation.

1. THE LAW OF VALUE TAKES FORM

The Genesis of the Problem: Smyth v. Ames.[1] When Justice Harlan handed down the opinion of the United States Supreme Court in 1898 in the now famous case of *Smyth* v. *Ames,* he rendered one of the most momentous and oft-quoted decisions in American constitutional history. The case affected, if it did not determine, all subsequent utility profits; albeit the decision settled nothing and bedeviled court and commission, public and industry, for almost half a century. It has been the bone of contention in the perennial battle between utility companies on one hand and commissions, councils, and legislatures on the other. It became a means by which economic values were created by judicial fiat and the Constitution was tied to the price level.

On the equivocal issue of value the Court took a firm and uncompromising fence-straddling position. It will be remembered that it listed no less than six considerations that must be given weight and added that

---

[1] *Smyth* v. *Ames,* 169 U.S. 466 (1898). See Chapter 3.

there might be other matters to be regarded. The requirements were not of a kind. Essentially, three methods of valuation were mentioned: (1) original cost, (2) the amount and market value of bonds and stocks, and (3) the present cost of construction.

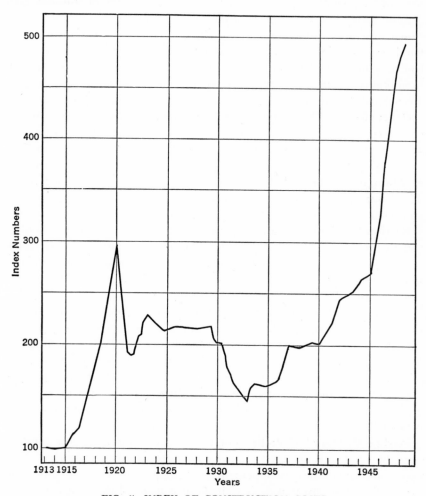

FIG. 5. INDEX OF CONSTRUCTION COSTS.

From the *Survey of Current Business*. Figures compiled by the American Appraisal Company. The index is made up of representative material and labor costs and is based on four types of buildings: frame, brick, concrete, and steel, in thirty representative cities.

Valuation and the Price Level. In *Smyth* v. *Ames* the railroads, facing the prospect of having three quarters of the value of their property wiped out, argued for rates that would protect their historical investment.

The "historical cost" doctrine was to be repudiated by the railroads in less than a decade and a half of rising prices, while the "present fair value" doctrine so ardently championed by the people's "Peerless Leader," William Jennings Bryan, was shortly to become the bane of existence of the public's regulatory bodies. After 1909 the cleavage of interests took definite form. The long upward trend of prices that began as the century closed won the utilities for the reproduction cost doctrine. On the other hand, public agencies saw their interests best served by using original cost as a method of valuation. Of the two theories of value, the Court, in ambiguous language, came to favor the former. "Fair value" came to mean "present fair value," which in turn meant "cost of reproduction."

Depreciation: The *Knoxville Water Company* Case.[2] The omission of depreciation from among the elements to be considered in valuation was remedied a decade later in the *Knoxville Water Company* case. The company urgently contended that depreciation from the time of construction should be added to the present value of the surviving plant. The Court denied the claim, pointing out that the company was only entitled to earn a sufficient sum each year to make good the annual depreciation. This was not only its right, but its duty, to its security holders and to the public. If it failed to make good these losses in value, value could not subsequently be enhanced by a consideration of past depreciation. In short, the value for rate-making purposes was to be the depreciated value.

Although the Court concerned itself largely with the matter of depreciation, one can discern a drift towards the cost of reproduction—present value theory. Depreciated value is a tacit, though needless, recognition of the elements of present fair value. The ultimate goal of the Court's reasoning was suggested more clearly in *Willcox* v. *Consolidated Gas Company*,[3] decided the same day. Here the Court spoke with approval of the value of the property "determined as of the time when the inquiry is made."

"Other Matters" of Value. The Court, the utilities, and the commissions, having tacitly accepted a more or less nebulous theory of value which gave some indeterminate weight at least to present value, utility companies started an insistent drive to include as many of the "other matters" as possible in the estimated cost of reproduction. Original cost is a fact, however difficult it may be to determine and no matter how inequitable it may be to apply in all instances. But once one begins to deal with the estimated present day value of a plant built years ago but hypothetically reconstructed today under hypothetical conditions which are a blend of the past and present in undecipherable degree, there is no end to the

---

[2] *Knoxville* v. *Knoxville Water Co.*, 212 U.S. 1 (1909).
[3] *Willcox* v. *Consolidated Gas Co.*, 212 U.S. 19 (1909).

many and interesting appurtenances of value that can be discovered. Lawyers and accountants began probing old records (and their imaginations) for such things as organization expense, interest during construction, early losses, good-will, going value, and intangible items of all sorts. It was a fertile field for those who could cultivate it skillfully.

Commissions were gradually forced on the defensive. They lacked the legal, engineering, and accounting talent the utility companies could command. They were without necessary records and statistics and did not have the staffs to compile them. They were probably not as diligent nor as ingenious in the pursuit of the public welfare as their rivals in the court room were in the pursuit of private profit.

Good-will and Franchise Values. Some early efforts to establish elements of value met with rebuffs. The *Willcox* case is also significant in that it excluded both good-will and a large part of the franchise value from the rate base. Of the first, the Court thought that there could be no such thing in the case of a monopoly, since customers were under compulsion to deal with the company. The value of the franchise was allowed only so far as it had been allowed in a commission-approved consolidation some twenty-five years previous. Value expressed in terms of excess earning power of the company was not allowed.

Land Values: The Second Minnesota Rate Cases.[4] The *Minnesota Rate Cases* of 1913 contributed the principle that the land of railways and public utilities was to be valued at the fair average value of similar land in the vicinity. The railroad had claimed land values based on what it would have cost to reacquire the land under the existing conditions. These values were thought to be consistent with the cost of reproduction. However, the railroad had not neglected to add additional amounts to represent the cost of acquiring the property. This figure was in turn increased by a "multiplier" supposed to represent the damages due to severing the property from the remainder, the cost of hypothetical improvements to the land, easements, and other general expenses. By these methods, lands costing $4,527,228.76 were to be valued at $17,315,869.45.

These extravagant claims gained no acceptance from Justice Hughes. Railroads and utilities were entitled to a reasonable share in the general prosperity of the communities which they served. That was all. In other words, they shared like other companies and persons in the enhancement of land values that comes with economic growth.

Paving Costs: The Des Moines Gas Company Case.[5] There were times when the artificial nature of present fair value became glaringly apparent. If the present cost of construction was the objective sought, couldn't it be reasonably argued that, if a street had been paved after the

[4] *Minnesota Rate Cases,* 230 U.S. 352 (1913).
[5] *Des Moines Gas Co.* v. *Des Moines,* 238 U. S. 153 (1915).

placing of gas mains, the value of the mains would be increased by the hypothetical cost of repaving the street? Such reasoning was too much for the Court, and its rejection was approved in the *Des Moines Gas Company* case in 1915.

Rising Prices and Going Value: The Galveston Electric Company Case.[6] Hardly had reproduction cost become the general and tacitly accepted basis for determining value than prices started sharply upward as a result of conditions of the First World War. Rate base values stood to become enhanced without limit. Under these conditions the Court could not quite accept what it had done.

In the *Galveston Electric Company* case in 1922, even the utility refused to claim "spot" reproduction costs, which were then more than double the 1913 costs. Prices would obviously fall, and the problem was to determine a relatively stable plateau of prices. To all the other ambiguities and complexities was now added the not inconsiderable problem of predicting the future.

The company contended that prices would stabilize at levels between 60 and 70 per cent above pre-war prices. The city of Galveston argued that it would return to the old level. The master and the lower court set the figure at 33⅓ per cent above pre-war prices. This rather democratic procedure of averaging the claims of the contending parties gained the approval of the Supreme Court. Such was valuation under the cost of reproduction.

The effect of this procedure was to set up myriads of possible rate bases, depending upon the particular set of prices chosen. Every rate case brought forth rate bases in wondrous profusion and variety. In the *Bluefield Water Works* case, a property valued by the West Virginia Commission at $460,000 was given values by the company ranging from $624,000 to $1,195,000.

The *Galveston* case is also significant in that certain vaguely described intangible elements of value, previously rejected under the name of "good-will," now made their appearance—in a slightly more concrete form—as "going value." In this instance, an attempt was made to include past losses in the rate base as development costs. Justice Brandeis said, "Past losses obviously do not tend to prove present values."

Valuation by Confusion: The Southwestern Bell Case (1923).[7] The line of the Court's decisions grew more twisted and tortuous. Within a few weeks in 1923 the Court decided three cases in diametrically different manners. Perhaps the Court attempted to make up in impartiality what it failed to give in definity.

Because it contained a most important separate opinion by Justice

6 *Galveston Elec. Co.* v. *Galveston,* 258 U.S. 388 (1922).
7 *Southwestern Bell Tel. Co.* v. *Public Serv. Comm.,* 262 U.S. 276 (1923).

Brandeis, the most significant of these cases was that involving the Southwestern Bell Telephone Company. The company submitted evidence to show that the cost of reproduction of its property, less depreciation, was $31,355,278. The book cost was $22,888,943. The Commission set the rate base at $20,400,000. The Court concluded that on the basis of the evidence a fair value would be $25,000,000.

The vigorous opinion of Justice Brandeis has long been a rallying point for the many critics of the Court. "The so-called rule of *Smyth* v. *Ames* is, in my opinion, legally and economically unsound. The thing devoted by the investor to the public use is not specific property, tangible and intangible, but capital embarked in the enterprise. Upon the capital so invested, the Federal Constitution guarantees to the utility the opportunity to earn a fair return." [8] Justice Brandeis went on to criticize the rule of *Smyth* v. *Ames* and to marshal the arguments for the "prudent investment" rate base.

The Split Inventory: The *Georgia Railway and Power Co.* Case (1923).[9] Here a new method of valuation was introduced to the Court. The Georgia Commission had found a rate base of $5,250,000. The value of the property in existence January 1, 1914 was valued at prices of that date, while the remainder of the property, which had been added during the war years, was valued at prices reflecting the new and higher costs. The commission gave "careful consideration" but apparently no weight to reproduction cost, which the company set at $9,500,000. The commission was sustained in an opinion written by Justice Brandeis, who had already established himself as the proponent of the "prudent investment" base. To this decision Justice McKenna took strong dissent, as Justice Brandeis had already taken to the *Southwestern Bell* decision. Justice McKenna would have accepted the company's contention that value should be based on reproduction cost.

Justice Butler and the *Bluefield Water Works* Case (1923).[10] The *Bluefield Water Works* case marks the beginning of the ascendancy of Justice Butler as the decade's greatest creator of public utility law. Justice Butler was a master at interlacing his decisions with obiter dicta which could later be cited with equal skill as authority in other decisions. He exercised great influence among the conservative and less liberal members of the Court. He came to the Court in 1922, after years of service as a railroad attorney. In the *Bluefield* case he got his first opportunity to hammer out a theory of value that for a long time prevailed over the views of Justice Brandeis that were so ably expressed as a separate opinion in the *Southwestern Bell* case. In this case the company claimed

---

8 *Ibid.*, 290.
9 *Georgia Ry. & P. Co.* v. *R.R. Comm.*, 262 U.S. 625 (1923).
10 *Bluefield W.W. & Imp. Co.* v. *Pub. Serv. Comm.*, 262 U.S. 679 (1923).

a value of $900,000, a figure that apparently reflected an approximate average of its value at pre-war and post-war prices. The West Virginia Commission found a value of $460,000, which was substantially the cost of the property. Justice Butler found the return inadequate on the rate base found, but worked in the dicta that the procedure used resulted in a valuation considerably less than that which would have been reached by a consideration of all the facts.

These cases taken together indicate that the Court had not yet placed its stamp of approval upon any one theory of value to the exclusion of all others. This outward uncertainty merely reflected the growing consolidation of two groups within the Court. Justice Brandeis had stated the case for original cost in his separate opinion in the *Southwestern Bell* case. Justice Butler had begun to lay the groundwork to make present cost the law of the land.

Prices for the Future: McCardle v. Indianapolis Water Co. (1926).[11] In this case are to be found the dicta that have been used to support cost of reproduction. Strangely enough there was no disagreement between the Indiana Commission and the utility as to the method to be used in valuation. Both sought a rate base founded on ten-year average prices. The utility selected a base period that yielded a considerably higher value than that selected by the commission. On appeal by the utility, the district court enjoined the commission's rates and found a value considerably higher. The position taken was that "spot reproduction cost" was tantamount to value.

The significant feature of the case was the language with which the Court threw its weight emphatically towards the cost of reproduction, not only at present or "spot" prices, but at future prices. ". . . in determining present value, consideration must be given to prices and wages prevailing at the time of the investigation; and, . . . there must be an honest and intelligent forecast as to probable price and wage levels during a reasonable period in the immediate future." And again, "It is well established that values of utility properties fluctuate, and that owners must bear the decline and are entitled to the increase."

And then as if to deny even the breath of certainty that these words vouchsafed, Justice Butler said:

> But this does not mean that the original cost or the present cost or some figure arbitrarily chosen between these two is to be taken as the measure. The weight to be given to such cost figures and other items or classes of evidence is to be determined in the light of the facts of the case in hand.[12]

The Identical versus the Hypothetical Plant. If the search is to be for present fair value, it would seem that it would be found in the cost

---

[11] *McCardle* v. *Indianapolis Water Co.,* 272 U.S. 400 (1926).
[12] *Ibid.,* 410.

of the plant that would be built today. In the competitive world, an old, inefficient plant, no matter how expensive, has no more value than a modern, efficient plant that would produce the identical service. The Court was unwilling to push the cost of reproduction doctrine to this logical extreme. In the *Indianapolis* case, city engineers had valued the utility's property on the assumption that a steam pumping plant would have been used instead of a more expensive canal. Justice Butler would accept none of this logic. "There is to be ascertained the value of the plant used to give the service and not the estimated cost of a different plant." [13] It is true that the acceptance of the theory of the hypothetical plant would lead the investigator far afield and encourage the unlimited use of the imagination, which was overdeveloped among valuation engineers as it was. Nevertheless, it did reduce the Court's theory of value to a hybrid and indeterminate mixture of elements pertaining to both the past and the present.

An Appraisal of the Court's Position. The Court's theory of value has been subject to a running barrage of criticism from the country's most able legal scholars. Here and there were found a few who would defend the Court's position, but they served their purpose more in confusing the issues than in rationalizing the law.

Is there anything good that we can say for the Court? When it rendered its decision in *Smyth* v. *Ames* in 1898, the Court was obviously feeling its way. The rule of *Smyth* v. *Ames* was nothing less than an attempt to keep open all possible avenues of legal reasoning across legal-economic terrain that was treacherous, strange, and difficult. No one could know to what demands of reason the Court might have to accommodate itself in the years to come. The elaborate formula of the case carried the proviso that there may be other matters. Thus *Smyth* v. *Ames* settled nothing. But if the Court must creep in 1898 it would not follow that it could not walk in 1926.

Into this ambiguous and uncertain situation stepped Justice Butler, an able, forceful lawyer, with a background of years of service as a railroad attorney. Justice Butler was vigorous, and to interpret his character with charity we must say that he knew what he believed. Given a number of conservative colleagues, he deftly shaped the law of valuation into a pattern of his own.

The rule of *Smyth* v. *Ames* is ambiguous and without substance. Insofar as the Court gave it content, fair value came to mean present value, and, in effect, cost of reproduction. But the Court refused to commit itself to any specific formula or theory.

The law of value was not fashioned from common cases. "Reasonable value," to use the term of Professor John R. Commons, was built from

[13] *Ibid.,* 417-418.

cases in which the representatives of the public came to the Court ill-equipped to argue their case on "reasonable grounds." The burden of proving confiscation was seldom an insuperable task. Under these conditions Justice Butler did not find it too difficult to fashion law that, at the most, was taken by lower courts and commissions to mean much more than could be fairly attributable to it, and, at the least, left them in complete confusion.

2. THE REGENERATION OF VALUATION LAW

The Court Changes. The 1930's. The flood of criticism directed against the Court came from such authority that the Court could not have been less than mindful of it. Many looking for the cause of the breakdown of regulation found it in the long chain of decisions on value. Finally, the Court itself was caught in the tide of the times that President Roosevelt so skillfully rode and directed. The conservative coterie of justices who had aided Justice Butler in hammering out the law of value found themselves to be more frequently in the minority. Later, they passed from the Court and their places were taken by younger and more liberal men who wrote new law.[14] Stratagems were devised by which the Court could escape the odious consequences of earlier decisions. The law and economics of the booming 1920's gave way to the new and more sober concepts of the depression-ridden 1930's.

1. The First Signs of the Disintegration of the Cost of Reproduction Doctrine.

Over the strong objections of Justice Butler and others, the Court began to pay less and less attention to reproduction cost. In the *Los Angeles Gas and Electric Corporation*[15] case of 1933, the Court held that where the utility had not met the burden of proving rates to be confiscatory, the procedure and method would remain in the jurisdiction of the commission. The following year in the *Lindheimer*[16] case, the Court found itself unable to accept the findings of a lower court, since they would have indicated rates so grossly confiscatory as to be at war with reality. Thus it seems that it is possible to prove too much. The same situation reoccurred in the same year in the *Dayton Power & Light Company* case.[17]

In the *Pacific Gas and Electric Company*[18] case of 1938, the California Commission, which had used historical cost during its entire history, con-

---

14 Justice Van Devanter retired in 1937, and Justice Sutherland in 1938. Justice Butler died in 1939. Justice McReynolds resigned in 1941.

15 *Los Angeles G. & E. Corp.* v. *R.R. Comm.*, 289 U.S. 287 (1933).

16 *Lindheimer* v. *Illinois Bell Tel. Co.*, 292 U.S. 151 (1934).

17 *Dayton P. & L. Co.* v. *Pub. Util. Comm.*, 292 U.S. 290 (1934).

18 *Railroad Commission of California* v. *Pacific G. & Elec. Co.*, 302 U.S. 388 (1938).

sidered the company's estimate of cost of reproduction, but found it so grossly excessive and conjectural as to be devoid of practical value. In effect it took a hasty look at the evidence, disregarded it, and continued on its way. The Court concluded that there was no reason to say that the Commission had not given the evidence "such weight as is just and right." Doggedly fighting back, Justice Butler in a dissenting opinion pointed out that the California Commission had persistently refused to apply the *Smyth* v. *Ames* criteria. It was a surly last-ditch stand. In the following year the Court sustained the Pennsylvania Commission on the company's failure to establish confiscation.[19]

Valuation by Index Numbers: The Chesapeake & Potomac Case (1935).[20] There was at least one important exception to this line of cases which loosened and revitalized the theory and practice of valuation. The Maryland Commission had arrived at a rate base for the Chesapeake & Potomac Telephone Company by taking the value of the plant as found in 1923 in an earlier case and adding to it the additions made in each subsequent year, corrected by a series of index numbers of prices. No physical appraisal of the property was made. The method was obviously a short-cut procedure designed to facilitate the rate-making process and probably made more urgent by a lack of funds, personnel, and time. Such simplicity outraged the Court's sense of decency and propriety. The method was new and unheard of, and was therefore to be damned. It was of no matter that Justice Stone in a dissenting opinion pointed out that the lowest value reached by the use of index numbers was only 23.4 per cent below the commission's valuation and the highest 10.6 per cent above, while company valuations ranged from figures of 25.0 per cent to 59.4 per cent above the Commission valuation.

The Natural Gas Pipeline Case (1942).[21] The first intimation of things to come appeared in 1942, when the Supreme Court in the *Natural Gas Pipeline* case sustained natural gas rates fixed by the Federal Power Commission. Gingerly the Court approached the task of rewriting the constitutional law of fair value. The issues were not brought into the clear and the Court was equivocal. Nevertheless, the company's contention that an amortization allowance for wasting gas reserves should be based on present value was not accepted. It would be sufficient, the Court said, if the owners received the cost of the property. With significance, it was said:

> The Constitution does not bind rate-making bodies to the service of any single formula or combination of formulas. Agencies to whom this legislative power has been delegated are free, within the ambit of their statutory au-

19 *Driscoll* v. *Edison L. & P. Co.*, 307 U.S. 104 (1939).
20 *West* v. *Chesapeake & Potomac Tel. Co.*, 295 U.S. 662 (1935).
21 *Natural Gas Pipeline Co.* v. *F.P.C.*, 315 U.S. 575 (1942).

thority, to make the pragmatic adjustments which may be called for by particular circumstances.[22]

The Court noted that the company was operating profitably and avoided denying the doctrine of *Smyth* v. *Ames*. Three justices, however (Black, Douglas, and Murphy), went further in a concurring opinion and concluded that the troublesome old ghost of *Smyth* v. *Ames* would haunt the Court no more.

2. New Law

The Hope Natural Gas Case (1944).[23] This case may well rank with *Munn* v. *Illinois* and *Smyth* v. *Ames* as landmarks in utility rate regulation. Here the Federal Power Commission, in valuing the property of a natural gas company, arrived at an "actual legitimate cost" of $33,000,000 after deducting depreciation and depletion. A $6\frac{1}{2}$ per cent rate of return was allowed. The Company contended for a $66,000,000 rate base and an 8 per cent rate of return. The Circuit Court of Appeals had set aside the Commission's order on the grounds that the rate base did not reflect "present fair value" and that depreciation and depletion should have been computed on a present fair value basis. Thus the issue was squarely presented. The Supreme Court reversed the lower court and repudiated a principle that was thought to have been well established. The principle of the *Natural Gas Pipeline* case that "the Constitution does not bind rate-making bodies to the service of any single formula or combination of formulas" was reiterated. Then the Court went on to say:

> ... And when the Commission's order is challenged in the courts, the question is whether that order "viewed in its entirety" meets the requirements of the Act.... Under the statutory standard of "just and reasonable," it is the result reached not the method employed which is controlling.... It is not the theory but the impact of the rate order which counts. If the total effect of the rate order cannot be said to be unjust and unreasonable, judicial inquiry under the act is at an end.[24]

The Doctrine of the End Result. The Court did not approve original cost or cost of reproduction. It did not approve any method. For all that was said, a rate-making body might use no formula at all—as long as the result was reasonable. This is the doctrine of the "end result." It is not the theory but the impact of a rate order that counts. The problems of selecting a method was returned to the legislatures and administrative bodies. The power of judicial review, which the Court had claimed so long for itself, was in part renounced.

22 *Ibid.*, 586.
23 *F.P.C.* v. *Hope Natural Gas Co.*, 320 U.S. 591 (1944).
24 *Ibid.*, 602.

If there was to be a concrete test, it was this:

> Rates which enable the company to operate successfully, to maintain its
> financial integrity, to attract capital, and to compensate its investors for
> risks assumed certainly cannot be condemned as invalid, even though they
> might produce only a meager return on the so-called "fair value" rate base.[25]

In this case the company's capitalization consisted of $28,000,000 of
stock of which $11,000,000 had been issued as stock dividends. The com-
pany had accumulated depreciation and depletion reserves of $46,000,000.
Earnings had averaged 12 per cent a year on the average of invested
capital. The Federal Power Commission order permitted it to earn
$4,191,314 annually, a return of almost 8 per cent on its stock. With the
better issues of bonds of natural gas companies selling to yield 3 per cent,
the Commission thought that the company could attract new capital.
This was the more so, since the company was well managed, its markets
firmly established, and its financial affiliations strong.

Significance of the Hope Case. The *Hope Natural Gas Company* case
yields two new guiding principles of regulation. (1) Allegiance to the
present fair value interpretation of the rule of *Smyth* v. *Ames* is no longer
required of commissions. (2) If there is to be any test of the fairness of
rates, it lies in the effect upon the holders of the utilities' securities. Under
these two standards, regulation has the power to move a long way forward.

Valuation in War Time. During the war, utilities generally abandoned
attempts to claim larger rate bases on a cost of reproduction value, both
because of public wartime policy and because of the fact that excess profits
taxes would take all but a small portion of any increased returns anyway.
In some instances, utilities even urged these "costless" rate reductions to
improve their public relations.[26]

The Two Rivers Case.[27] The *Hope Natural Gas Company* case did not
free commissions from all adherence to standards of value. In 1947 the
Wisconsin Commission in the so-called *"Two Rivers"* case stated that it
did not believe it necessary to make any finding of value and concluded
that $12,500 was a reasonable profit for the company. The court of review
asked the pertinent question "reasonable profit on what?" This off-hand
regulation was attacked in a vehement decision which reversed the commission.

[25] *Ibid.,* 605.

[26] For a good discussion see John Bauer, "Relation of the War Taxes to Utility Rate-
making," *33 Pub. Util. Fort.* 211 (Feb. 17, 1944).

[27] *City of Two Rivers* v. *Commonwealth Tel. Co.,* 70 P.U.R. (N.S.) 5 (1947); *Commonwealth Tel. Co.* v. *Wisconsin Pub. Serv. Comm.,* 71 P.U.R. (N.S.) 65 (1947). The latter
reference is to the court decision and provides an interesting discussion of administrative
procedure and of the institutional background of regulation in Wisconsin.

3. AN EVALUATION OF THEORIES OF VALUE

Every writer in the field of valuation—and their number is legion—
every utility lawyer, every commission counsel has his own workable
theory of value—workable in every respect save that the Supreme Court
would have none of them. Each theory may be applied in innumerable
ways.

For our purposes, historical or original cost is taken to mean the fair
cost of the property at the time of construction or first use in public
service. Sometimes it has been taken to mean the purchase price, which is
something else. Book cost may reflect some other value. Allowance must
be made for subsequent additions and retirements. Generally, the value
of the property is reduced by depreciation.

Appraisers may shut their eyes to records pertaining to property costs
and look instead to the securities issued as a measure of value. If consideration is to be given to the wisdom of the financing, the so-called
"prudent investment" standard would be adopted.

Reproduction cost constitutes an estimate of the value of the existing
plant at existing prices under current conditions (with some exceptions).
Depreciation is always deducted from the estimated value when new.

Arguments for or against these standards fall into two classes: (1) those
based on economic theory and (2) those based on administrative procedure. Let us examine some of these arguments.

The Purchasing Power Argument. It has sometimes been claimed for
the cost of reproduction standard that it tends to yield utility investors
an income of constant purchasing power. If prices rise and the value of
money declines, the rate base will be increased and utility investors will
receive a greater return in monetary units of smaller purchasing power.
On the other hand, a stable rate base tied to original cost would give
investors enhanced real income in times of low prices and small real income when prices are high.

This argument has been laboriously conceived and its proponents have
done little more than further bemuddle a confused problem. The most
simple and most practical objection to the argument is that as long as
utilities are financed by both debt and equity capital, no group of investors would receive an income of fixed purchasing power. Investors in
bonds would receive the same monetary income regardless of any change
in the rate base. In times of price inflation, the entire increment of income
arising from the upward revaluation of all the company's property would
go to the relatively small group of stockholders. Hence stockholders would
get much more than they would be entitled to in theory. On the other
hand, a decline in prices might not merely reduce the real income of
stockholders; it could conceivably destroy all their income.

Finally it may be said that if an income of constant purchasing power is to be sought, it can be obtained more easily by means of varying the rate of return.

Approximating Competitive Conditions. In a broad sense, the objective of public utility rate regulation is to achieve through regulation the same result that would be achieved by competition. Common fairness would dictate such a policy. In competitive enterprise the value of the fixed plant tends to rise and fall with earnings and with the price level. It is argued that the cost-of-reproduction standard tends to gear the returns in the public utility industries with those expected in other industries.

This argument has more than equity to sustain it. Capital resources are not distributed properly in our economic system if the return in one industry is artificially forced out of line with those in other industries. More concretely, if a utility is held to a low rate of return in times of rising prices and general prosperity, it will find difficulty attracting capital. Thus the public will be denied needed services and capital will flow into less useful fields. But here again the problem could be met by means of a variable rate of return.

This argument has also been seized upon by some students of the business cycle who attribute the cause of a depression to the inflexible prices of some industries. We could go far, so the argument runs, to eliminate depressions by making all prices immediately responsive to the forces of demand and supply. This price flexibility argument, however, is but one of innumerable explanations of the causes of the business cycle. It is an old argument, afflicted with many infirmities, and to be accepted with the utmost circumspection.

To evaluate this argument it must be remembered that neither cost of reproduction nor original cost bears any necessary relation to cost on the competitive market. All the costs of Christendom, past or present, cannot give value to a business property that has no earning power. If the argument is to be driven to its logical conclusion, the value sought would be that of the hypothetical substitute plant that would be built today rather than the identical plant.

Risk. Justice Brandeis and others have argued that, under the cost-of-reproduction standard, risk and the cost of capital are increased. There can be little doubt of this, for a fluctuating rate base increases the risk of investors. The long-run cost of risk or equity capital is greater than the cost of debt capital. This is particularly true if the common stock equity is thin. Not only is a higher earnings rate necessary to attract investors in equity securities, but, by the same token, the debt securities are made more insecure and a higher rate of interest must be paid. A stable, original-cost rate base that protects the interests of investors might do much to decrease the cost of capital, even if it denies speculative profits to security holders.

Risk and Earnings as Affected by Administrative Policy. Justice Brandeis' argument does not cover all the ground. From a practical standpoint the risk to investors under a cost-of-reproduction standard is not as great as might be supposed. With a falling price level, a utility commission might not deem it desirable to reduce rates by the full measure of the contracting rate base. To do so might be to throw the utility into bankruptcy —in which event all regulation would have to be foregone. Utility commissions are also required by law to safeguard the credit of utilities. In practice, a utility would tend to get a cost-of-reproduction or an original-cost rate base, whichever would be higher.

Since there is no certainty that commissions will adopt any such policy, it is unlikely that investors are influenced to any great degree by the possibility. Hence, utility rate payers are placed in a position of paying in the capital market for a risk that is non-existent.

On the other hand, it is even more possible that utility companies will be injured in somewhat the same manner by the adoption of original cost as a rate base. In times of prosperity and high prices utility companies will be held to a low, original-cost rate base. There is no guarantee, however, that they will be able to earn a fair return on the same rate base in times of depression or adversity. The public demand for lower rates and the pressure from publicly financed plants may be so great as to force utilities to accept returns considerably below the standard of a fair return on a fair original cost.

Both evils may be avoided in part, but not entirely, by a stable rate base and a fluctuating rate of return. The rate of return can be made to fluctuate in unison with, but not as much as, the rate of return in competitive industry. In good times, the utility rate of return might be one or two per cent less than that of other industries; in bad times, possibly a per cent more. On the whole, the return would probably be slightly less because the degree of risk is lower.

Standards of Value and the Appraisal Process. The most telling arguments against the cost of reproduction have to do with administrative efficiency. If original cost as determined from the utility's books and records is not to be the measure of value, an appraisal to determine the reproduction-cost value becomes virtually necessary. The Court has refused to countenance the conversion of book costs into reproduction cost by the use of index numbers. Appraisals yield uncertain results and are productive of much bickering and disagreement. Endless argument and litigation sap the vitality of regulation. By this means, the ends of regulation are defeated.

Once the valuation expert leaves the relatively firm ground of actual costs and begins to deal with the hypothetical cost of a hypothetical plant constructed under hypothetical conditions at hypothetical prices, the result becomes completely unpredictable. The imagined definity of the valuation appraisal vanishes into thin air. There is almost no limit to the range of values that competent experts might reach for one and the same piece of property. Even the opinions of experts hired to guess for the same litigant will differ widely in their estimates of reproduction-cost value. Examples have already been cited.

The Valuation of Intangibles. To the various and sundry estimates of the hypothetical value of the physical plant, the valuation expert in search of reproduction-cost value will seek to add allowances for intangibles—good-will, going value, franchise value, water rights, and other will-of-the-wisp figments which on examination "disappear without being seen," but which nevertheless can be made to produce claims of value.

Thus, into a darkness made more rather than less confusing by expert testimony, a commission must perforce stretch its hand and pluck reasonable value like a rabbit from a hat. Some commissioners have frankly admitted that, in reality, the rate base is determined by some such procedure as averaging all the possible values, adding a certain amount, and subtracting another amount, and then coming forth with a round figure without explaining in too much detail how the figure is computed. If this is too much effort for the wearied commissioners, they may simply go into a trance and, after communing with the ghost of *Smyth* v. *Ames,* give forth a figure on value that is probably just as accurate and just as acceptable or non-acceptable to a Court as most of the others.

Time and Cost of Appraisals. If estimates of the cost of reproduction are obscure, ambiguous, and conflicting, it is not for want of the time and energy that has been spent upon them. Property units have to be inventoried, classified, and priced. Each step of the process may be a source of dispute. If the utility company is recalcitrant or if it chooses to stand on its legal rights, it may be in the courts more often than it is out. The New York Telephone Company litigation lasted nine years, accumulated 62,864 pages of testimony, and cost at least $5,000,000. There were six different valuations, all based on principles laid down by the Supreme Court. An appraisal of the Chicago telephone properties in the *Lindheimer* case cost $1,200,000, while the cost of making refunds after the case cost $2,500,000, with much of the task remaining. This case was based on an order issued in 1923 and was decided by the Court in 1933.

These cases are exceptional. Most rate cases are promptly disposed of without resort to the courts. However, a case involving a large utility can be made extremely expensive if the utility chooses to exercise all of its legal rights. A utility company can almost invariably charge the costs back to the ratepayers; a commission must operate on its limited budget. In no way can it present the array of technical, legal, and accounting talent commonly called upon by utility companies.

The delay and expense of rate litigation plays into the hands of the utility companies even if but a few cases are carried to the courts. Regulatory commissions, knowing their own limitations, will take what they can get in the way of rate adjustments rather than attempt to play an unequal game.

Reliability of Books and Records. The ultimate aim of regulatory commissions is to have the evidence of value easily available on the books of the companies. For this reason, original cost as shown on the books lends itself better to the purpose of regulation than reproduction-cost estimates, which must be made anew whenever a rate base is sought. However, utility financing has been notoriously free and easy, and little credence could be given to book costs. For this reason, commissions were frequently forced to accept the cost of reproduction as determined by an appraisal. Later, the use of the cost-of-reproduction standard contributed to the ill-repute of book costs. With every rise in the price level, utility companies contrived to get the resulting increments of value onto the books to justify new security issues and to buttress their claims for higher rates.

Substantial accounting reforms have been effected in recent years. When these are completed, valuation on an original-cost basis will be speeded up immeasurably.

Capitalization as a Rate Base. The real test of fairness of earnings lies in the effect upon the fortunes of investors. The question might then be raised as to why a utility's capitalization should not be used as a rate base. The answer is that the standard is practical only if the issuance of securities has been adequately regulated from the first. Corporate financial histories reveal that such regulation is seldom found.

Thus in the early *Knoxville Water Company* [28] case the Court noted a large variation between the real value of the property and the capitalization. Substantially all the preferred and common stock had been issued to contractors for the construction of the plant in amounts far in excess of the true value of the work. Part of the plant was constructed at a cost of $125,000 in return for $125,000 in bonds and $200,000 in stock. The contractors themselves were officers of the company or in some manner controlled its policies.

Only a few states have exercised continuous control over security issues. In Massachusetts, close control dates to 1885. Returns have been based on capital honestly and prudently invested. Studies have indicated that the utilities of the state have managed to earn very liberal returns on their paid-in capital. California has not controlled security issues for as

[28] *Knoxville* v. *Knoxville Water Co.*, 212 U.S. 1 (1909).

long a time but has perhaps done it more effectively on a prudent investment basis.

Recent Trends. For all this the end-result doctrine of the *Hope Natural
Gas* case points to a greater reliance upon capitalization as a measure of
the fair return. In other instances, many utility depressions tested the
fairness of temporary rate orders during depression years by their effect
upon the stockholders of the utility. Earnings which permitted a utility to
meet interest charges and preferred dividend requirements, with enough
left to pay a reasonable dividend upon the common stock plus perhaps
a certain amount for surplus, were thought to be adequate. The whole
troublesome problem of valuation was by-passed.

The Market Value of Stocks and Bonds as a Measure of Value. The
market value of stocks and bonds was included among the factors to be
given consideration in determining fair value in the rule of *Smyth* v.
Ames. The statement indicates circular reasoning on the part of the
Court. Market values reflect earning power—the greater the earnings, the
greater the value investors will place upon the securities in the market.
But in public utility regulation, it is precisely the earning power that has
to be determined. By this standard, any level of earnings could be justified
by the market value of the securities. In spite of this obvious fact, one
finds references to this criterion creeping into court decisions.

The writer suggests that market values of securities are useful in determining the fairness of earnings in exactly the opposite way from the
manner just mentioned. Rates so low as to reduce the value of securities
below the fair original investment value are unfair, if not confiscatory.
If utility stockholders originally subscribed $1,000,000 at $100 share for
the capital stock of a utility, rates which would cause that stock to sell
at $80 instead of at the $100 par value would be of questionable fairness.
Such a condition would probably (but not always) indicate that the utility
is not receiving a return comparable to that received in other industries.
Investors are avoiding its stock. On the other hand, if the stock is selling
for $150 a share, it is not evidence that the company has a value of
$1,500,000, but that its rates have been set too high.

4. THEORIES OF VALUE: A RÉSUMÉ

1. Original versus Reproduction Cost

The so-called rule of *Smyth* v. *Ames* has been found, in the words of
Justice Brandeis, "legally and economically unsound." However, in the
heavy hands of Justice Butler, that most able and diligent blacksmith of
the law, it was hammered into the rule of present fair value that has
bound and hamstrung commission regulation for almost five decades. The
rule was flimsy material from which to fashion such binding doctrine.

The weight of disinterested authority has been strongly against both the rule and its corollary, that fair value means present value. Justice Jackson in the *Hope* case has pointed out that the rule is in general disrepute. Professor Bonbright has said, "The attempt to regulate rates by reference to a periodic or occasional reappraisal of properties has been tested long enough to confirm the worst fears of its critics. Unless its place is taken by some more promising scheme of rate control, the days of private ownership under government regulation may be numbered." [29]

The baneful effects of the reproduction-cost theory have permeated almost every aspect of utility regulation. Commission regulation has been devitalized. Higher rates have been forced upon consumers. Stock watering and the growth of holding company monstrosities have been encouraged by it with the consequent loss of millions of dollars to investors in the stock market crash of 1929. The country has moved towards government ownership as an alternative. In fairness to the theory and the law that sprang from it, it can be said that it has provided a great deal of work for lawyers who otherwise might have been unemployed.

The choice seems to lie with some form of original cost. It is equitable in theory and relatively easy to determine. Once determined, it may be recorded on the books of the utilities and becomes available with a minimum of effort. It safeguards the interests of investors and ratepayers alike.

Two important points remain to be stressed. A fixed and stable rate base does not necessarily imply a return that is completely inflexible. Adjustments can and should be made in the rate of return rather than in the rate base. Second, it must be pointed out that the acceptance of original cost does not mean that all costs must be included in the rate base. Original cost may be modified for imprudent investments. If accounting and security controls are adequate, satisfactory methods may be worked out for determining a fair rate base from either property accounts or from the capitalization.

2. The Non-conformity of Some Commissions

Many of the stronger commissions have successfully flouted the Court's interpretation of value. The California Commission has consistently used the prudent investment basis to the ire of Justice Butler. The Wisconsin Commission has regulated its state's utilities on the basis of book values which substantially reflected original cost.[30] The Massachusetts Commis-

---

[29] J. C. Bonbright, *Valuation of Property* (New York, McGraw-Hill Book Company, Inc., 1937), Vol. II, p. 1190.

[30] The Wisconsin Commission's procedure was successfully challenged by the Wisconsin Telephone Company. See *Wisconsin Telephone Co.* v. *Pub. Serv. Co.*, 287 N.W. 122 (1939). Other Wisconsin utilities have been content with rate bases as found by the Commission.

sion has used prudent investment as measured by the securities issued. The strong Oregon Commission has favored original cost and, strikingly enough, "has considered cost of reproduction only when an appeal to the courts was anticipated." The Connecticut Commission has considered "fair value" in formal cases, while informal negotiations were conducted on the basis of undepreciated book cost.[31]

3. The *Hope* Case and the Future of Regulation

It has already been pointed out that the *Hope* case apparently leaves the states and the regulatory commissions free to adopt whatever method of rate base determination they may see fit. But this does not free commissions from the restraints of proper administrative procedure as the *Two Rivers* case so plainly indicated. In both the *Natural Gas Pipeline* and *Hope* cases there were findings of a rate base. The end result must be reasonable, and the effect upon earnings and financial condition may be a test of reasonableness. Commissions will also be limited by the statutes of their own states. But those seeking to upset a rate order must carry the heavy burden of proof in showing the order to be unjust and unreasonable.

Statutory Limitations on Commissions. The *Hope* decision will not assuage all the ills that have afflicted rate regulation in general and rate base determination in particular for these past many years. The Federal courts will presumably place fewer restrictions on regulatory commissions. State commissions, however, may be limited by the statutes under which they operate as interpreted by the state courts. Carl I. Wheat lists the following states in which commissions, by decisions of their highest courts, must give weight to reproduction cost: Illinois, Indiana, Montana, New Hampshire, New Jersey, Oregon, Oklahoma, Virginia, West Virginia, and the District of Columbia.[32]

Charles A. Esser, after a survey of state statutes, summarizes his findings as follows: [33]

The statutes fall roughly into the following four categories:
(1) In about half the states, the written law would seem to allow the commissions to use their own methods in obtaining a rate base. (This may well open the doors wide under the *Hope* decision.)

[31] Twentieth Century Fund, *The Power Industry and the Public Interest* (1944), pp. 36, 37.
[32] Carl I. Wheat, "Impact of the Hope Natural Gas Decision on Commission Regulation," 33 *Pub. Util. Fort.* 139, 149 (Feb. 3, 1944).
[33] Chas. A. Esser, "State Laws in Relation to the Hope Natural Gas Decision," 34 *Pub. Util. Fort.* 69 (July 20, 1944).

(2) Nine state commissions must find some sort of "fair" or "reasonable" value.[34]

(3) Commissions in nine other states are required by law to consider reproduction cost, but in no state is it required to be the exclusive or controlling consideration.[35]

(4) The scattered balance do not regulate gas or electric utilities.

The Attitude of the Commissions. Of the Supreme Court it has been said that, like Pontius Pilate, it washed its hands of a troublesome controversy. Certainly, the controversy has been returned to the commissions by the *Hope* decision, and theirs will be much of the responsibility. Those more skeptical observers of regulation will ask if the many commissions that have hidden behind the courts in innocuous desuetude for so long will suddenly be revised and will acquire what Professor Glaeser calls "the élan vital."

A picture of the general attitude of state commissions may be gained from a survey made by the *Wall Street Journal* in 1937. Of those replying, seven state commissions approved of the position of the courts; fourteen commissions appeared to favor prudent investment or historical cost; sixteen commissions stated that they followed the principles laid down by the Supreme Court; six state commissions reported that they used prudent investment or historical cost.[36] One can conclude from this survey that there are many commissions which are satisfied with things as they are.

Some conception of the effect of the decision can be gained from another telegraphic survey of state commissions made by the same paper.[37] Of the twenty-four state agencies answering the queries of this paper, eleven reported that they saw no possibility of any general reduction in utility rates in their own states, and most of them further asserted that there would be little change in their own policies as a result of the decision. Some of these states were already regulating on other than a cost-of-reproduction basis. At least five state commissions (Maryland, Oregon, Connecticut, California, Indiana) thought that the decision would be helpful. Spokesmen for at least two commissions expressed some concern over the decision. The chairman of the Arizona commission thought that the lack of a rule would be dangerous, while the chairman of the Illinois commission was somewhat concerned over the possibility of injecting social and economic theories into rate-making policies.

[34] States included in this classification by Mr. Esser were Connecticut, Kansas, Maine, Maryland (telephone), Michigan, New York, Pennsylvania, Washington, and Texas (gas only).

[35] States in this classification include Alabama, Indiana, Kentucky, New Mexico, North Carolina, Oklahoma (constitutional), Nebraska (telephone), Ohio, and North Dakota.

[36] As reported in the issue of December 28, 1937.

[37] As reported in the issue of February 7, 1944.

From the opinions quoted, few radical or immediate revisions in utility rates can be expected as a result of the *Hope* decision. Given the statutory power and the approval of the state judiciaries, the bargaining position of the commissions in rate negotiation will be materially strengthened. Over a period of time the more able commissions may make regulation considerably more effective. A wise regulatory program must now be worked out in the legislatures, in the commissions, and to a now lesser degree in the courts.

8. Valuation Procedure

VALUATION BY APPRAISAL

VALUATION AND ACCOUNTING RECORDS

CONCLUSION

The Appraisal Process and Accounting. Attention has been given to the theories of value and depreciation. In this chapter we shall be concerned with the valuation procedure.

Not every rate case requires a physical appraisal of the property. To save time and money, and if all parties are willing, the value of the company's property may be determined from the company's books. Since book records are not always accurate, they will probably be spot-checked in the field. If a physical appraisal has been made in the not too distant past, it may be brought down to date from accounting records. This method is frequently used since it is cheap and quick. Some utility companies have recently established continuous inventory records by which a running account is kept of all property items. In such instances specific information on costs and installation dates is available and the valuation procedure is reduced to comparative routine. In general, more rigid accounting regulation has made utility records more accurate and thus reduced the work of making physical appraisals or eliminated the need for them.

If a physical appraisal is made it will often be made by the utility company's engineers. Regulatory commissions seldom have sufficient funds and they will thus often content themselves with spot-checking the results—or in the worst cases—accepting them *in toto*.

VALUATION BY APPRAISAL

1. THE VALUATION OF PHYSICAL PROPERTY

1. The Inventory

The first step in the valuation process is to make an inventory of all the utility's property. This should be more detailed than the classification of accounts. Certain general property categories are established, such as poles, meters, wire, mains, etc. These may be broken down by size and date of installation. Large property units, such as electric generators, may be handled separately.

Non-Utility Property. Only property used in the utility business is included in the appraisal. If a utility owns an office building and rents part of the space to other concerns, the proportionate value of the rented space is excluded. An amusement park operated by a street-railway company, even for the purpose of stimulating business, is non-utility property.

Used and Useful Property. To be included in the rate base, utility property must be used or useful. Excluded property is of several kinds.

Dismantled, obsolete, and abandoned equipment no longer useful and not likely to be useful in the near future will be excluded. In practically all cases the utility company will claim that such property is necessary for standby service. In some cases it will be claimed that the equipment is necessary to guarantee continuous or special service to some large customer, as for example to a large power or gas consumer, or to the fire department in the case of pumping equipment or auxiliary engines. Even if this property can be shown to be useful for this purpose, it is decidedly questionable whether the general consumers should be required to bear the costs.

Important factors in determining the disposition of such property include (1) the relation of its capacity to the maximum demand it might be required to meet. If it is greater than such demand, or if on the other hand it falls too far short of meeting it, the equipment might be excluded. (2) The time necessary to place such equipment in operation. There are instances of old boilers carried as standby equipment which could not have been fired up without an explosion. (3) The existence of alternative sources of supply. Standby generating equipment may not be considered necessary if two or more power lines serve the community. (4) The length of time that the equipment has been idle.

Another type of problem is found in the case of property that is in perfectly good condition but is no longer used because of a decline in demand. Suppose a depression leaves a utility with a large amount of excess capacity. If the utility had shown reasonably good judgment in installing the equipment, it seems unfair to penalize it, particularly since it was obligatory to render adequate service at all times. On the other hand, if there is little likelihood that the property will ever be used again or even in the near future, there is little reason to leave it on the books as a permanent burden upon the ratepayers. Elimination of this property does not necessarily place an unconscionable burden on the utility, since its value is generally deducted from both the property accounts and the depreciation reserve, so that there is no change in the depreciated rate base. The saving to the consumer arises out of the decreased depreciation expense as an item of operating costs.

Property Acquired for Future Use. Utilities, like other business enterprises, must plan for expansion. This is in the public interest, but can ratepayers be required equitably to pay a return upon all such property acquired in anticipation of future needs? As a general principle, the acquisition must be a reasonable one and the need for the property must be reasonably imminent. Otherwise it will not be included.

Donated Property. Many utility companies carry a considerable amount of donated property on their books. Customers in rural areas may contribute the cost of extending facilities for their use. Equitably, this property should not be included in the rate base.

2. Applying Unit Prices

The next step in the appraisal is to apply unit prices to each of the property classes. The following schedules (Tables 19 and 20) indicate some of the detail of the inventory work sheets.

TABLE 19

SELECTED ITEMS FROM THE APPRAISAL OF THE TRANSMISSION POLES,
TOWERS AND FIXTURES, ACCOUNT 331-a

CONOWINGO POWER COMPANY

	Units	Unit Price	Total
20 ft. poles, chestnut, class 1	4 @	$ 12.85	$ 51
35 ft. poles, chestnut, class 1	10 @	19.17	192
40 ft. poles, chestnut, class 1	23 @	28.32	651
60 ft. poles, chestnut, class 1	1 @	56.09	56
10 ft. cross arms, single, wood, 4" x 5"	1292 @	4.08	5,271
Line guys	264 @	5.68	1,500
Keystone truss pins	6559 @	.70	4,591
Acres, right-of-way clearing	4.82 @	100.00	482
TOTAL			94,641
Miscellaneous construction expense, 6%			5,678
TOTAL, Account 331-a			100,319

TABLE 20

SUMMARY OF THE APPRAISAL OF THE CONOWINGO POWER COMPANY

As of June 30, 1934

Account Number	Title	Reproduction Cost New	Reproduction Cost New Less Depreciation
311	Land	$ 29,838	$ 29,838
312	Structures	21,191	18,650
328	Substation Equipment	50,041	42,530
330	Underground Conduits	374	350
331	Poles, Towers and Fixtures		
	(a) Transmission	100,319	80,300
	(b) Distribution	277,609	208,200
332	Overhead Conductors		
	(a) Transmission	81,614	81,500
	(b) Distribution	165,970	157,700
333	Underground Conductors	1,012	1,000
335	Services	27,592	23,500
336	Line Transformers and Devices	109,290	100,000
337	Line Transformer Installation	9,683	9,683
338	Consumers Meters	48,935	41,600
339	Meter Installation	5,230	5,230
342	Street Lighting Equipment	10,529	9,480
344	General Equipment	17,906	13,500
	TOTAL DIRECT COST	$ 957,133	$823,061
301	Organization and Legal 3%	28,714	24,692
351	Engineering, Superintendence and Contractors Profit, 9% of Direct Cost less Land and General Equipment	81,845	70,175
353	Injuries and Damages 1%	9,571	8,231
		$1,077,263	$926,159
355	Interest during Construction 3%	32,318	27,785
	TOTALS	$1,109,581	$953,944

Unit costs may be obtained from several sources. Appraisal companies and well-staffed utilities and regulatory commissions maintain them on file. Otherwise, catalogue prices, old work orders, or contractors' estimates may be used. It may be extremely difficult to obtain these prices for specific years of installation. In that event various expedients may be used to estimate them.

Direct unit costs include (1) the list price, (2) the cost of freight, (3) the labor cost of installation, and (4) certain indirect overhead costs which may be estimated on a unit basis and attributed to the specific installation of the piece. Specific overhead includes such items as workmen's compensation insurance, job superintendence down to and including the foreman's salary, the cost of trucking and small tools; storeroom, tool, and supply expense; and some engineering expense. This expense is separate from the allowance for general overhead applicable to the construction of the plant as a whole.

Unit prices may represent original cost, present value, or some modification of either. To meet the requirements of *Smyth* v. *Ames,* two or more systems of prices may be used to produce several figures of final value.

3. General Construction Overheads

In the case of appraisal value, but not necessarily in the case of book value, it is necessary to allow an additional amount for general construction overheads. Book values are supposed to reflect all costs incurred in constructing the utility, the burden of proving the contrary being on the company. Construction overheads have their origin during the period in which the utility is organized and established as a "going concern" and include expenses that cannot be attributed to specific items of property. They are considered the expenses of promotion.

The provision for overhead is generally made in the form of a flat percentage-loading of total value of the physical property new. Fifteen per cent is a frequent allowance. A typical distribution is as follows:

Organization and legal expense	1.5%
Interest during construction	5.0
Engineering and superintendence	5.0
Taxes during construction	1.5
Omissions and contingencies	2.0
TOTAL	15.0

The hypothetical nature of these expenses furnishes opportunities for lawyers and appraisers to load property values with everything that the mind is capable of comprehending. The above percentages were adopted by the Wisconsin Commission. They are relatively conservative. Higher allowances have been granted, and utility companies will claim percentages upward to 100 per cent.

A strong commission will not accept these or any other flat percentage figures without question. Many of the listed expenses have never been incurred by promoters or by anyone else; many have been charged to the customers as operating expenses. If the property is small and poorly constructed, the allowance for engineering and superintendence may be reduced. Small companies generally do not maintain the same construction standards as large companies. Interest during construction may be reduced if there is reason to believe that the construction period is somewhat shorter than normal. The allowance may be increased by evidence of other items. The work may have been done by a contractor who charged the usual fee of ten per cent. Various kinds of insurance may have been carried. Larger promotion and financing costs may be included. Five to ten per cent is not an unusual range of financing costs during construction.

In computing interest during construction, it is generally assumed either that the property is placed in use as it is completed, or that funds are borrowed only as construction proceeds. Thus, if the construction takes two years, it is assumed that the equivalent amount of capital must be borrowed for an average of only one year.

4. Depreciation

Once the physical property has been appraised as new, depreciation is deducted. It is sometimes assumed that depreciation is to be deducted only in the event that cost of reproduction value is obtained. This is incorrect. Depreciation may be a legitimate deduction even if original cost is sought, and it is not always deducted even if cost of reproduction is used. The real issue turns on the accounting procedure adopted and the amount and source of funds collected from the ratepayers in the form of operating expenses. Although there are many older cases in which the courts have held that depreciation accounting methods have nothing to do with valuation procedure, the greater freedom given the commissions under more recent cases permits the determination of the rate base in accordance with more equitable principles. This problem is discussed in the chapter on Depreciation.

It should also be pointed out that all overhead and costs associated with construction are depreciable. These costs include such expenses incurred during construction as interest, engineering and superintendence, taxes, legal expenses, etc. Construction work in progress, however, is not depreciable, nor is plant held for future use. Temporary, emergency, or spare plant may be depreciable. The depreciation of property leased to or from others is largely determined by the nature of the lease.

5. The Valuation of Land

To the depreciated value of the physical property obtained so far, the value of the land must be added. Land differs from other physical property in that it is not subject to depreciation but rather tends to appreciate in value in growing communities. Under the doctrine of the *Minnesota Rate* cases, land is to be valued at its present fair value, irrespective of what weight might be given to the original cost of other types of property.

The application of the present fair-value standard to land offers as many, if not more, problems as its application to other types of property. Land defies simple classification; each piece is a peculiar unit. It is frequently the first property acquired by a utility and all past records have been destroyed, so that the appraiser lacks even the original cost as a point of departure. In some instances it will have been acquired from promoters for securities of indeterminate value. Under these circumstances lawyers and appraisers vie with each other in the number of cost-producing situations they can devise. A broad and sweeping imagination is of great value, and any sense of the ridiculous is more likely to be a drawback than otherwise. It may be assumed that the land, if acquired today, would be occupied by costly and extensive structures. These would have to be purchased and torn down—a costly procedure. The owners, knowing the necessity of the utility, could be imagined to be reluctant to sell. Condemnation proceedings would be expensive. The owners might claim severance damages—that is, a decline in the value of the remaining property as a result of the removal of integral parts. If not this, the property may have a sentimental value to imaginary original owners. These and many other claims have been pressed before commissions.

Such claims are seldom accepted by commissions, although nothing prevents the lawyers from trying. In general, lands are valued at the fair market value of adjacent land.

The rule is not universally applicable. The Federal Power Commission values the land of hydro-electric projects at original cost if it is a fair measure of the market value at the time of acquisition.

Natural Gas Lands and Leaseholds. Natural gas lands and leaseholds present peculiar problems in appraisals. In many instances, the properties were acquired before the utility was subject to regulation. A portion of the gas from any particular leasehold may still be sold under conditions of competition for industrial or for other non-regulated use. If the gas is a by-product of the production of crude oil, it is impossible to separate the costs of production. If the lands are producing at all, it is quite likely that their market value is far in excess of their fair original cost. On the other hand, the same natural gas company will probably have spent large sums of money in acquiring and developing properties that produced nothing except dry holes.

The wide divergence between market values and original cost is well illustrated in the *United Fuel Gas Company* cases. The company claimed a market value of their properties of more than $36,000,000. The West Virginia Commission allowed only book costs of less than $7,000,000. The commission was sustained, and the cases have come to have controlling weight.[1]

Recent cases have strengthened the principle. In the *Hope Natural Gas Company* case, the Court sustained a rate order based on the actual legitimate cost against insistent claims that the gas-producing properties should be given a value reflecting the market price of gas.[2] This case resolved still

---

[1] *United Fuel Gas Co.* v. *Pub. Serv. Comm. of W. Va.*, 278 U.S. 322 (1929). See also *United Fuel Gas Co.* v. *R.R. Comm. of Ky.*, 278 U.S. 300 (1929).

[2] *Hope Natural Gas Co.* v. *FPC*, 320 U.S. 591 (1944).

another significant problem. The Federal Power Commission refused to include in the rate base some $17,000,000 of drilling expenses that had been charged to operating expenses previous to 1923. (After that date the West Virginia Commission had required the company to capitalize these expenses.) The Court sustained the Federal Power Commission.

The boldness with which the Commission set forth its policy did not quiet the many disturbing questions raised by the problem. Such was the effect that an investigation of the entire natural gas industry was instituted by the Commission. The investigation revealed no definitive answers, except perhaps that the many problems of value can be settled only by more or less arbitrary pronunciamentos by those with authority to set them forth.[3]

2. THE VALUATION OF INTANGIBLES

The utilities have claimed, and both courts and commissions have admitted, that the value of a going business enterprise is something more than the value of its physical properties. But how much more? Let us examine in detail the specific claims for something more that may or may not be added to the physical value to arrive at the proper rate base.

1. Franchise Value

It has already been pointed out that in the *Willcox* [4] case, the United States Supreme Court had admitted that a franchise had value but had denied that this value was to be measured by the capitalized excess earning power that it gave the utility. The franchise was included in the rate base only to the extent that the state itself had accorded it some value in previous consolidation proceedings.

Clearly, the *Willcox* case was not the last word. In the *Cedar Rapids* [5] and *Georgia Railway* [6] cases in 1912 and 1923 respectively, the Court came forth with opinions that are now regarded as controlling. Allowances for franchise values are properly excluded from the rate base. No commission would permit the inclusion of a franchise at its monopoly value today. To do so would nullify all regulation, for regulation seeks to eliminate monopoly profits. General practice permits the inclusion of certain legitimate costs sustained by the utility in securing its franchise.

---

[3] The investigation is discussed in Chapter 13.
[4] *Willcox* v. *Consolidated Gas Co.*, 212 U.S. 19 (1909).
[5] *Cedar Rapids Gas Light Co.* v. *Cedar Rapids*, 223 U.S. 655 (1912).
[6] *Georgia Ry. & P. Co.* v. *R.R. Comm.*, 262 U.S. 625 (1923).

2. Good-will

Denied the right to capitalize monopoly earnings as franchise values, the valuation experts sought out other vehicles by which the self-same intangibles could be hauled into rate-base proceedings. Good-will, a recognized element of value in competitive business enterprise, appeared to fill the needs of the situation. Good-will was defined in the *Des Moines Gas Company* case as "that element of value which inheres in the fixed and favorable consideration of customers, arising from an established and well-known and well-conducted business." [7] In simpler language, it is the value of the tendency of customers to return to the old stand. The counter habits of millions of soft-drink customers is an asset of immense value to the Coca-Cola Company and possibly worth as much as the company's physical property.

On the other hand, there is a general distrust of good-will even where it is recognized to be substantial. It has been too often used to capitalize exaggerated expectations of future earnings. Conservative accounting practice is to write it off the balance sheet, even in the instance that actual considerations have been paid for it. [8]

In spite of commercial practice and the efforts of the lawyers, good-will is not accepted as a constituent element of the rate base. Where the utility is obliged to serve and where the customer has no choice but to return to the same stand, there can be no special or differential value to the company-customer relationship that might exist if competition prevailed. The issue has been settled—good-will is not an element of public utility value for rate-making purposes.

3. Going Value

Suppose a new gas utility is started in a community previously unserved. In order to build up a load quickly, a house-to-house canvass is made to acquaint householders with the advantages of gas. Advertisements are put out. Dealers are urged to push the sale of gas ranges. Demonstrations of gas cooking are organized. The public adjusts its way of living to take advantage of the new service. A working force is acquired and trained. Managers are oriented in their duties. Routines and procedures are established so that the various parts of the organization can work together as an efficient whole. The program is costly, but the utility builds up an active business and an organization to take care of it. If the utility were sold immediately thereafter, the first owners would undoubtedly

---

[7] *Des Moines Gas Co.* v. *Des Moines*, 238 U.S. 153, 165 (1915).

[8] See T. H. Sanders, H. R. Hatfield, and U. Moore, *A Statement of Accounting Principles* (American Institute of Accounting, 1938), p. 14.

demand payment for the expenses incurred. Can these expenses be included in the rate base as an intangible element of value?

Going value, or going concern value, may be defined as "the value which inheres in a plant where its business is established as distinguished from one which has yet to establish its business." [9] The notion has appealing qualities to utility lawyers, and they have labored with resourcefulness, ingenuity, and some measure of success to have it included as an element of value in the rate base. It does not depend upon the existence of competition as good-will does, nor is it invalidated by the existence of monopoly as are franchise values. It accrues to any business that is established and earning profits.

It is easier to admit that there is a special and intangible value to a going business than it is to measure it. The so-called Wisconsin method was originated by the Commission of that state in the early days of regulation.[10] It has long since been repudiated by that Commission and by the courts. Under this method, going value was measured by the capitalized deficits of the utility during its development period. The excess earnings of later periods were to be credited against the deficits. The measure of going value was also sought in the costs of developing the business as shown in old company records or as developed by hypothesis. Some "experts" have attempted to measure going value by setting it equal to the difference between the earnings of the existing enterprise and one without its business attached over the period required to develop the equivalent business. This is known as the comparative plant method. Some engineers, in despair of establishing any substantive basis for an allowance, have fallen back upon the expedient of asking a flat ten per cent of the property value. Ten per cent possesses a certain mystic fascination for the experts in this respect. All of these methods are subject to refinements and elaborations which peculiarly enough never fail to enhance the amount to be claimed. One engineer confessed with commendable frankness that he did not use any formula in determining the claim for going value, but that he looked over the property "just as a horse-trader looks at a horse and decides what it is worth." Ranking high among the descriptions of going value is that of an accountant who, in testifying of the nature of a write-up of $18,000,000, spoke of it as a "sort of essence permeating the whole situation."

A long series of cases beginning with the *Des Moines Gas Company* case established the judicial theory that going value was a property right upon

[9] *Des Moines Gas Co.* v. *Des Moines*, 238 U.S. 153, 165 (1915).
[10] Set forth in *Hill* v. *Antigo Water Co.*, 3 WRCR 623, 705-723 (1909). Repudiated in *Re City of Chippewa Falls*, P.U.R. 1927A 545, 558 (1926), and by the U.S. Supreme Court in *Galveston Electric Co.* v. *Galveston*, 258 U.S. 388 (1922).

which the owner had a right to a return.[11] The doctrine has been weakened considerably in recent years.[12] Going value cannot be perfunctorily read into every rate base.[13] There must be consideration of the history and circumstances of the particular enterprise.[14] There is no constitutional exaction that going value has to be separately considered and added to the cost figures attributable to the physical property, if there is a reasonable allowance for the overheads that seem to be appropriate in the value of the physical property.[15] The amount to be allowed is minimized if the company is a new company,[16] if the customers have been clamoring for service, and if the market is assured.[17]

Other objections can be urged to the going value allowance. The excess earnings through the years of a seasoned utility are likely to have more than offset any early deficits and development costs. Although going value is figured as a percentage of the company's present value, going value properly applies only to the expenses incurred during the early development years when the company was much smaller. Subsequent expenses incident to the company's expansion are more than likely to have been easily absorbed in operating expenses.

To summarize the discussion, where going value is claimed the company is charged with the burden of showing that development costs were actually incurred and that these costs were not absorbed in operating expenses, covered in other allowances for the value of the physical property, or their equivalent returned to the company in the form of excess earnings. These are substantial obstacles to hurdle if a commission should choose to place them in the way of a company. Not all commissions have chosen to do so. The Court's present position appears to be sound. There is no objection to an allowance for going value where its equity can be clearly shown. If it is not thought desirable to incorporate the allowance in the rate base, some consideration can be given in setting the rate of return.[18]

11 *Des Moines Gas Co.* v. *Des Moines,* 238 U.S. 153, 171 (1915); *Denver* v. *Denver Union Water Co.,* 246 U.S. 178, 191 (1918); *McCardle* v. *Indianapolis Water Co.,* 272 U.S. 400, 414 (1926), and other cases.

12 *Driscoll* v. *Edison Co.,* 307 U.S. 104, 117 (1939), and other cases.

13 *Dayton P. & L. Co.* v. *Commission,* 292 U.S. 290, 309 (1934).

14 *Los Angeles G. & E. Co.* v. *R.R. Comm.,* 289 U.S. 287, 314 (1933).

15 *Dayton P. & L. Co., op. cit.; Colorado Interstate Gas Co.* v. *F.P.C.,* 324 U.S. 581 (1945).

16 *Dayton P. & L. Co., ibid.*

17 *Columbus Gas Co.* v. *Comm.,* 292 U.S. 398, 412 (1934).

18 For other material on going value see E. W. Bemis, "Going Value in Rate Cases in the Supreme Court," 27 *Columbia Law Rev.* 530 (1927); M. G. Glaeser, "Some Aspects of the Going Value Concept in Utility Valuation," 1 *Jnl. of Land & Pub. Util. Econ.* 435 (1925); B. W. Lewis, "Going Value and Rate Regulation," 26 *Michigan Law Rev.,* 713 (1928); also "Going Value," 17 *Am. Econ. Rev.* 657 (1927); W. W. Potter, "Going Value," 24 *Michigan Law Rev.* 232 (1926); J. D. Sumner, "Interpretation of

3. WORKING CAPITAL

In most instances, a certain amount must also be included in the rate base as working capital. Working capital is defined as the amount of capital necessary to bridge the gap between the time that expenses for production of service must be met and the time of collection of the revenues from the same service. The United States Supreme Court recognized this element of value when it somewhat ambiguously spoke of the "sum required to meet operating expenses." Materials and supplies must be bought, salaries and wages must be paid, while the customers may not be required to pay for weeks or even months later.

There are two chief methods of determining working capital allowances. One is to analyze the current asset and current liability accounts on the balance sheet of the utility company. The other is to consider the operating expenses involving cash outlays during the time elapsing between production and payment.

Analysis of Balance Sheet Accounts. Balance sheets must be considered with caution and a certain degree of skepticism. Figures may not reflect normal conditions or they may be window-dressed. Average figures should be sought. It is also quite likely that the utility may actually have working capital far beyond any reasonable needs.

Gross working capital is measured by the company's current assets, which include such items as cash and bank deposits, accounts receivable, materials and supplies, and prepayments. This amount is reduced by the amount of the current liabilities to obtain the net working capital which is generally considered the more proper measure of the allowance. Certain observations must be made about these constituent elements.

The utility must have some cash on hand at all times, although the amount may be more than necessary to carry on the business efficiently. Accounts receivable represent the value of the service supplied but not paid for. The real measure of working-capital needs is the cost of service to the utility, rather than its selling price or selling value. A certain quantity of materials and supplies must be kept on hand. Amounts necessary for new capital construction cannot be included in this amount, as the utility will receive a return on them when interest during construction is capitalized and included in the rate base. Any prepayments for materials, taxes, etc., will increase the working-capital needs. It is much more likely that tax accruals will reduce the working-capital needs, since they are generally paid as much as a year after they are accrued. During that period the utility has the use of the funds.

Going Value," 4 *Jnl. of Land & Pub. Util. Econ.* 59 (1928); also "Validity of Going Value," *ibid.*, 113 (1928); M. C. Waltersdorf, "Going Value in Utility Valuation," 17 *Am. Econ. Rev.* 26 (1927).

Expenses During the Billing and Collection Period. Under this method, the utility's operating expenses are estimated for the average period elapsing between production and collection. If a utility bills its customers every month and requires payment within fifteen days, its working capital requirements will approximate one month's operating expenses—that is, an average period of production of 15 days between production and billing, plus 15 days for collection. An allowance equal to the operating expenses for 45 days or one-eighth of a year is sometimes made. This is rather high.

Billing and collection methods affect working capital requirements and differ between utilities. Telephone companies require payment in advance and hence their customers supply much of their working capital. Street-railways also require small amounts of working capital, since their patrons either pay when they use service or purchase their tickets in advance. Gas and electric utilities generally bill their customers every month. At the other extreme are found the water companies which bill their customers quarterly or semi-annually. They would require a large amount of working capital in relation to their operating costs.

Modifications to this procedure may be necessary. The company itself may purchase on credit. It may require its customers to make deposits to guarantee the payment of its bills. These amounts supplement the utility's working capital. Taxes are seldom paid until quite a while after they have accrued. On the other hand, materials and supplies must frequently be purchased a considerable period before they are used for production. A frequent procedure is to add an amount equal to the average value of materials and supplies kept on hand to the amount computed as above for operating expenses.

The Courts and Working Capital. Although the question of working capital comes up in virtually every rate case, there is little discussion of the principles involved. The courts are even uncertain whether materials and supplies are to be included in the term working capital. In the *Los Angeles Gas & Electric Company* [19] case, the United States Supreme Court upheld the California Commission, which based an allowance on operating costs rather than on sales value and reduced the amount because the company purchased natural gas on thirty-days' credit.[20]

A Summary of the Appraisal Process. The appraisal process thus includes the following steps:

[19] See *Los Angeles Gas & Electric Co.* v. *California Railroad Commission*, 289 U.S. 287, 317 (1933), and the lower court decision in 58 Fed. (2d) 256, 262 (1932); *Ohio Utilities Co.* v. *Commission*, 267 U.S. 359, 363 (1925), and *McCardle* v. *Indianapolis Water Company*, 272 U.S. 400, 412 (1926).

[20] A list of readings on this topic is to be found in the references section for this chapter.

1. Inventorying the property by classes of units.
2. Applying unit prices (which include certain overheads) to each class.
3. Adding construction overhead.
4. Deducting depreciation.
5. Adding land values.
6. Adding a certain amount for intangible values in some instances.
7. Adding an allowance for working capital.

It is apparent that the process of valuation is expensive. An appraisal may cost from one to two thirds of one per cent of the final value of the property, and may be even more for very small properties. These expenditures have been made necessary in the past by the Court's interpretation of *Smyth* v. *Ames* and by the inadequacy of accounting records. If fixed property records can be cleaned up, the second of these obstacles to sound regulation can be eliminated. We turn next to the significant developments in fixed-property accounting.

VALUATION AND ACCOUNTING RECORDS

4. THE RECLASSIFICATION OF FIXED PROPERTY

1. Origin of the Problem

The Problem of Fixed Property Accounting. So far in this chapter we have been concerned with value as determined by an appraisal of the property. The problems of fixed-property accounting are not necessarily related to those of the appraisal process. Accurate and adequate property records, however, reduce the need for appraisals and simplify the problem of determining the rate base. All too often these records are not available to commissions—or anyone else. An investigation begun by the Federal Trade Commission in 1928 revealed that the assets of utility operating companies had been written up by approximately one and one-half billion dollars.[21] Aside from the problem of determining whether these write-ups were justified in any sense, utility commissions were faced with the first problem of determining exactly what the property accounts did show. Was it original cost? Or the purchase price? Or the value at some unspecified date at which properties changed hands or were appraised or had the values adjusted?

[21] Federal Trade Commission, *Utility Corporations* (70th Congress, 1st Session, Senate Document 92, Part 72-A, 1935), p. 302.

The Nature of the Write-ups. The evils complained of go back to the earliest days of the century and before, although they did not appear in full flower until roaring boom days of the 1920's. The century was just turning when many farsighted entrepreneurs who realized the full value of the potential wealth locked up in the nation's water power resources began acquiring title to them all over the country. Many sites were acquired for little more than the fee required to make the contract binding. These men were later to become the nation's utility magnates of fortune and fame. As time went on they acquired other properties—gas, electric, street-railway, water, and telephone. Golden opportunities were opening up. Markets were expanding, service was becoming a necessity, monopoly conditions were ideal. The small, original owners of the properties scarcely realized—or in some instances they realized too well—the full value of what they had. By 1920 the time was ripe to really capitalize on the developing situation. The holding company age had arrived. With all the dexterity of a magician, these men shifted properties from one hand to another, shuffling and reshuffling so adroitly that even the eyes of a trained accountant could scarcely tell what was going on. With each shift the value was increased. Meanwhile, the fiction was maintained that the right hand knew not what the left hand was doing. If Company A of the left hand sold property costing five million dollars to Company B of the right hand for ten million dollars, was it necessary for Company B to know that they were both arms of the same holding company and of the aforesaid utility magnate who was shortly to achieve fortune and fame. Even if there was less than one arm's length between them, there were two arms. So what under other circumstances would have been nothing more than an intracompany transfer now became an intercompany purchase and sale with ten million dollars as the new book value of the property.

A typical procedure would run as follows: The holding company would acquire the property (or securities) of some operating utility and transfer it to its own operating subsidiary, which might be organized for that purpose alone. The operating company would surrender securities consisting of bonds, preferred stock, and common stock to the holding company in return for the property and far in excess of its original or any other fair value. The operating company would set up its plant accounts on the basis of the fictitious par value of the securities. The holding company would market the bonds and preferred stock for an amount approximately equal to its own investment. The common stock would be retained. If the inflated values of the operating company's properties were accepted by the regulating commission, and they frequently were under the reproduction-cost standard, the holding company would reap handsome dividends on its common stock equity which cost it nothing at all. If not, all sorts of pressure would be placed upon the operating utility to pay dividends anyway.

Sales, purchases, and consolidations came so rapidly upon the heels of each other in the 1920's that there was scarcely time for the utilities to correctly enter new properties on their books. One accounting authority has stated that it was not unusual to find 50 per cent or more of a utility's fixed investment carried in a single account called "Fixed Plant Not Classified by Prescribed Accounts," or "Cost of Plant and Equipment Purchased." [22] The fault rested too with regulatory commissions that were lax in requiring utilities to classify their property specifically. Some items of value were legitimate. Others were more than a little bit on the questionable side.

2. The New Property Accounting Requirements [23]

The reclassification of property accounts thus became one of the most important—and one of the most controversial—features of the new accounting systems prescribed in the 1930's. In general, fixed property accounts were broken down into sub accounts. The Federal Power Commission classification of accounts for electric utilities, for example, provided for the following accounts:

Account 100.   Electric Plant
        Account 100.1   Electric Plant in Service
        Account 100.2   Electric Plant Leased to Others
        Account 100.3   Construction Work in Progress
        Account 100.4   Electric Plant Held for Future Use
        Account 100.5   Electric Plant Acquisition Adjustments
        Account 100.6   Electric Plant in Process of Reclassification
Account 107.   Electric Plant Adjustments.

Account 100.1 includes the actual legitimate cost of electric public utility property to the person first devoting it to public service. That is, if public utility A purchased property from public utility B, it is the cost to B rather than the cost of A that goes into A's account, if B had already devoted it to public service. Where the accounting utility has purchased an operating system in arms-length dealing for more or less than this original cost, the difference is classified in sub account 100.5, Electric Plant Acquisition Adjustments. Account 107, Electric Plant Adjustments, is designed to include all other write-ups, and other fictitious amounts injected

[22] A. R. Colbert, "Advantages of Original Cost Classification of Plant," 35 *Pub. Util. Fort.* 333, 336 (March 15, 1945).

[23] An extensive list of readings on this topic is to be found in the reference section for this chapter.

into property accounts. One account represents increases in book values incident to sale and purchase; the other represents more deliberate write-ups without change in ownership.

This method of original cost accounting dates back at least to 1931, when the Wisconsin Commission revised its accounting systems to require utilities to record property at the cost to the first person devoting it to public service. The FPC system is practically similar to that recommended by the National Association of Railroad and Utilities Commissioners for electric utilities. It is slightly different from that prescribed for gas utilities. Practically all commissions have prescribed accounting systems similar to that of the FPC or N.A.R.U.C.

The Controversial Issues. The objective of the new system is to segregate property write-ups in separate accounts, 100.5 and 107. There are two controversial issues: (1) whether the particular write-ups are to be placed in Account 100.5 or Account 107, and (2) how, in turn, are the amounts in these two accounts to be disposed of?

The first question is important, for presumably a utility company can expect much more sympathetic treatment from a regulatory commission in respect to amounts in 100.5 than for amounts in Account 107. Amounts in the latter are clearly suspect, and it is unlikely that they will be given any consideration at all in determining the rate base. On the other hand, if the utility company purchased properties at arms-length dealing, the full purchase price might conceivably be included in the rate base even if it included a write-up in value. The question has attained greater importance, since by the *Hope Natural Gas* decision regulatory commissions have greater freedom in selecting the method of valuation.

The first issue is also important, since the manner of disposing of amounts in these two accounts is different. Amounts in Account 100.5 arising from purchase transactions may be left on the books indefinitely or they may be depreciated or amortized at the expense of the ratepayers. Amounts in Account 107 will quite likely be amortized against income or surplus at the expense of the stockholders.

The Federal Power Commission has considered itself to be charged with the duty of adjusting the books of utilities under its jurisdiction to squeeze the very last drop of water from the capital structures. It has gone about its job with grim determination. Its policies have been bitterly contested by many utility companies who have aligned a substantial array of accounting talent on their side. Some state commissions have also taken violent exception to the Commission's policies. However, since the *American Telephone and Telegraph* [24] case, its power to prescribe accounts has been incontrovertible and it gained additional powers in the *Northwestern Electric Company* case.

[24] *Amer. Tel. & Tel. Co.* v. *U.S.*, 299 U.S. 232 (1936).

Northwestern Electric Co. v. FPC (1944).[25] Shortly after the organization of the Northwestern Electric Company in 1911, it issued shares of $10,000,000 par value to the promoters of the company for no cash or any other consideration. Later, the company set up an account entitled Land and Water Rights to offset the stock issued. It carried on operations in the states of Oregon and Washington and subsequently built up its properties. In 1925, the American Power & Light Company purchased its stock for more than $5,000,000. The value of the stock was later written down on the Northwestern Company's books to $3,500,000 and the value of the assets reduced accordingly. The Federal Power Commission ordered the company to reclassify its accounts and put the entire $3,500,000 of so-called property in Account 107, and to amortize the amount by applying all income after preferred dividend requirements had been met.

The United States Supreme Court upheld the order of the Federal Power Commission. It was admitted that the procedure might not be in accord with best accounting practice and that it interfered to some extent with the function of management. But the Court did not find the plan arbitrary. The Court noted that the company could keep other books that would show the appreciated present value of the property. However, the substantial effect of the order would be to prevent the company from paying dividends to its common stockholder, the American Power & Light Company, until the amount was amortized.

What Is a Purchase Acquisition Adjustment? To return to our original illustration involving transfers between the right hand and the left hand, should a write-up in such an instance go into Account 100.5 or Account 107? There was a purchase and there were two separate corporate identities. Will a commission "look behind the corporate veil"? The Federal Power Commission has taken the position, against great opposition from some utilities, accountants, and state commissions, that where there was no "arms-length" bargaining there can be no purchase acquisition adjustment. In short, the write-up is a write-up and nothing less. Profits realized by an affiliate in an intra-system transfer of properties are amounts to be included in Account 107.[26] This is consistent with the Commission's established policy of excluding affiliate's profits from the legitimate costs of licensed hydro-electric power projects.[27] The Com-

---

[25] *Northwestern Elec. Co.* v. *FPC,* 321 U.S. 119 (1944). See also 52 P.U.R. (N.S.) 86 and for the lower court and commission cases 48 P.U.R.(N.S.) 65; 36 P.U.R.(N.S.) 202; 43 P.U.R. (N.S.) 140 and 148.

[26] *Re St. Croix Falls Minnesota Imp. Co.,* 43 P.U.R.(N.S.) 1 (1942); *Re California-Oregon Power Co.,* 47 P.U.R.(N.S.) 193 (1943).

[27] In this the Commission has been sustained in the courts. *Alabama Power Co.* v. *McNinch,* 94 F. (2d) 601 (1937); 21 P.U.R.(N.S.) 225. *Niagara Power Co.* v. *FPC,* 137 F. (2d) 787 (1943); 51 P.U.R.(N.S.) 40. *Alabama Power Co.* v. *FPC,* 134 F. (2d) 602 (1943); 47 P.U.R.(N.S.) 257. *Puget Sound P. & L. Co.* v. *FPC,* 137 F. (2d) 701 (1943); 50 P.U.R.(N.S.) 375. *Penn. P. & L. Co.* v. *FPC,* 139 F. (2d) 445 (1943); 52 P.U.R.(N.S.) 275.

mission has also included in Account 107 such items as expenses in marketing preferred stock, the capitalized costs of rate investigations, and certain costs of amending a company charter.[28]

Is "Arms-length Bargaining" a Controlling Consideration? Consolidations and mergers represent another type of the same problem. Suppose two or more companies, each a distinct group acting entirely in its own interests, consolidate to form a new company. There is considerable negotiation, bargaining, and jockeying for position in the new company. Each wants to get as much as possible. In a case such as this, two distinct interest groups consolidated to form the Niagara Falls Power Company. Each group, prior to consolidation, wrote up its plant accounts. The Federal Power Commission refused to accept the new values and concluded that the subsequent transaction was not a sale, but only a pooling of interests.[29]

The *Montana Power Company* Case.[30] The Federal Power Commission met the same situation in the reclassification of the accounts of the Montana Power Company in a case that involved an interesting historical background. The Montana Power Company had been formed in 1912 by a consolidation of several Montana utility companies. More than $51,-000,000 of the total plant valuation of $81,000,000 represented "intangibles," such as water rights, contracts, and franchises. John D. Ryan, a famous copper magnate, used his position as the head of powerful copper mining interests which purchased electric power to gain a strategic bargaining position for himself in the organization of the new company. In return for hydro-electric and other properties which he owned and transferred to the new company, he obtained a highly valuable and controlling stock interest. There was, however, a substantial amount of bargaining and negotiation between Ryan and the other groups. The significant fact in this instance, as in that of the Niagara Falls Power Company, was that there was no party to the bargaining whose interests would have been served by the reduction of the capitalization.

Other properties had been acquired at enhanced prices to eliminate competition. These new and larger "nuisance values" had appeared on the new company's books. Some properties had been acquired from affiliates in transactions in which there could have been no "arms-length" bargaining. Other inflationary items included bond discount and expense, amounts representing credits to the contingency reserve, fees paid to affiliates and capitalized, capital stock expense, unrecorded retirements, and amounts previously written off to expense. All in all, the Federal Power

---

28 *Re Minnesota P. & L. Co.*, 48 P.U.R.(N.S.) 1 (1943).

29 *Niagara Falls Power Co.* v. *FPC*, 137 F. (2d) 787 (1943).

30 *Re Montana Power Co.*, 57 P.U.R.(N.S.) 193 (1945). The Montana Commission took decided exception to the Federal commission's procedure. See also 56 P.U.R.(N.S.) 193 (1944).